War Came to The Philippines

War Came to The Philippines

*Being an Account
Chiefly of Events Which Transpired
During the First Year of the
Japanese Occupation of the Philippines*

by

Arnold H. Warren

Old Guard Press

Published in the United Kingdom in 2018
for Old Guard Press by
Shearsman Books
50 Westons Hill Drive
Emersons Green
BRISTOL
BS16 7DF

Shearsman Books Ltd Registered Office
30–31 St. James Place, Mangotsfield, Bristol BS16 9JB
(this address not for correspondence)

ISBN 978-1-84861-646-2

Copyright © International Philippine Philatelic Society, 2011, 2018.
Epilogue and Addendum copyright © Douglas K. Lehmann, 2011.
Editorial matter copyright © Old Guard Press, 2018

CONTENTS

Preface   10
Introduction   11
Foreword   12

1. Concerning Baguio, Where I Resided at the Outbreak of the War with Japan   13
2. The War Comes to Baguio   18
3. We Flee from Baguio to Manila   29
4. Concerning Events in Manila during the last ten days of December, 1941   33
5. The Japanese Occupy the City of Manila   41
6. I Am Interned at Santo Tomas   45
7. I Am Interned at the Red Cross Hospital in the Ateneo University   57
8. Concerning Some of the Patients in the Men's Ward   60
9. Concerning Captain Winship   64
10. Concerning the Miner and Planter   67
11. Concerning the Manner in Which Internees Were Permitted to Receive Visitors   72
12. Concerning "Honest Abe"   75
13. Concerning Our Food at the Ateneo Hospital   79
14. Concerning the Retired Navy Cook   82
15. Concerning Tommy, The Club Manager   85
16. Concerning the Banker   88
17. Concerning the Women at the Ateneo Hospital   90
18. Concerning Jack, the Sailor   94
19. Concerning the Automotive Mechanic   96
20. Concerning the Jesuits and the Manner in Which They Ministered to Us   100
21. Concerning Certain Persons Who Sought and Were Granted a Refuge at the Ateneo University   105
22. Concerning Charlie, the Policeman   108

23. Concerning the Marine Chief Engineer	111
24. Concerning the Professor	113
25. Concerning the Manner in Which We Obtained News of the War	115
26. Concerning Ford, the Editor	118
27. Concerning Ira, the Surveyor	120
28. Concerning the Mining Engineer	124
29. Concerning Japanese Visitors at the Ateneo	126
30. Concerning USAFE's Defeat and Surrender to the Japanese	128
31. Concerning Slim and His Family	134
32. Concerning the Suffering and Death of USAFE War Prisoners from Bataan	137
33. Concerning the Auditor and His Wife	139
34. Concerning the Playboy	141
35. Concerning the Activity of the Jesuits in the Underground Movement	148
36. Concerning a Secret Hospital for Guerrillas	151
37. I Obtain a Brief Glimpse of Manila During the Early Months of Japanese Occupation	154
38. Concerning Mr. Koontze	158
39. Concerning the School Teacher	161
40. I Quit Smoking and Do Some Profitable Reading	163
41. Concerning Robert, the Movie Director	165
42. My Health Deteriorates and I Undergo an Operation	166
43. The Red Cross Closes the Ateneo Hospital and We Are Transferred to Red Cross Hospital No. 4	168
44. Concerning Frenchy, The Retired Sergeant, and Mr. Em	169
45. Concerning Guy White, the Two Johns and the Scotsman	171
46. Concerning the Internee Nurses	173
47. Concerning Red Cross Hospital No. 4	177
48. I Visit Santo Tomas and Secure a Pass Interning Me in My Home for Ten Days	181

49. Concerning the First Ten Days of My Internment at Home	188
50. I Am Granted a Pass Authorizing My Internment in My Home for One Month	194
51. I Visit Several of My Former Internee Companions	197
52. My Wife Recovers My Valuable Collection of Philippine Stamps	199
53. The Japanese Military Administration Seeks to Curb the Dissemination of Uncensored News	201
54. The Son of Our American Neighbor Dies and a Wake is Held Over His Body	203
55. The Commandant of the Santo Tomas Internment Camp Assumes Control of the Public at the Remedios Hospital	204
56. Concerning Substitutes for Wheat Flour	206
57. My Pass is Renewed for Two Months	211
58. I Sell Some Postage Stamps	216
59. Concerning Various Occurrences During August and September	222
60. Concerning the Neighborhood Associations and the Distribution of Rice	224
61. I Visit the Internees at the Ateneo University and Obtain Authentic News of the War	226
62. Concerning Mrs. Bowers and Her Daughter, Bessie	228
63. Concerning the Smuggling of Rice into Manila	231
64. Concerning Wartime Transportation in Manila	233
65. I Make Cup Cakes of Rice Flour, Cornstarch and Coconut Milk for My Friends Interned at the Ateneo	239
66. Concerning Chaotic Conditions on the Island of Negros	242
67. Concerning a Superstitious Belief	244
68. I Do Some Errands and Hear Some News	246
69. My Pass is Renewed for Another Two Months	250
70. Concerning Japanese Attempts to Suppress the Guerrillas by the Use of Filipino Constabulary Soldiers	253
71. Concerning the Danger of Being Overheard When Discussing the War	255

72. *I Meet Captain Winship*   257

73. *Several Red Cross Hospitals are Closed*   259

74. *Concerning the Manner in Which the Japanese Permeated the City of Manila*   260

75. *Concerning Hard Times for Many People in Manila*   264

76. *Financial Assistance is Given to Some of Those Interned in Their Homes*   267

77. *My Wife Seeks Another Source of Income to Replace the Salary Which She Would No Longer Receive from the Red Cross*   271

78. *We Have Visitor from Baguio*   273

79. *Concerning the High Prices Which Collectors Paid for Stamps*   276

80. *Concerning the Arrest by Japanese Military Police of Three Prominent Business Men of Manila*   278

81. *Concerning the Stagnation Which Gripped Manila after the Japanese Occupation of the City*   279

82. *The Tide of War Turns in Favor of the Allies*   287

83. *My Son has a Birthday*   292

84. *We Again Receive News from Baguio*   294

85. *My Wife is Permitted to Withdraw a Small Sum of Money from Her Frozen Accounts in the National City Bank*   296

86. *I Report Again at the Santo Tomas Internment Camp*   298

87. *I Call on Tom Hawkins Once More and Obtain from Him the Latest War News*   300

88. *I Am Reinterned at the Santo Tomas Internment Camp*   302

Epilogue   307

Addendum   309

To the people of the Philippines, who lost their homes and other property, their loved ones, and even their own lives as the result of brutal Japanese aggression—and to the soldiers, both Filipino and American, who fought, suffered in prison camps, and died, in order that the aggression might be driven from Philippine soil—this volume is humbly dedicated.

Preface

The author of this diary, Arnold H. Warren, was a prominent member of The International Philippine Philatelic Society (IPPS). The IPPS posted the original of this typed diary on their website. It is available to all. I felt it should also be available in book form, as an important window into events in the Philippines during the Japanese Occupation. These efforts have the full backing of the IPPS.

In preparation, the original typed copy was kindly re-typed at Filipinas Heritage Society. We work closely together on the largest collection of books, articles and monographs on World War II in the Philippines. The proof reader and editor's comments on the book were so interesting that I asked her to write a few words on her impressions. Thanks also to Karen Hall who has 'shepherded' these efforts. Tony Frazer of Shearsman Books takes the final manuscript and turns it into the final published book, with its own ISBN, available for purchase on any online bookstore. Tony and I have collaborated on the publication of six books, mainly diaries of war experiences. War Comes to the Philippines can now be added to the body of work providing first hand insight into every day life during the war.

Roderick Hall

Introduction

It has been a great privilege to work with this archival document. Initially I prepared for a depressing and grim read, but the more I worked with it the more I have been moved by its humanity rather than its inhumanity.

Each chapter stands alone and can be read entire. However, those reading the complete archive will be aware of considerable repetition which, because of the intrinsic nature of what is essentially a diary, has not been modified or edited out. This was a critical decision as this repetition heightens those details which Warren must constantly have been worrying over and, more importantly, holding on to, vividly illustrating the fragility of his circumstances and consequent state of mind.

Against the backdrop of ever advancing and pervasive fear, both real and imagined, the once comfortable status of the author's family life is continually undermined and becomes increasingly vulnerable.

The elements which shine through are those of dignity, generosity, fairness, ingenuity, charity, determination, harmony and huge personal restraint. These behaviors gradually become apparent through the record of minutely observed and recorded details which describe the appalling and mounting strain initiated by tedium, monotony, boredom, dependence, ill health and that excruciating poverty of body and spirit which results from the removal of all stimulus and erosion of responsibility. Despite every one of these instances, documented throughout with a necessary suppression of emotion, there are moments of poignancy which cause the reader to maintain the same focus which Warren relentlessly kept.

Towards the end of the account Warren discovers that maintaining his pride as a breadwinner lies in the cultivation of a garden. We feel the power this has on his feelings of self worth and sanity. We cannot help but be reminded of Voltaire in his great work, *Candide*. This diary is not a great work but it does provide us with an important insight into the ability of ordinary human beings to cope with extraordinary circumstances.

The Editor/Proof Reader

Foreword

This volume is devoted almost exclusively to events which transpired during the first year of the Japanese Occupation of the Philippines. Occasional brief reference has been made, however, to events which occurred during the second, third, and the beginning of the fourth, years of Japanese oppression.

While it is the true that the suffering of the Filipino people did not reach its peak until the beginning of the fourth year of the Japanese occupation, their suffering was great enough during the first year. I have chosen to write concerning the first year because it was during that year that I had the greatest opportunity both to witness the suffering of the people, and to talk with persons who witnessed occurrences which did not come within the range of my personal observation.

The first draft of this volume was written in 1942, when the events described therein transpired. Immediately prior to my reinternment in Santo Tomas, in December of 1942, the manuscript was concealed in the attic of my mother-in-law's house in Manila, where it remained until I brought it to the United States. The manuscript has been rewritten and occasional reference has been made to events which transpired subsequent to the writing of the first draft.

Arnold H. Warren
Spreckels, California,
February 22, 1946

Chapter 1.

Concerning Baguio, where I resided at the outbreak of the War with Japan

I am an American. I arrived in the Philippines on June 6, 1914. Thereafter, for almost twenty-one years, I was a resident of the Philippines and never at any time outside its boundaries. I married Socorro Rosado, a native of the Philippines, in 1922. We have one child, a son, born ten years later. Although I have never given up my United States citizenship and consider it one of my most cherished possessions, I have come to look upon the Philippines as my country and its people as my people.

During the decade prior to the birth of our son in 1932, I earned a comfortable income as a sugar technologist. My wife was a successful life-insurance agent. During the period between 1929 and 1932 my wife invested the greater part of her savings in stock of the two largest gold mines in the Philippines. The dividends from this fortunate investment provided us with a comfortable income such that, subsequent to the birth of our son, it was not necessary for either of us to engage in gainful employment. My wife devoted her time to the care of our son and I became a prospector of gold. In 1935 I became the president of a small mining corporation which owned a promising gold-silver property about sixty miles north of Baguio in Benguet Province of the Philippines. I also became a collector and student of Philippine postage and revenue stamps. Eventually I came to be recognized as an authority on Philippine stamps. In 1941, I became a member of the Rotary Club of Baguio, with the classification, unusual in that organization, of "Philatelist."

We moved to Baguio in 1933 and continued to make it our home until the outbreak of the war with Japan in 1941.

Baguio is located on a pine-clad plateau, almost 5,000 feet above sea level, in the midst of the richest Philippine gold mining district. There were seven producing gold mines within fifteen miles of the business center of Baguio. Two of these mines were rated as among the half dozen richest gold mines in the world. But Baguio was not only a mining metropolis, it was also one of the world's most beautiful resorts. It was famous as the Summer Capital of the Philippines long before it became an important mining center.

The mild temperate climate of Baguio is very similar to that of Puget Sound in the State of Washington, and there is a remarkable similarity in the flora of these two widely separated regions with pine trees, oaks, wild roses, strawberries, huckleberries, and the ferns called "brakes".

Baguio was not a large city. The permanent population was only about 25,000. Nor did it have the social characteristics of the modern city. Rather, it was a large village, where the permanent residents were as well known to each other as are the residents of a rural village in the United States.

A favorite place for the exchange of news, particularly mining news, was the Shamrock Hotel. The proprietor, Mike Ryan, was an Irish-American veteran of the Spanish-American war. He had been a resident of the Philippines for more than 40 years. Each day there gathered in the barroom of the Shamrock Hotel a slowly dwindling group of American Old Timers, who played a card game called solo whist—or simply solo—and discussed the news. On Saturdays and Sundays, American miners from nearby mines dropped in with news of the mines, which was carefully appraised by the assembled Old Timers. Among other frequent visitors were the paymasters and other members of the staffs of the more remote mines, officials of nearby sawmills, travelling salesmen from Manila, the Igorrote owner of a large and prosperous bus transportation business, the British manager of the local cold stores, the Vice Mayor and the Chief of Police of the city, a local stock broker who dealt in mining shares, the Russian manager of another hotel, the American manager of two local moving picture theaters, American non-commissioned officers and civilian employees of the nearby Camp John Hay.

The dean of the Old Timers was J.D. Highsmith. What his initials stood for I never learned. Everyone called him "High." He was a native of Georgia who had come to the Philippines as a soldier during the Spanish-American War. For more than 40 years he had resided in Baguio. He married a Filipino woman and by her had a son, Tom, now about 30 years old. Tom had married an American girl and by her had a daughter.

For years High had earned a living by hunting deer and wild pigs. The game which he killed he sold in Baguio. He was also a prospector and acquired several valuable mineral claims. For a number of years, while it was still a struggling prospect, he was employed as a miner at the Balatoo Mine. Because there was not sufficient money to pay all of his wages in cash he accepted a small interest in the prospect as part payment for his services. When Balatoo became one of the world's richest gold mines High's small interest in the mine made him a wealthy man. He also acquired an interest in two other gold mines in exchange for several of his mining claims. At one time he was probably worth a quarter of a million dollars. But he and his son, had spent the money freely. High had reinvested a considerable portion of his fortune in a hardware and machinery firm. Knowing nothing about the business himself, he placed too much confidence in the man employed as manager. The store failed with a loss to High of almost his entire fortune. About all that was left was the motor service station which was operated by Tom and the two homes in which High and Tom lived. High now received a pension as a Spanish-American War Veteran.

Until he was past fifty years of age, High had been a heavy drinker, but a serious illness caused him to give up alcohol. He said that he either had to quit drinking or start pushing up the daisies. He had preferred to quit drinking. Although now past seventy he was still very vigorous for a man of his years. With his son, he still hunted frequently. Tom had won the trap-shooting championship of the Philippines but High could still outshoot his son when it came to bagging game. The two were among the outstanding sportsmen of the Philippines.

High usually arrived at the Shamrock Bar at about nine o'clock in the morning. He returned to his home at noon. But at three o'clock in the afternoon he was usually back in the Shamrock Bar, where he remained until dinner time at seven o'clock in the evening, never touching alcohol. The bar was his club and office. In it he had concluded many business transactions. Because of his shrewd common-sense he was frequently consulted, not only concerning the mines, but also concerning many other matters of public and private interest. People knew that he could be found in the bar of the Shamrock Hotel and came to see him there.

When not otherwise engaged, High played solo whist with the other Old Timers who frequented the Shamrock Bar. The players changed throughout the day but a game was always in progress. When one player dropped out another took his place. Among the players were two young men—High's son, Tom, and Joe Icard, the son of another Old Timer. Both were successful young businessmen and usually joined the game after business hours late in the afternoon. Among other players were Jake Albright, a retired Master Sergeant of the United States Army who had made a small fortune in the mines; Mike Ryan, the proprietor of the Shamrock Hotel and Bar; Bill Reese, for twenty-five years construction foreman in Baguio's Department of Public Works, but now retired and living on his pension as a Spanish-American War veteran and the rent from two apartments which he owned; Elinger, a Spanish-American War Veteran whom we called "Carabao" and who was employed as a foreman in one of the nearby gold mines; Shevelin, who earned a comfortable living by mining free gold on a small property which he owned and O'Brien, who for the past fifteen years, had been a sergeant stationed at the nearby Camp John Hay and who had been a captain during the First World War.

No money was wagered on the game, but at the end of each game the loser bought a round of drinks for the players. Often a single game lasted two hours. Hence drinks were not purchased very frequently! About half of the players, including High, Mike Ryan, and myself, did not take alcoholic drinks. Thus, although we played in a barroom, the drinks most frequently served to the solo players were Coca Cola, orangeade, and lemonade. The abstemiousness of the solo players was a frequent subject for amused and, be it said, admiring comment by other patrons of the Shamrock.

When I came to Baguio to prospect for gold in 1933, I knew nothing about mining. I sought acquaintance with the Old Timers because many of them were old miners and from them I might learn something about prospecting. They introduced me to the game of solo whist and I soon became accepted as one of them even though I was a newcomer to Baguio and had not been a resident in the Philippines for as long a time as most of the others. By most I was regarded as still a young man, in whom they took a kindly paternal interest.

Late in the afternoon Colonel Van Schaick usually visited the Shamrock. He was a retired officer of the United States Army now employed as an executive of the two largest gold mines near Baguio. The colonel had won the Congressional Medal of Honor for exceptional gallantry during the Philippine campaign of the Spanish-American War. He was now a wealthy man as a result of his investment in Philippine gold mines. He had organized and had become the first president of the Baguio Rotary Club. Like myself, he was an enthusiastic collector of Philippine stamps and we spent many happy hours together discussing our stamps. The colonel did not play solo whist. I usually got another player to take my place in the game while I visited with Colonel Van Schaick whenever he dropped in at the Shamrock.

There were rumors of impending war with Japan throughout the early part of 1941. The United States Army and Navy had ordered the return to the United States of the wives and children of personnel stationed in the Philippines. Both Army and Navy in the Philippines were making feverish preparations for the war which it was believed would come.

In April of 1941, Colonel Van Schaick came to my home and informed me that he and his wife would leave for the United States. Several warts on his face and neck has been diagnosed by his doctor as cancers. The colonel was going to the Mayo Brothers' Hospital to have these cancers removed.

"But I am coming back," he said earnestly. "I have never yet run away from a war and I am not going to run away from this war."

True to his promise, the colonel did come back. He and his wife returned to the Philippines late in November of 1941 on almost the last United States Army transport to arrive before the outbreak of the war. He had encountered great difficulty in persuading the United States military authorities to permit him, and particularly his wife, to return to the Philippines. It had been necessary for him to make a trip to Washington, D.C., in order to obtain passage on the transport. Several cancers had been removed from his face and neck. He said that he was feeling fine.

The colonel told us about his trip to the United States at the first luncheon of the Baguio Rotary Club after his return. I was initiated as a member of the club at that meeting, which occurred early in December, only a few days before the outbreak of the war.

Chapter 2.

The War Comes to Baguio

On that fateful Monday of December 8, 1941 (Sunday, December 7, in the United States), I arose, as usual, at about five-thirty and as usual at six fifteen am I tuned in to the Manila Radio news broadcast. "We are at war with Japan!" shouted the announcer. This was followed by a brief account of the attack on Pearl Harbor.

My first reaction was one of intense anger at my wife. For more than a year I had been convinced that war would come to the Philippines and had sought to impress upon her the need to build up a considerable reserve of cash in our bank account. She had ignored my warnings and had continued to play the mining stock market. About the middle of November, at my urgent request, she had sold some of her holdings and had placed the proceeds in our bank account. But on December 6 she informed me that she had reinvested the money in shares of a mine which had declared a large dividend, payable during the latter part of December. Thus, when the radio announced that war had come, my first reaction was one of rage because my wife had ignored my repeated warnings to get out of the stock market and build up a cash reserve. Unable to contain myself, I immediately awoke my wife, told her that war with Japan had come and upbraided her for ignoring my warnings. She very discreetly remained silent and having vented my anger in harsh words, I was able to eat my breakfast with equanimity.

After breakfast, as usual, I drove my son to his school. Then I drove to the Shamrock Hotel to discuss the news of the war. The Old Timers had also come early with the same intent. Bill Reese, Mike Ryan, and I sat down to play a game of solo.

"Do you suppose the Japs will attack the Philippines?" said Mike, as he shuffled the cards.

"They probably will," said High, as he filled his mouth with a generous portion of chewing tobacco.

At that moment we heard several explosions.

"What was that?" I asked nervously.

"Can't you recognize the sound of blasting in the rock quarry?" asked Bill Reese caustically.

"Maybe the Japanese have bombed Camp John Hay," said High quietly.

We rushed out into the street and scanned the sky for planes. But none could be seen, either in the direction of Camp John Hay or elsewhere. We returned to our game.

"About an hour ago I saw a squadron of planes pass over Baguio flying very high and going north," I said. "I assumed they were American planes going north on patrol. I counted sixteen."

"I counted only twelve," said Bill.

"Tom and I saw them and counted seventeen," said High.

About fifteen minutes later Mike was called to the telephone.

"Those explosions we heard were Japanese bombs alright," said Mike when he returned. "O'Brien just telephoned from Camp John Hay to report that a few minutes ago the camp was bombed by Japanese planes. Ten persons were killed and many more were wounded. One bomb struck the barracks occupied by Filipino scout soldiers."

At that moment we heard several more explosions, apparently from the direction of the Camp. Again we rushed out into the street and scanned the sky, but not a plane could be seen.

A little later Sergeant O'Brien telephoned to say that the last explosion had been caused by four or five bombs dropped by a solitary Japanese plane just outside the main gateway into the Camp. At least one civilian had been killed and several others injured.

This was followed by news that three Old Timers, John Mueller, T. J. Nill, and W. M. Weidmann, were among those injured. It appeared that the three were chatting in Nill's store when the sound of the first bombs was heard. Nill immediately called a taxi and the three set out for the Camp to see what has happened. At the main gate they were turned back by the sentry. They then took the road which skirted the Camp to the right of the main gate in an attempt to enter by another gate. They were turned back at that gate also. However, returning by the same road from which they had just come, they unfortunately arrived in front of the house near the main gate at the same instant as the bombs exploded. One bomb, striking the road beside the taxi, tore off the door, broke both of John Mueller's legs and slightly injured the taxi driver and both of the other Old Timers. A fourth Old Timer, who arrived on the scene a few moments later in his own car, took the injured to the hospital.

Another of the bombs fell upon a concrete court between two houses. The wall of the lower floor of one of the houses was blown in, killing the father of the household and injuring two of his servants. The force of the explosion cut down two pine trees, each about ten inches in diameter and located fifteen or twenty feet from the spot where the bomb exploded. The trunks of the trees were severed about six feet above the ground.

During the afternoon of that day my son picked up, in our flower garden, two brass gadgets about 3 ½ inches in diameter and shaped like four-bladed propellers with a threaded hole through the hub. Seven or eight of these gadgets were picked up in the vicinity of our home. We associated them with the Japanese bombing planes but did not know what they were for. I showed one of these gadgets to my next-door neighbor, a Japanese building contractor who was a naturalized Philippine citizen. He informed me that this propeller-like device was screwed over the firing pin of the bomb to prevent an accidental explosion when handling it. As the bomb falls, after being released from the airplane, the air pressure causes the firing-pin guard to spin until it is unscrewed from the bomb and falls free. These propeller-like firing pin guards would land at a distance of about a mile from the point where the bombs would strike. The bombers would pass directly over the spot where the firing-pin guards fell and the noise of a firing-pin guard striking a tree would be heard a moment before the explosion of the bomb.

The schools were closed by the order of President Quezon's on December 8. On the morning of December 9 my son went with me to the Shamrock Hotel, where we met a young newspaper woman, Yay Panlillo, who was in Baguio on vacation when the bombing occurred on December 8.

She had already forwarded an account of the bombing to her newspaper, and was gathering material for a more detailed report. My son showed her the firing-pin guard which he had found. She immediately wanted it as a souvenir for her boss and asked my son to give it to her. When he declined to do so she offered to pay one peso ($0.50) for it. This proposal was satisfactory to my son and the deal was closed. He refused, however, to sell his one remaining firing-pin guard, although she pressed him to do so.

There were two other bombings of Camp John Hay between December 9 and 25, but I do not recall the exact dates. The second bombing caused one death and injuries to several other persons. None were killed and only two were injured by the third bombing.

After the third bombing Sergeant O'Brien took us to Camp John Hay to show us the result of the three bombings. I was amazed at how relatively little damage had been done. About 40 bombs have been dropped. The location of each bomb crater was indicated on a map of the Camp. This map indicated that the aim of the Japanese bombers was accurate, since the craters were very well distributed over the area containing the most important buildings. The Japanese were unlucky, however, and only three or four direct hits were scored out of the 40 bombs dropped.

The exigencies of military transportation and communication caused a suspension of both mail and telegraph services between Baguio and Manila on December 5. We were, therefore, dependent for news upon the radio and upon such news as was brought in by persons coming by private automobile from Manila. To disseminate this news, Ms. Halsema, the Baguio representative of the *Manila Daily Bulletin*, issued a daily mimeographed sheet which was paid for by voluntary contributions.

An executive of one of the gold mines had been returning by automobile from Manila to Baguio on December 8. He had reached the vicinity of Clark Field in Tarlac Province at midday—the time Clark Field was being bombed. When he reached a roadside hotel at San Miguel, his car had been requisitioned by several USAFE officers. At their command, he drove them to Clark Field, where he witnessed the bombing. He reported that Clark Field had apparently been caught napping, in spite of the fact that the bombing did not occur until some four hours after the bombing of Baguio. He said that many planes had been destroyed on the ground; that gasoline was stored in drums piled beside the hangar; that this resulted in the burning of both gasoline and hangar when the gasoline was hit and that apparently no fighter planes had got into the air to repel the attack. He was very indignant and said that in view of the fact that news of the attack on Pearl Harbor had reached the Philippines more than six hours earlier, the air force at Clark Field should have been more alert.

Reports concerning the attack on the Iba Zambales airport indicated that the USAFE Air Force had also been caught napping on December 8. A squadron had been out on a routine patrol during the morning, but had returned and landed for lunch. The men of the air force were in their barracks when the attack came at about midday. All but about 30 of the 200 American members of the air force had been killed in the bombing and machine-gunning of the barracks, and many planes were destroyed on the ground.

A similar report came in concerning the first attack on Nichol's Field near Manila, which also occurred on December 8. Many planes were destroyed on the ground and there was considerable loss of life from the bombing and machine-gunning of barracks.

Reports came in of Japanese landings at Vigan on the northeast coast of Luzon and at the extreme northern tip of Luzon.

The USAFE Air Force—what was left of it—swung into action. The landing at Vigan was effected only after the loss of several transports and a considerable number of Japanese soldiers. A daring USAFE flyer single-handedly destroyed a number of Japanese planes on the ground at Appari and shot down one in the air. Captain Kelly sank a Japanese war ship off the coast of Luzon. He brought his plane back safely but died of machine-gun wounds which he had received in the encounter. He was awarded a posthumous Congressional Medal of Honor. Likewise, Captain Villamor was awarded the Congressional Medal of Honor for his daring exploit in attacking a much superior Japanese force and shooting down several Japanese planes during the encounter. For another daring victory in the air he was awarded the Distinguished Service Cross.

The Cavite Navy Yard, across the bay from Manila, suffered a disastrous midday air attack, which practically wiped out the naval ships with very heavy loss of life. The naval planes were absent on patrol duty at the time.

Baguio was full of wild rumors during the first two weeks of the war. There were chiefly rumors of aid arriving from the United States. Some of the rumors were spread by American Army officers from Camp John Hay, perhaps to bolster the morale of the people, or perhaps in the hope that the rumors would reach the Japanese and cause them to delay any offensive land action until they could land a stronger force. At any rate, a U.S. Army major reported at the Shamrock Hotel that 24 U.S. transports had arrived at Corregidor in Manila Bay and had been safely unloaded. There were other rumors of a similar nature.

The USAFE force at Camp John Hay was small—not more than 300 officers and enlisted men—and was poorly equipped to repel an attack, either by land or by air. There were no planes, no anti-aircraft guns and no artillery of any sort. The only weapons available were rifles and a few 30 caliber machine guns. These were entirely ineffective against air attacks. But nevertheless soldiers blazed away at the Japanese planes with both rifles and machine guns during each of the three air attacks upon Baguio.

During the third air raid I took refuge with my son under a pine tree on the hillside across the street from the People's Bank. At the Baguio branch of the University of the Philippines a company of cadets had two machine guns. They blazed away at the Japanese planes as they flew overhead after the bombing of Camp John Hay. Soldiers patrolling the park near the business center blazed away with their rifles as the Japanese planes flew over the park. I heard the "plop" of bullets as they struck the sidewalk perhaps fifty feet from where we were sitting beneath the pine tree. I thought that we were being machine-gunned by the Japanese planes. But later I learned that the bullets which I heard fall near us were spent machine-gun bullets fired by the cadets at the Japanese planes.

After this air raid orders were issued by the Colonel in command of Camp John Hay to refrain from firing at the Japanese planes because this might cause the Japanese to retaliate by machine-gunning the civilian population of the city.

Meanwhile, the military authorities had commandeered most of the motor trucks in Baguio and had requisitioned dynamite from the mines to be used to mine bridges in Central Luzon in order to retard the anticipated Japanese advance from the north. Experienced miners drawn from the staffs of the mines were placed in charge of this kind of work. Both the Kennon

Road and the Naguilian Road connecting Baguio to the seacoast were also mined. A guard was maintained on each of these roads at the points where mines had been laid. Each evening several truck loads of Filipino soldiers were sent to mine fields on the Naguilian Road to oppose any attempt of the Japanese to come up that road by night. These Filipino soldiers of the Philippine Scouts were in fine spirits as they rode past our house each afternoon. They shouted greetings to us and held up two fingers forming a "V" for victory.

There were nearly 1,000 Japanese residents of Baguio and its vicinity. Most of these were interned two or three days after the outbreak of the war. The men were interned at Camp John Hay in the barracks which had received a direct hit during the bombing of December 8, killing six Filipino soldiers and wounding many more. The Japanese internees were permitted to send some of their number to market each day to purchase food.

Major Speth, the vice mayor of Baguio, was Austrian by birth but was a naturalized citizen of the Philippines. He was a retired major of the United States Army and a veteran of the First World War. He was very assiduous in his attendance upon President Quezon whenever the latter was in Baguio. At the beginning of December President Quezon, who was in very poor health, came to Baguio for a few days rest. When he returned to Manila immediately after the outbreak of the war the vice-mayor accompanied him.

Two or three days later, when I went to the Shamrock Hotel immediately after breakfast, Mike Ryan and Mr. Mills, the manager of the moving picture theaters in Baguio, took me by the arm and led me out to the middle of the street in front of the hotel.

After peering cautiously about to make sure that no one else was within earshot Mike said, "Major Speth came to the Shamrock Hotel last night. He had just returned from Manila and was slightly intoxicated. Murphy was in the bar and Speth told him that General MacArthur does not intend to defend Baguio. Speth said that General MacArthur's plan is to attempt to hold Central Luzon from Clark Field and Cabanatuan southward to Manila. Speth has a letter which he said described MacArthur's plan of defense. He asked Murphy to read it, but Murphy refused."

Murphy was a Spanish-American War veteran who, for many years, had been office manager of the Heald Lumber Company while at the same time making himself wealthy by managing several successful business enterprises of his own.

"So you think the Japanese can take the Philippines?" asked Mike anxiously, after again peering up and down the street to make sure no one else was within earshot.

The Japanese army had already landed in Vigan, north of Baguio, but had not yet begun its advance southward.

"I believe that they can, if they are willing to spend sufficient men and materials in the venture," I replied slowly.

"Yes!" exclaimed Mr. Mills, who was an ex-soldier.

Mike turned and walked slowly back to the Shamrock Bar. Mr. Mills and I followed him. By mutual, but unexpressed, agreement we did not again mention the subject.

But the rumor that General MacArthur did not intend to defend Baguio spread rapidly throughout the city and was carried to the neighborhood mines. That day a mass exodus from Baguio began. Hundreds and thousands of people taking such few personal belongings as they could carry, fled in panic to the lowland plain of Central Luzon where General MacArthur's USAFE forces were deployed. Within three days 15,000 people fled from Baguio and from the neighborhood mines. Several of the mines were forced to suspend operations because most of their miners fled.

Each day, while the exodus from Baguio continued, the Old Timers at the Shamrock Hotel played their card game as usual. The number of patrons visiting the Shamrock Bar doubled, tripled, quadrupled. Ostentatiously they came to slake their thirst. But I noticed that many of them glanced curiously toward the table where the Old Timers were playing. Some of those glances expressed relief. The world has not yet fallen apart. The Old Timers were still playing solo. In other glances there was admiration. The Old Timers were still playing solo in spite of the fact that their world *was* falling apart. A few old men who still played cards in the midst of war comforted a city which was terrified and knew not where to turn for safety.

About a week after the outbreak of war Sergeant O'Brien informed us that Colonel Horan at breakfast that morning had told his officers to prepare to enter an internment camp and had instructed them not to keep any large sum of money on their persons or in their baggage. O'Brien gave Mike 1,800 pesos to be placed for safe-keeping in Mike's safe.

A day or two later Colonel Horan came to the Shamrock Bar in a state of considerable agitation. It so happened that when he entered the bar Mike, High, Jake Albright and I were the only occupants. Colonel Horan came to our table and informed us in a voice which betrayed his emotion that he had been told rumors were circulating to the effect that the morale at Camp John Hay was not as high as it should be. He wished us to know that the morale of his men was splendid and that he and his men would fight to the last ditch. Without another word he turned away and left the bar.

"He has made us and himself a promise, and he will keep it," said High understandingly.

When it became evident about two weeks later that a greatly superior Japanese force was marching upon Baguio, Colonel Horan retired with his men to the mountains. For five months he out-maneuvered and inflicted very annoying losses upon the Japanese who pursued him. On the evening of May 8, just after the surrender of Corregidor, I heard Lieutenant General Wainwright in a radio broadcast order Colonel Horan to surrender.

On about December 15 I accepted an invitation to join a group of civilians in Baguio who proposed to form a volunteer corps of guards to repel airborne Japanese troops. The leader of this group was Doctor Walker, a dentist. The group included, among others, Joe Icard, Tom Highsmith and his father, J.D Highsmith. When Colonel Horan was approached with this proposal he said that he would not approve the organization of such a force unless it was organized and equipped as a regular unit of the United States Army, and since he did not have weapons with which to equip such a force he could not approve its formation.

Baguio has an airport. In order to prevent any attempt by the Japanese to land planes in Baguio sections of large concrete pipe were placed in rows upon the landing field and for the same purpose sections of concrete pipe were also placed in Burnham Park.

A house next door to our house in Baguio was owned by the Honorable Ramon P. Mitra, who represented Baguio in the lower house in Philippine legislature. When he was in Baguio he occupied the upper floor of this house. The lower floor was leased to a Japanese building contractor who was a naturalized citizen of the Philippines and whose two eldest sons were lieutenants in the Philippine Army.

At the beginning of December Mr. Mitra came from Manila to Baguio and proposed that he and I become partners in the building of an air-raid shelter. "War with Japan is very near," he gravely told me. "I must return to Manila immediately. But if you will build an air-raid shelter large enough to accommodate your family and mine I will be glad to pay one-half of the cost."

I suggested that we drive a tunnel into the hill at the back of my house and he agreed to this. The site of the proposed tunnel was public land, well covered with pine timber. Mr. Mitra believed that there would be no difficulty in obtaining from the city engineer a permit to build the tunnel and that permission would be granted to cut down sufficient pine trees for the timbering of the tunnel. Mr. Mitra returned to Manila but I did nothing about the air-raid shelter until after the first bombing of Baguio.

I believe it was on December 10 that I obtained from the city engineer a permit to build the tunnel and to cut, at the site of the tunnel, timber for posts and caps for timbering the tunnel. I purchased a truck load of pine slabs for lagging and contracted the service of three Igorrote boys each about fifteen years old, to cut down the trees and dig the tunnel. They knew nothing about driving a tunnel, so I was compelled to supervise the work and to personally cut and fit the posts and caps. As a result of my previous work as a prospector I had all of the necessary tools and some knowledge of how to drive a tunnel. The work progressed at the rate of about five feet per day and by the December 20 we had driven 40 feet of tunnel. After 20 feet into the steep hillside we made a right-angled turn and drove 20 feet farther.

The Japanese building contractor who lived on the lower floor of Mr. Mitra's house took a great interest in our tunnel. I granted his request for permission to use it as an air-raid shelter for himself and his family. A few days after we began driving our tunnel the Japanese contractor brought a Chinese merchant to see the tunnel. As a result of this visit the Japanese contractor was engaged to drive a similar tunnel as an air-raid shelter for the Chinese merchant.

The work of driving the tunnel kept me away from the Shamrock Hotel during the greater part of each day. Hence I had no firsthand knowledge of an incident which occurred while I was busy on the tunnel. But I was told about it by Mike Ryan and Jake Albright, who were present at the Shamrock Bar when the incident occurred.

It seems that one morning Major Speth, the vice mayor of Baguio, came to the Shamrock for a glass of beer. The Old Timers were, as usual, sitting at their card table and there were several other customers in the barroom.

Major Speth, while standing at the bar to drink his beer, announced that he was going to get a prominent Japanese merchant who was interned in Baguio to accompany him on a visit to the commander of the Japanese force north of Baguio. Major Speth left the Shamrock saying that he was going to look for the Japanese merchant. About half an hour later Major Speth, accompanied by the Japanese merchant, returned to the Shamrock Hotel. They ordered beer and while they were drinking Major Speth ordered the bar-boy to bring several sandwiches and bottles of drinking water which the major had ordered during his earlier visit to the bar. Before leaving the barroom Major Speth shook hands with Mike Ryan, the proprietor of the Shamrock Bar, and with Colonel Van Schaick who happened to be present. Major Speth said that he and the Japanese merchant were going out to visit the commander of the Japanese force north of Baguio. They departed in Major Speth's car.

Immediately after their departure someone at the Shamrock called Camp John Hay by telephone and informed the military authorities of the vice-mayor's departure, his Japanese companion, and his announced destination. As a result, about an hour later, the military authorities arrested the vice-mayor and his Japanese companion when they reached Bauang on the coast of La Union Province about 60 kilometers (40 miles) from Baguio. Both the vice-mayor and his Japanese companion were brought back to Baguio.

According to one rumor, Major Speth was confined at Camp John Hay. According to another rumor, he was confined in his home. At any rate he was not seen in public until after the Japanese occupied the city of Baguio at about the end of December. It is said that he then resumed his duties as vice-mayor for several months under the Japanese military administration.

An investigation of the vice-mayor's conduct was made by the United States military authorities immediately after his arrest. It was rumored that he was exonerated of any disloyal intent, and that his objective was to have Baguio declared an open city. He was bitterly condemned, however, by a large majority if the people in Baguio, both Americans and Filipinos.

Beginning on December 9, there were each day eight to ten air-raid warnings, one or two of which usually occurred after nightfall. When each alarm sounded we hurried out of our house and took refuge near the air-raid tunnel. On each of the three occasions when Baguio was bombed the Japanese planes passed directly over our refuge en route to bomb Camp John Hay. There were many other occasions when Japanese planes appeared but did not bomb Baguio. After we began driving our tunnel into the hill my wife and son spent most of each day with me at the site. My son, who was about nine years old, and several other boys of about the same age, took a great interest in the work of digging the tunnel. They were permitted, much to their delight, to wheel dirt out of the tunnel on a wheelbarrow. At other times they amused themselves by digging miniature tunnels in which they placed their toys. Several times at night, when the sirens sounded, I lifted my sleeping son out of his bed, wrapped a blanket around him, and carried him out to the tunnel. It is cold at night in Baguio and clad as we were only in our night clothes we suffered from the cold. Frequently also we stumbled in the darkness during our hasty flight to the tunnel.

The proprietor of the Shamrock Hotel also operated a beach resort, known as the Long Beach Hotel, at Bauang about 40 miles from Baguio. The manager of this resort was Mr. Cole, an Englishman, who was also in charge of the wharf and warehouse of the Lepanto Consolidated Mining Company at the port of San Fernando, about three miles from the Long Beach Hotel.

A few days after the outbreak of the war Mr. Cole came to Baguio. He informed us that a British merchant ship had made port at San Fernando and that he had brought to Baguio a letter from the captain of the merchant ship to the commander of Camp John Hay. Mr. Cole reported that there were several British warships and merchant ships off the coast of San Fernando. However, this was never confirmed.

There was a regiment of USAFE troops stationed at San Fernando. About ten days after the Japanese landing at Vigan, a USAFE patrol clashed with a Japanese patrol a few miles north of San Fernando. Mr. Cole telephoned that several Japanese soldiers were captured and brought to the Long Beach Hotel.

Mr. Perriam, the superintendent of the Lepanto Consolidated Mining Company's copper mine, located about 60 miles north of Baguio, arrived in Baguio on Friday, December 19. He reported that Japanese patrols had been on the road leading from the coast inland to the town of Cervantes, which it located about 10 miles northeast of Lepanto. He also reported that the bridges had been destroyed between Cervantes and Bontoo and that the old Spanish trail between Cervantes and Lepanto had been blocked by setting off charges of dynamite. This action had been taken to retard the anticipated Japanese advance inland toward Bontoo, the capital of the Mountain Province, and toward Baguio. I was informed by Dave Foster, who also came from Lepanto, that the dynamiting of the old Spanish trail was done by miners sent from Lepanto by the superintendent of the Lepanto Consolidated Mining Company.

Chapter 3

We Flee from Baguio to Manila

On the morning of Sunday, December 21, I went to the Shamrock Hotel as usual to learn the latest news. Mr Cole had telephoned from Bauang that the USAFE military authorities had set fire to the gasoline and crude petroleum storage tanks near the wharf at the port of San Fernando, La Union Province. He said that heavy fighting was in progress between USAFE and Japanese troops a few miles north of San Fernando. An American officer from Camp John Hay had told me that during the preceding night several truck loads of USAFE troops had passed through Baguio en route to Bontoo. He said that the troops had stopped at Camp John Hay for a hot meal.

The fact that the stocks of gasoline and crude petroleum at San Fernando had been set afire by the USAFE authorities convinced me that the USAFE commander doubted his ability to stop the Japanese advance within two days or less. I went home immediately and told the news to my wife. She was greatly alarmed and proposed that we travel to Manila without delay.

We had not driven our car for two weeks because the Mayor of Baguio had requested all car owners to economize in the use of gasoline. When I tried to start the car I found the battery dead. I called Tom Highsmith, who came with his service car and took our car to his shop. A grounded cut out was found to be the cause of the trouble. As no service battery was available, an attempt was made to do a quick job of recharging my battery. It was 11 a.m. when my car was taken to the shop. At 2 p.m. I called for it. The battery was still too weak to start the car. The engine was started by temporarily connecting the starter to a battery taken from another car. I could keep the engine running until we reached a hill where gravity would start the car. Fortunately Baguio is a very hilly city and the road in front of my home had sufficient gradient for us to start the car.

We had to obtain a military pass which would permit us to go through the USAFE lines between Baguio and Manila. We also had to select and load into our car foodstuffs, clothing and a few of our least bulky and most cherished possessions, since it was not probable that we would be able to return until the war was over. It took some time both to obtain the military pass and to load the car. So it was not until about 6.30 p.m. that we pulled up before a service station to fill our tank with gasoline.

The American manager of the filling station reminded us that we would not be permitted to drive at night without covering our head and tail lights.

He very kindly rigged up an emergency covering made from paper wrapping he removed from an automobile tire. This paper cover was fastened over the light with strips of gummed Manila paper commonly used in the wrapping of packages. A small hole about ½ inch in diameter was made through the center of the paper covering each headlight. With this very meager illumination we started for Manila at about 7 p.m. For the first 33 kilometers the road descended 4,000 feet in almost continuous loops and sharp curves. With so little light I was forced to drive very slowly.

We were also very heavily laden. There were six passengers—myself, my wife, my son, and three servants—and about 700 pounds of luggage and foodstuffs, including 50 pounds of wheat flour and 250 pounds of rice. Because the US Army had requisitioned almost all transportation facilities there was likely to be a shortage of foodstuffs in Manila. Such a shortage has already developed in Baguio. The gardener, who had accommodation in the basement of our house, was left behind in charge of the house. With him were his wife and infant son. The three servants who accompanied us—two young girls and a 15-year-old boy—we took only because their relatives lived far from Baguio and they begged not to be left behind. We had to reduce the quantity of foodstuffs carried in order to make room for them.

No military guard was encountered until we reached the lowland plain about 40 kilometers from Baguio. Here we were stopped at the toll gate of a bridge and were required to show our military passes. Most of the sentries were Filipino civilian volunteer guards. I was impressed by the unfailing courtesy which they manifested when stopping us to examine our passes.

When we reached Sison, about 50 kilometers from Baguio, we met a convoy of USAFE troops and artillery files moving north in an attempt to stem the Japanese advance. During the next 100 kilometers we met many such convoys. Each convoy was preceded by an American soldier on a motor cycle who required us to put out our headlights and park our car at the side of the road until the convoy had passed. All the convoys were mechanized. Each truck was provided with very dim blue headlights. It was amazing how fast they travelled with so little light. There was no moon and the sky was overcast with clouds so that there was not even starlight to illuminate the darkness.

From a huge truck opposite our car the American driver called out, "Where are you going?" I replied, "To Manila." He answered, "OK," and his truck passed on without stopping. Sometime later, while our military pass was being examined by a volunteer guard, another truck going north was stopped by the guard and asked if we had come from Baguio. We answered, "Yes." He then inquired where we were going. We answered, "To Manila." He asked if there were many Americans still in Baguio. We answered that most of the American residents of Baguio were still there. He then told us that he and his fellow soldiers were going to Baguio. We asked no questions and he returned to his truck, which started north again.

We were supposed to use only our dimmed lights. But the illumination through the 1/2 inch holes in the paper covering our headlights was so little that I was forced to drive very slowly. Several times I turned the lights on full in order to travel faster. But each time I was ordered to dim my lights by the next guard who stopped us. After the third warning I resigned myself to using only the dimmed lights and travelled on at a snail's pace.

It was one o'clock in the morning and we had been on the road six hours when we reached Tarlac, 130 kilometers from Baguio. In the southern outskirts of the town we were stopped by a USAFE sentry, who told us that he had orders not to permit any civilian car to pass, and must therefore refuse to honor our military pass. My wife asked the name of his commanding officer and where the latter might be found. The sentry replied that his commanding officer was a Filipino major, whose name he gave, and stated that the major could be found at his quarters in Tarlac. I proposed that we park our car at the side of the road and wait for daylight. But at my wife's insistence we returned to Tarlac and got a policeman to guide us to the major's quarters, where we awakened him. He was very courteous and wrote on our military pass a note to his sentry instructing the latter to permit us to pass. Upon our return the sentry warned us that a tank convoy was on its way north and advised us to park our car at the side of the road when we heard it coming.

We proceeded slowly until we reached the Bamban Hotel, located on the site of a sugar factory. We had come 153 kilometers from Baguio and were still 104 kilometers from Manila. It was 3 a.m. and we had been on the road for eight hours. There were several USAFE camps within a few kilometers, both north and south of us, and we were only a few kilometers from Clark Field. Thus we were in the midst of a military zone which was being subjected to almost daily bombing attacks from the Japanese. Nevertheless it was so dark, and driving by our dim lights was so difficult, that I decided to park our car beneath the grove of trees in front of the hotel and wait for dawn. The parking space was about 100 yards from the road and the interlocking branches of the trees completely screened it from the air.

At about 3.30 a.m., we heard the approach of the tank convoy going north. The tanks proceeded in three groups of about 5 or 6 tanks each. Some two kilometers separated the last tank of one group from the first tank of each subsequent group and were spaced around 300 meters apart. In spite of having only dim blue headlights, the tanks travelled at an amazing speed and their rapidly rolling treads made a tremendous noise. We could hear the din of the approaching tanks when they were still half a kilometer distant. The rapidly mounting crescendo of noise reached its peak when the tanks passed our parked car and then rapidly faded away as they sped northward. Before the sound of the first tank had completely faded we could hear the next group approaching. There was a brief period of complete silence after the last tank of one group had passed and before the din of the first tank of the following group could be heard.

At about 5 a.m., about an hour before dawn, we heard two or three USAFE planes from Clark Field flying overhead and caught a glimpse of their wing lights. A few minutes later we heard a single plane approaching from the north. This was apparently a Japanese scouting plane because the USAFE planes from Clark Field returned to meet it. There was a short burst of machine gun fire almost directly above our car. The lone Japanese scout turned tail and fled back north. The planes from Clark Field were apparently content to drive the invader off. They did not pursue it.

At about 5.40 a.m., when the approach of dawn brightened the sky sufficiently for me to see the road without lights, we set out once more for Manila. We passed an almost continuous stream of military trucks and automobiles heading north into the battle zone. About 20 miles north of Manila we found traffic halted by an air-raid alarm. We pulled up behind the last car in the line and hurriedly took refuge among the trees at the roadside. The hum of Japanese planes could be heard faintly from some distance to the east. We could see them flying quite low along a range of hills. The planes soon disappeared in the direction of Manila and the volunteer guards permitted the stream of traffic to proceed. We were halted by similar air raid alarms four or five times before we reached Manila at about 11 a.m.

It had taken us more than five hours to drive the 65 miles from Bamban to Manila. We reached Manila 16 hours after leaving Baguio. The normal driving time from Baguio to Manila was four to five hours.

Chapter 4

Concerning Events in Manila During the Last Ten days of December, 1941

We proceeded at once to the home of my wife's mother in Pasay, a suburb on the southern boundary of Manila. We had received no word from my mother-in-law since the war began and had been worried about her safety. Her home was located only about a mile northeast of Nichol's Field, a military airport which had been subjected to several severe bombings. We had heard that many civilian homes were destroyed in the bombing of Parañaque, a suburban town adjoining Nichol's Field on the western side. We were therefore greatly relieved to find my mother-in-law uninjured and her home intact. There was an air raid alarm about an hour after our arrival. We took refuge in the dugout beneath a mango tree in her next-door neighbor's yard.

We got to work that afternoon digging a trench beneath the banana trees in my mother-in-law's back yard. It was finished within three days. We dug the trench about 4 feet deep, 3 ½ feet wide and 20 feet long. It was roofed with branches from a large tree which had been cut down for firewood in a neighbor's yard. Sheets of galvanized iron were laid on the timbers and the roof was then covered with about two feet of earth. A floor of loose boards covered with buri mats was laid inside the dugout.

There were six or more air raid alarms each day. Late one afternoon, before our dugout was completed, Japanese planes arrived in our vicinity before the siren sounded. We hastily laid down on the concrete ground floor of my mother-in-law's house. From the direction of Nichol's Field we heard the sounds of exploding bombs and of planes coming our way. We could feel the vibration from the exploding bombs. The last bomb struck quite near our house. We heard the rattle of small fragments falling on the corrugated iron roof above us. When the sound of the receding planes could no longer be heard we ventured out into the street to investigate. The last bomb had struck about 300 yards from our house. One house, whose occupants fortunately were absent at the time, had been completely demolished. The adjoining house was almost as badly damaged and two children asleep in the house were injured. An old man sitting at the window of his house across the street was killed by a flying fragment. The injured children had already been taken to the hospital when we arrived on the scene. Apparently the target which the raiders had sought to bomb was an electric sub-station located about 400 yards from the spot where the bomb actually struck. Upon our return to our house, one of our neighbors showed us a small steel bomb splinter which narrowly missed his head and had imbedded itself in the wall of his house as he stood watching the raiding planes.

We had arrived in Manila on the morning of December 22. In spite of the war and in spite of the daily air raid alarms, people were doing their Christmas shopping. We had spent Thanksgiving week-end with my wife's mother during the latter part of November. On the Saturday following Thanksgiving I had purchased in Manila a set of toy military mechanized units for my nine-year-old son. I had ordered this to be delivered on the day before Christmas to my mother-in-law's house, where we planned to spend our Christmas holidays. Fearing that the delivery might not be made, I went to the store and took delivery of the toys on December 23. This was fortunate, because delivery had been suspended, due to the exigencies of the war.

We had brought from Baguio a small pine for a Christmas tree. My wife had thought of this in spite of her fears and the haste of our departure from Baguio! As usual, we set up the tree and decorated it with colored electric lights on the day before Christmas. We were not permitted to light the tree on Christmas Eve, however, because of blackout restrictions.

As usual, on Christmas Eve my son hung his stocking at the front of his bed.

"Will Santa Claus come when there is a war?" he inquired anxiously.

I assured him that Santa Claus would come and his face lit up with happy relief.

"Put me in my bed," he said.

When I had tucked in his mosquito net, he knelt upon his bed and recited that familiar prayer of childhood,

"Now I lay me down to sleep. I pray the Lord my soul to keep. If I should die before I wake, I pray the Lord my soul to take. Amen."

Since we might be bombed out of existence before morning, that simple child's prayer held for me that Christmas Eve an especially solemn significance.

As usual, my son arose at dawn on Christmas morning. He was delighted with the toys and candy which Santa Claus had left for him. The mechanized army set brought forth shouts of satisfaction. I reflected rather sadly, "Was there ever a small boy who did not delight in playing at war?" And yet war at best is such a sorry business. Must men always be destroying one another? Is this one of the basic instincts of human race?

As usual, we had a turkey for our midday Christmas dinner. But we did not have the usual number of guests. In fact, we had only one. Sam Deebel, who had been my intimate friend for almost twenty-eight years, came in his car from Manila. We had also invited an American neighbor and his family who lived next door. But they declined to come because his wife, who was very nervous, feared that the usual midday air-raid would occur during dinner. We sent some of our Christmas dinner to their home, and they ate it there.

An air raid alarm did sound while we were eating, but for once we refused to seek shelter and no bombs were dropped in our vicinity.

As usual, Sam stayed a while after dinner to talk over old times. But he refused to stay for the evening meal. Late in the afternoon he drove back to his apartment. The headlights of his car were not shrouded as required for night driving. I did not see him again until we met in the internment camp late in January.

On December 23, I went to General MacArthur's headquarters at Fort Santiago to volunteer for military forces. I thought that I might be of some service in the engineer's corps because of my previous experience in construction work and mining. Colonel Bonham of the engineering corps was absent and I was requested to return the following morning. When I returned Colonel Bonham referred me to another colonel in the engineering corps. The latter said that they were closing up shop to get ready for action and there was no civilian job available for me. I answered that I was ready to enlist in the army as a private. He then gave me a letter addressed to the colonel in charge of personnel, who had just returned to his quarters. A major seated at the adjoining desk said that he would be back in a few minutes.

While waiting, I watched an American soldier pulling documents from a steel filing cabinet and burning them on the concrete floor of an interior court. Another soldier filled a small trunk with stationery and then placed a typewriter on top of the trunk.

The personnel colonel returned carrying his bed roll, which he placed on the floor. He greeted me kindly and asked what he could do for me. I said that I wished to enlist as a private.

"You and 130,000,000 other Americans!" exclaimed the major seated nearby.

"I can't take you," the colonel replied gravely. "We are taking to Nichol's Field this morning and I don't feel very happy about the situation. The best thing for you to do is to go home and be a good citizen."

"The Japanese are going to make it pretty tough for you for a while," I said as we shook hands in farewell. I did not see him again.

At the entrance to Fort Santiago an American soldier, whom I knew, was on sentry duty. I stopped and talked with him for a few minutes.

"I have been in the Philippines for three years and I was scheduled to go back to the United States next month," he said rather mournfully.

A lieutenant whom I had met in Colonel Bonham's office was waiting for a taxi when I reached the street outside Fort Santiago. He accepted my offer of a lift in my car. I took him to Villamor Hall at the University of the Philippines, where one of the military headquarters was located.

After delivering the lieutenant, I was driving on Taft Avenue when the air raid siren sounded. I pulled up to the curb and got out of my car as required by the air raid regulations. The Japanese planes were already overhead. I hurriedly spread a newspaper upon the ground beneath a hibiscus bush—to prevent my white suit from becoming spoiled—and laid down on the newspaper. This was on the lawn of the legislative building. A moment later a young Filipino took shelter under the same bush. Then came the explosions of the bombs, whose concussions could be felt as brief breaths of air striking our cheeks. Later I learned that the bombs had fallen in the vicinity of the military shops and warehouses in the port area, about a kilometer distant from where we lay. A number of civilian employees of the army were killed and many more were injured. Considerable damage was done to both military and commercial establishments in the port area.

An American friend, who was the civilian engineer in charge of the military power plant in the port area, witnessed this bombing. He lived next door to us in Pasay. Early that evening, Christmas Eve, he came to our house and gave us a first hand account of the bombing. He showed us a fragment from the shell of the bomb, which was about the size of the palm of his hand. It was made of steel, about ½ inch thick. He estimated that this fragment came from a 500-pound bomb. He said that he was lucky. The army laundry had sustained a direct hit with considerable loss of life. He had left the laundry only a few minutes just before the bomb struck.

The news from the fighting fronts during the three days before Christmas was discouraging. On December 22 the Japanese landed a considerable force in La Union Province, north of Manila, where they were reported to have recaptured several towns which they had previously taken. But Japanese control of the air soon forced the USAFE forces to retreat on both the northern and southern fronts. The proposal to withdraw the USAFE forces from Manila and its vicinity and to declare Manila an open city was announced in the daily newspapers in the days leading up to Christmas, and on December 24 it was announced by General MacArthur and President Quezon that the USAFE forces had been withdrawn and that Manila was henceforth declared an open city.

The Japanese command in the Philippines refused, however, to consider Manila an open city. Thus the withdrawal of the USAFE forces merely resulted in an intensification of the bombing of Manila during the last week of December. Furthermore, since the Japanese knew that Manila was not defended, further bombing attacks were concentrated upon the port area which was bombed a second time, upon Fort Santiago, and on the piers and shipping both in the harbor and along the Pasig River.

The Japanese planes usually came in from the south and passed directly over our house in Pasay en route to the waterfront of Manila. A few minutes after the planes passed over we could hear the explosions of the bombs.

On December 27, the Japanese airplanes apparently concentrated their attack upon shipping berthed in the Pasig River, but they missed their targets. Instead they caused great damage to buildings, with about 400 human casualties, in the portion of the old walled city adjacent to the river. Several bombs struck the Intendencia Building (treasury) on the bank of the river. Another bomb partially wrecked the ancient Santo Domingo Church across the street from the Intendencia. A girl's convent school near the Santo Domingo Church was also bombed. The resulting fires completed the havoc.

On December 25, Japanese planes again bombed the Walled City. The printing establishment of the Peoples Press, publishers of the *Philippine Herald* and other daily newspapers, received a direct hit and was completely destroyed by the resulting fire. Because it was Sunday and working people were in their homes, there were very few human casualties. The damage to property, however, was great. This raid, like that of the preceding day, was apparently aimed at ships in the Pasig River, but the bombers missed their target and instead struck the adjacent Walled City.

Unable to obtain crews to take the ships out of the Pasig River and in to Manila Bay, the authorities made frantic efforts to scuttle several of the ships during the night of December 28. The river was so shallow, however, that the superstructures of the sunken ships projected above the surface of the piers.

It was on the morning of December 29 that my wife and I drove down town. I took my wife first to the Wilson Building on Juan Luna Street. There was no parking space nearby, so I waited in the car with the engine running while my wife entered the building to pay the annual premium on my life insurance. While I waited in the car a single Japanese plane flew very low over the Wilson Building. My wife came out of the building and climbed into the car a few moments later. We then drove to a repair shop to pick up a typewriter which I had left for repair. The air-raid alarm sounded while we were in the repair shop. We hurried out of the shop and took refuge in the lobby on the ground floor of the Great Eastern Hotel.

There we met a number of people from Baguio who had left that city subsequent to our departure. From a number of the staff of the Itogon Mine I learned that a group of automobiles carrying staff employees of the Itogon and Suyoc Consolidated Mines had left Baguio for Manila on the afternoon of Tuesday, December 23. They were machine-gunned by Japanese planes near Sison, about 50 kilometers south of Baguio, and a little more than 200 kilometers north of Manila. Fortunately no one was injured. They witnessed several dogfights between USAFE and Japanese planes over Sison. Their party was, they believed, the last to come from Baguio to Manila by car. The Japanese advanced south into Pangasin and closed the Baguio-Manila road on the night of Tuesday, December 23.

Another evacuee told of leaving Baguio about December 24. Since the automobile roads were closed their party hiked out over a mountain trail. Some of the American women and their children were left behind in Baguio because they were not strong enough to hike. The party was three days on the trail before reaching a point on the automobile road near Bamban, Nueva Viscaya Province, from which they were able to come to Manila by autobus. The party included members of the staffs of several of the mines in the vicinity of Baguio.

Joe Icard, a young stock broker from Baguio, told us that he brought his wife and three children from Baguio to Manila in his car on Tuesday, December 23. In the haste of their departure he had neglected to bring his own clothing. He arrived in Manila with no clothes except those on his back. He then went from Manila to Bamban, Nueva Viscaya, by car and attempted to return to Baguio for his clothes by way of the Bamban–Baguio trail. A day's journey out on the trail he met the party of Baguio residents who hiked out over that trail. They told him that Baguio probably would be occupied by the Japanese forces before he could reach there, so he returned with them to Manila. From other sources I learned that Baguio was occupied by the Japanese on December 27.

As soon as the all-clear signal was sounded we left the Great Eastern Hotel and went to a safe-deposit vault, where my wife deposited her watch and diamond rings. We then purchased some groceries and drove back to my mother-in-law's house in Pasay. We put the car, a 1928 Ford, in the garage of the house across the street. There it remained until it was confiscated by the Japanese military authorities a couple of months later. We did not use that car again after the morning of December 29.

Most of the people of Manila were kept in ignorance of the state of affairs at the fighting fronts and of the rapidity with which General MacArthur's forces were being withdrawn from both northern and southern fronts and concentrated on the Bataan Peninsula during the last week of December. This was a military necessity in order to keep such information from reaching the Japanese. A newspaper editor told me later that he knew the true situation but was not permitted to publish it. The communiques from General MacArthur's headquarters announced each day that our troops were being pressed and were retiring slowly, but that our lines were holding.

In the meantime General MacArthur was hurriedly moving supplies, equipment and troops into the Bataan Peninsula by every means of transportation at his disposal. Supplies were conveyed to both Corregidor and Marivelis (Bataan) by water. Supplies were moved to Bataan by truck. Troops retiring to Bataan from the southern front detoured Manila by way of the new circumferential road in order to keep the move as secret as possible and to avoid the congestion of Manila's down-town traffic. These troop movements took place at night. Thus most of Manila's residents were unaware of them at the time they were actually occurring.

My wife was told by a friend that the Japanese had announced by radio that they expected to occupy Manila by January 1,1942. But even as late as December 29 most of the residents of Manila were not aware of how near the Japanese would come to fulfilling that boast.

Nevertheless, as the month of December 1941 drew inexorably to its close, the people of Manila were filled with foreboding, and with resignation. That the Japanese forces would occupy Manila appeared to be inevitable. The only question was how soon the occupation would come.

General MacArthur's daily communiques carefully concealed from the people the actual rate of progress of the Japanese forces toward Manila on both the northern and southern fronts. The communiques seemed to indicate that the USAFE lines, although under terrific pressure, were holding in the vicinity of Lucena, Tayabas, south of Manila. But a truck driver returning from the south brought back the report that the Japanese had already reached Candelaria, some distance north of Lucena, and that no USAFE troops were opposing them. A few hours later the Japanese forces were rumored to have reached San Pablo, only about 100 kilometers south of Manila. This was, I believe, on December 30. On December 31 it was rumored that the Japanese forces had reached Calamba, only about 50 kilometers south of Manila.

All day on the December 31 we heard the explosions of the demolition of Fort William McKinley by the retiring USAFE forces. The sound of similar explosions came from Nichol's Field. Columns of smoke were seen rising from Fort William McKinley and from Nichol's Field. A huge column of intensely black smoke rose from the vicinity of Pandagan indicating that the crude petroleum storage tanks has been fired. The gasoline storage tanks had been fired about a week earlier.

Wholesale mob looting seems to have begun in the port area of Manila on the afternoon of December 31. It was preceded by the opening of the military warehouses and the free distribution of the contents to all persons who could remove the goods from the warehouses. The mob, not content with the free distribution of goods from the military warehouses, began to loot privately owned merchandise which was stored in the port area. The looting of the waterfront continued throughout the night of December 31. Late that night the stock of military cold stores in the government-owned ice plant on the Pasig River was thrown open and the public was invited to help itself to anything which it could carry away. When it became evident that the public could not remove the immense stock of butter before morning, kerosene was sprayed upon the butter and it was set afire.

That same night the USAFE military authorities set fire to the barracks adjoining the government ice plant. Other fires which occurred that night across the river from the military barracks are supposed to have been the work of looters.

On the morning of January 1, 1942, the looting became general throughout the city and its suburbs. Gangs of looters roamed the streets, smashing the window and doors of retail stores and boldly carrying off the merchandise found within. Chinese merchants were the principal, but not the only, victims of the looting. The police, who had been disarmed in preparation for the impending Japanese occupation of the city, made no attempt to prevent the looting. By nightfall the entire stock of mainly Chinese-owned retail stores in the city had been looted.

After I entered the Santo Tomas Internment Camp I became acquainted with the American civilian employee who was in charge of the government-owned cold stores at the government ice plant on the Pasig River. He told me that he and his staff worked until midnight of December 31 loading cold stores aboard boats and trucks for shipment to Bataan and Corregidor. He then opened the doors and invited the public to help itself to the remainder of the stock of cold stores. He said that he gave several truck-loads of cold stores to an American civilian who promised to place them in a warehouse and turn them over to the Red Cross, but he doubted that these supplies had ever reached the Red Cross.

We did not leave the yard of my mother-in-law's house in Pasay during the period that the looting was in progress. But at noon on January 1 our American next-door neighbor who had gone down town that morning, returned and reported that all of the Chinese stores has been looted and that he witnessed the looting of some of them.

Chapter 5

The Japanese Occupy the City of Manila

The Manila daily papers on the morning of January 1 announced that Japanese troops had been seen only a few kilometers both north and south of the city. Emissaries of the Philippine government, headed by Jorge B. Vargas, had made contact with the leaders of the Japanese forces and arrangements were being made for the Japanese forces to enter the city without bloodshed. The formal entry of the Japanese forces, although expected on January 1, did not actually occur until the afternoon of January 2.

I did not witness the entry of the Japanese forces. Obeying the instructions of the local police, we remained at home, about a mile from the route taken by the Japanese troops who entered Manila from the south.

I believe that it was not until the morning of January 3 that we, ourselves, first saw Japanese soldiers. My mother-in-law's home is located near the road leading from Pasay to Fort William McKinley and from the rear windows of her house it was possible to look across a neighbor's lawn to the Pasay-Fort William McKinley Road. On January 3 we saw trucks loaded with Japanese soldiers going towards Fort William McKinley. All through that day we heard the rumble of Japanese military traffic passing on the Pasay-McKinley Road. When we peered cautiously through the screen of banana trees which filled our back yard, we saw military automobiles, buses filled with Japanese soldiers, motor cycles, trucks filled with drums of gasoline, tanks which made a tremendous racket and all the other motorized equipment of an army on the move.

Although our rear boundary was not more than 100 yards from the Pasay-McKinley Road along which Japanese military traffic was continually passing, the narrow parallel street on which our house fronted was not visited by Japanese soldiers until several days after the occupation of Manila. When Japanese soldiers eventually appeared on our street they were evidently off-duty and on a sight-seeing tour. Two or three such Japanese soldiers passed by our house each day thereafter.

As we heard that Americans in Manila were being rounded up and interned by the Japanese military authorities, I was careful to keep out of sight and remained indoors throughout the day. But after nightfall I took my daily walk in the banana grove of our house.

Our next-door neighbor was an American veteran of the Spanish-American War. His wife, like mine, was a Filipina. He was small, wizened and darkly tanned. When he wore his black Spanish beret he looked like a blue-eyed Spaniard. His house was separated from ours by the lot of an elderly Filipino woman who, at the outbreak of the war fled to the home of a relative, leaving her house unoccupied. We had cut holes through the two fences separating our lot from that of our American neighbor, so that we could pass from one house to the other without going into the street. This pathway was well screened from the street by a tall hedge of hibiscus. In the late afternoon my American neighbor usually came to our house for a game of cribbage. Usually, also, he was slightly drunk. I feared that his loud talk would attract the attention of any Japanese soldiers who might happen to be passing. Both he and I were, of course, in hiding. I entertained him in a bedroom at the rear of our house in order to minimize the danger of his voice being heard on the street.

One day my American neighbor went to visit another elderly American who lived on our street about a half mile distant. Upon his return he encountered several Japanese soldiers with whom he exchanged bows of greeting. These soldiers, who appeared to be friendly, walked with him to the gate of his home. The next day two of these same soldiers returned and knocked at my neighbor's gate. He admitted them. Of course, they were without rifles, evidently off-duty and on pleasure bent, curious but friendly. My American neighbor showed them through his house and then provided chairs for them beneath a mango tree on his lawn. He offered them both food and drink, which they refused with signs indicating they feared the food and drink might be poisoned. Members of my neighbor's household were two young girls, nieces of his wife about 16 and 15 years of age, who evidently aroused the interest of the visiting Japanese soldiers.

After this first visit, one or both of these Japanese soldiers, usually accompanied by one or two other Japanese soldiers, visited my American neighbor daily for about a week. They soon lost their fear of poison and partook of the food they were offered. One day they brought my neighbor a kilogram of Irish potatoes, on another day a gallon tin of candies. The tin of candy, we later learned, had been given to them by the Chinese manager of a candy factory located across the street from our house.

On the occasion of their third visit there were only two Japanese soldiers and they were both slightly intoxicated. Their host, my American neighbor, was also, as usual, slightly intoxicated. They sat under the mango tree, their host talking noisily and endeavoring by signs to acquire some knowledge of spoken Japanese.

Suddenly the two Japanese soldiers rose, hurried to the hole in our fence and entered our yard, climbed the stairs and rapped on our front door. When no one appeared in answer to their knock, they came to the kitchen door at the rear of the house, where they were met by my mother-in-law.

One of the Japanese soldiers waved an automatic pistol as he inquired belligerently, "Americanos (Americans)?"

My mother-in-law and a Filipino neighbor, who stood nearby, both answered, "No—Filipinos."

My mother-in-law, who was a small, white-haired woman of more than 75 years, timidly reached out and stroked the cheek of the gun-waving soldier, saying as she did so, "Amigo, amigo (friend, friend)."

The two Japanese soldiers then returned hastily through the hole in the fence to the yard of our American neighbor. After the Japanese soldiers had departed the American neighbor came to our house. He said that the gun-waving soldier, immediately after his hasty departure from our yard, went to our neighbor's kitchen and vigorously washed his face. Apparently he considered the touch of my mother-in-law's hand upon his cheek to be a bad omen. Our neighbor also said that the automatic pistol which the Japanese soldier carried was not loaded and was an American army officer's weapon which the Japanese soldier had probably picked up on some battlefield.

About a week after their first visit these Japanese soldiers informed my American neighbor that they had been ordered to the fighting front in Bataan. They did not come again.

Prior to the outbreak of the war we owned two automobiles—a 1920 Model Ford, registered in my name, and a 1940 Model Lincoln Zephyr, registered in the name of my wife, Socorro R. Warren. The Ford was kept in the garage of my mother-in-law's house in Manila. The Lincoln Zephyr we kept in Baguio. In December, soon after our arrival from Baguio in the Lincoln Zephyr, we removed the Ford to the garage of a neighbor across the street and placed the Lincoln Zephyr in my mother-in-law's garage.

When rumors reached us during the second week of January that the Japanese had already begun to confiscate the automobiles of American internees we removed the wheels and tires from the Lincoln Zephyr and concealed them in the attic of my mother-in-law's house. If the Japanese came to the house and inquired concerning my automobile we would show them the Ford in the neighbor's garage across the street. If they discovered the Lincoln Zephyr and inquired concerning the missing wheels and tires we would say that we had sold the wheels and tires in order to obtain money for food.

On January 14,1942, the commander in chief of the Japanese army issued a proclamation requiring all persons who owned motor vehicles, or who had motor vehicles in their custody, to register all such vehicles at the office of Mr. Jorge B. Vargas, the Filipino head of the Japanese-controlled provisional government of Manila. We decided to register the Lincoln Zephyr in my wife's maiden name, Socorro Rosado. We hoped in this manner to prevent its confiscation by the Japanese. The 1928 Model Ford, which was of little value anyway, we would register in my name. We hoped that if the Japanese were shown the Ford when they came to take my car they would not make a search for any other car.

Chapter 6.

I Am Interned at Santo Tomas

The newspapers of Manila had suspended publication on January 1, 1942. But the *Tribune*, a Filipino-owned daily in English, almost immediately resumed publication under Japanese censorship. In this daily were published the decrees of the Japanese military administration and such news as the Japanese censors permitted.

On about January 12 an order was published instructing all American and other enemy nationals who were not already interned to register with the Japanese military administration on or before January 15. I went to the old Bureau of Printing building, across the street from the City Hall, and registered on January 14. It was the first time I had ventured outside of our yard since December 29. As evidence of my registration, I was given a lithographed Bay View Hotel baggage label. On the back of this label were written the date, "1/14"; my registration number, "3442"; and several Japanese characters, presumably conveying the same information in Japanese. Much to my relief, I was told to go home.

A few days later there was published in the *Tribune* an order instructing all Americans and other enemy nationals who were not already interned to report to the commandant of the University of Santo Tomas Internment Camp for further instructions.

On the morning of January 20 two Filipino young men called at our house in Pasay. They were strangers to us and they did not make clear the exact purpose of their visit. They informed us, however, that they had been members of a regiment of Filipino soldiers which had been disbanded and left in Manila when General MacArthur withdrew his forces to Bataan.

When these young men arrived a tartanilla, a covered two-wheeled horse drawn cart, which we had called was waiting at our gate. Socorro and I were about to depart for the Santo Tomas Internment Camp, where I would report for instruction in accordance with the military order published in the *Tribune*.

When we informed the young men of our destination, they told such tales of Americans being maltreated in the internment camp that my wife was frightened and begged me to delay reporting until the last day specified in the order, which was three days hence. I could see no good reason for delay, however. Among other tales, the young men told us that two American women had died at Santo Tomas the preceding day.

Before going to Santo Tomas, we went to the office of Jorge B. Vargas at Malecanan, where my wife sought to register her automobile, as required by an order of the Japanese military administration. There was a huge crowd of people waiting to register their automobiles. After waiting for some time, we learned that the supply of blank forms for registration had been exhausted and were told to return the next day.

While waiting at Malecanan, we met a prominent Filipino of our acquaintance, who said that he had been taking food to several of the American internees at Santo Tomas. He told us that persons who brought food to the internees were being assaulted by the Japanese guards. He, himself, had some difficulty when delivering food on his last visit. This information reinforced my wife's anxiety. Again, she begged me to go home and wait a day or two before reporting.

But still I could see nothing to be gained by delay. In the end I would have to report and it might as well be now. So we went to Santo Tomas, arriving at the gate shortly after midday. There I was told by the Japanese officer of the guard to go home, get my clothes, and report for internment on the following day, January 21.

When we returned to our home, my wife's mother told me that a Filipino soldier had come from Bataan to visit his parents, who were our near neighbors. He had arrived by boat the preceding night, accompanied by an officer. He was returning to Bataan that night and was willing, my mother-in-law said, to take me with him.

I replied that I was not a soldier and did not have any military training. I had already tried twice to join the army and had been rejected. I felt that, instead of being a help to the USAFE forces in Bataan, I would only be a burden upon them and another mouth to feed where food was sure to be scarce. It was better for all concerned that I enter the internment camp.

This Filipino soldier who offered to take me to Bataan was, I presume, one of the USAFE spies who frequently entered Manila during the siege of Bataan. In a futile effort to stop this traffic, the Japanese military administration had issued a decree prohibiting the navigation of boats upon Manila Bay after nightfall. Heavy penalties were imposed for violation of this decree.

On the morning of January 21, I loaded my suitcase, bed-roll, and a basket of food into a *tartanilla* and, accompanied by my wife, set out for Santo Tomas. I kissed my nine-year-old son goodbye at our gate.

"When are you coming back, daddy?" he asked.

"When the war is over." I replied.

At the gate of Santo Tomas I inquired of the Japanese interpreter whether or not I would be provided with food in the internment camp. He replied that the Japanese army did not provide food for the internees but that they were permitted to purchase food and have it delivered to them at the camp.

Then he added contemptuously, "If you are poor the Red Cross will feed you."

I kissed my wife goodbye at the gate of Santo Tomas and followed the cart bearing my baggage along the driveway leading to the main building of the university. In the lobby of this building there were several Japanese officers and a civilian Japanese interpreter, who recorded my name in their list of internees. They also carefully inspected my baggage to make certain that I was not bringing in any deadly weapon or intoxicating liquor. This done, no one paid any further attention to me. I waited in the lobby for several hours, during which period I watched a steady stream of new arrivals coming into the camp. I was told later that more than 200 arrived that day and that there were already more than 4,000 in the camp.

About the middle of the afternoon, a friend, who had been a resident of the camp for about two weeks, saw me standing in the lobby. He told me that the camp was, to a very large extent, governed by the internees themselves. He took me to an office manned by internees, where I was registered and told to return at 4 p.m. to be assigned sleeping quarters and to receive a temporary meal ticket which would entitle me to dinner at 4.30 p.m. that afternoon and breakfast at 5 a.m. the following morning.

Together with some 50 other new arrivals, I was assigned sleeping quarters in the gymnasium. This was a large room with interior balconies around its four sides. On two sides, beneath the balconies, were "bleacher seats" consisting of tiers of two-inch by twelve-inch planks rising from the floor in stair like succession, much like the familiar bleachers of baseball parks. Bedding was prepared upon these bleachers, and I wondered how the occupants were able to sleep without rolling off the 12-inch wide planks.

More than 500 persons were already quartered in the gymnasium. The place was so crowded that I wondered where space could be found for the new arrivals to spread their beds. I reported to the "monitor" of the gymnasium and was told to deposit my baggage on the porch until a place for me to sleep could be found.

It was by this time 5 o'clock in the afternoon and half an hour past the dinner time. The friend who had assisted me to find quarters and to secure a temporary meal ticket took me to the building which served as the dining room. Here we took our places at the end of a long line of people who were awaiting their turn to enter the dining room. After standing in line for perhaps half an hour we were admitted to another dining room. The dinner consisted of a very generous helping of corned beef, a small quantity of green string beans and one piece of *pan de sal* (salt-risen bread) about one-half the size of a fist. A second piece of *pan de sal* was given to each person who asked for it. A second helping of corned beef was also available if one asked for it. The quantity of food was sufficient but more than one-half of the total weight of the rations consisted of corned beef. I heard one of the cooks say that he alone had opened more than 500 tins (12 ounces each) of corned beef for that one meal, and I was told that about 2,000 persons were fed. I wondered how long the supply of canned meat would last. It seemed to me that a less expensive, and better balanced, ration could be provided by serving twice as much bread and only one-half as much meat. I was told, however, that the kitchen had been in operation only a few days and that arrangements for the purchase and delivery of foodstuffs had not yet been completed. The kitchen was being operated by the internees themselves and the food was provided by the Red Cross. It was intended to feed only those internees who were unable to provide their own food. At this time only about half the internees were eating at the camp kitchen.

The rest of the internees had their food sent in to them by friends or servants from outside of the camp. I observed dozens of little cooking fires where coffee or tea was being prepared. Fuel was scarce and some of the furniture from the gymnasium was being broken up and used for fuel, even then.

From 3 to 4 o'clock in the afternoon was the hour for receiving food, laundry and other supplies from outside the camp. Just inside the gate was a row of tables. Those bringing supplies to the internees formed a line and in turn deposited their packages on the tables where they were opened and inspected by Japanese guards. The internees waited in a line some 50 feet from the tables. Four or five internees assigned to the duty picked up each package after it was inspected and called out the name of the internee to whom it was addressed. If the addressee did not immediately present himself, the package was deposited upon the ground to await delivery. Packages not collected at the expiration of the hour fixed for delivery were taken to the "lost and found" office and a list of the addressees was posted on the bulletin board. There were, I was told, some unscrupulous internees who waited in line and claimed packages addressed to internees who failed to present themselves. So it was best to be present in the line and claim one's package at the time it arrived.

It was 7 p.m. before a place was found for me to bed down on the floor of the gymnasium. Not without some grumbling, four internees were required by the "monitor", himself an internee, to move their beds closer together in order to provide sufficient space for me to spread my mattress upon the floor. We were terribly crowded. More than 550 men slept in the gymnasium that night. Two nights later 700 men slept in the gymnasium.

The crowding was almost equally great in the main building. I visited a room, perhaps 20 by 35 feet, in which 29 men were quartered. A few of them had cots or narrow beds, but most of them slept on mattresses and blankets spread on tables and desks which had been shoved against the walls of the room.

The floor of the gymnasium was divided into sections and a section monitor was in charge of each section. The section monitor had a list of the men in his section and they were required to report to him each evening for roll-call at 7 p.m.

Four internees were assigned to night guard duty at the gymnasium. They slept in a small porch, apart from the rest of the internees, and took turns as night guard. A monitor was also on duty all night at the entrance to the gymnasium. I was told that a Japanese guard visited the night monitor once or twice each night but did not enter the gymnasium.

There was a locker room with shower stands and toilets at one end of the gymnasium. The half dozen showers were sufficient. But there were only two toilets for the more than 500 men quartered there. Each morning there was a long line of men waiting to enter the toilets. In order to relieve this distressing congestion, the internees had obtained the necessary bowls and were setting up four additional toilets in an enclosure at one side of the gymnasium. In this enclosure a long trough provided running water for washing dishes and clothing had already been set up. In one corner of this enclosure, coffee for 200–300 men was made over an open fire. This coffee was supplied gratis by the internee who made and distributed it. Any one who desired it was welcome to bring his cup and get a free cup of coffee each morning.

The things which made the most vivid impression upon me during my first 4 hours in the internment camp were: (1) the terrible crowding of so many people into such limited sleeping quarters; (2) the apparent cheerfulness of the great majority of the internees; (3) the deep suspicion with which some of the internees regarded their fellow internees; and (4) the wild and absolutely baseless rumors concerning the arrival of military aid for the Philippines which were passed eagerly from one internee to another.

Groups of internees sat beneath the shade of trees on the camp. Laughter and the hum of cheerful conversation could be heard on every hand. A softball game was in progress almost constantly. Food was being prepared and eaten in the open air. Children were laughing and shouting and scampering about. The internment camp seemed at first glance to be a picnic ground.

The only newspaper accessible to the internees was the *Manila Daily Tribune*, a four-page tabloid sheet published under the direction of the Japanese propaganda corps. Such war news as the *Tribune* contained was highly favorable to Japan and its allies. The internees of course regarded this source of war news as extremely unreliable. In order to satisfy their craving for information as to the progress of the war, they listened avidly to the wild rumors which continually circulated throughout the camp. The internees were as credulous in accepting rumors of allied successes as they were quick to reject the *Tribune's* claims of Japanese and Axis victories. Everyone longed so desperately for U.S and Allied success. I was told that 20,000 American Negro troops had landed at Appari in Northern Luzon and were marching southward, driving the Japanese before them. I was told that a convoy of 80 U.S. transports had arrived at Atimonan in Tayabas Province south of Manila, and that 80,000 U.S. troops had landed and were marching north to Manila. I was told that a convoy of U.S. transports had reached Bataan and had successfully unloaded troops and munitions to reinforce General MacArthur's besieged army. The report of the landing at Atimonan was given in considerable detail. A Filipino truck driver had been sent to Atimonan to get a load of merchandise. In the outskirts of the town he had been stopped by American sentries and told to return the way he had come. He had looked out over the sea and had seen a large number of U.S transports anchored off the coast of Atimonan. Needless to say, there was not the slightest grain of truth in this yarn.

These rumors were not confined to the internment camp. They circulated throughout the city of Manila and were accepted as eagerly and credulously by the Filipino population as by the internees. The rumors circulated from mouth to mouth in the public markets under the very noses of Japanese guards.

Apparently one source of these wild rumors of United States aid reaching the Philippines was a group of Filipino young men who claimed to have been members of two regiments of General MacArthur when he withdrew his forces to the Bataan Peninsula. These young men circulated throughout the city and frequently hinted that they constituted a volunteer secret service for General MacArthur.

Sometimes I wondered if fictitious rumors of United States aid reaching the Philippines were started by the Japanese themselves, for the devastating effect which it was hoped the rumors would have upon Filipino morale when subsequent events proved the rumors were false.

Scarcely less amazing than the rumors of the United States aid reaching the Philippines were the rumors of internees acting as Japanese spies. One of the internees quartered in my section of the gymnasium warned me that some of the internees were spies for the Japanese. "You would not believe what they are doing," he said. He then informed me that several guns had been found that day hidden among the weeds at the back of the gymnasium and that one gun had been found fastened beneath a truck which was parked behind the gymnasium. A group of internees had been cleaning the yard that morning and it was suspected that one of these internees had informed the Japanese guards in the hope of winning favor with the Japanese. The truck beneath which a gun had been found was said to belong to the Marcman Trading Corporation. The following morning a Japanese from the Commandant's office called at the gymnasium and inquired if a member of the staff of Marcman, whose name he gave, was quartered in the gymnasium and said that this person was requested to report to the Commandant's office. The person requested was not in the gymnasium. We wondered if this visit of a member of the Commandant's staff was in connection with the rumored finding of a gun beneath one of Marcman's trucks.

One effect of these rumors of internees acting as spies for the Japanese was that many internees regarded each other with suspicion. Apparently, all new arrivals were regarded with suspicion until they were vouched for by internees whose good standing in the camp was already established. I noticed several internees eyeing me with apparent suspicion.

The University of Santo Tomas is located on a nearly square campus whose area is perhaps 24 hectares (about 60 acres). There are ten buildings on the campus, but not all of them were being used for the process of the internment camp. One large two-story concrete building was the home of the Dominican Fathers who had served as professors in the university. The Fathers continued to occupy the building. Most of them were Spaniards and were not, therefore, subject to internment. The two-story concrete education building was at that time (January 1942) occupied by a group of Catholic nuns whose own home had been occupied by the Japanese forces. A one-story concrete building in one corner of the campus, which housed the University of Santo Tomas Press, was also not occupied by the internment camp. The operation of the press had been suspended and the building had been sealed by the Japanese military authorities. This left seven buildings which were occupied by the internment camp. These consisted of the large four-story concrete main building, in which were located the offices and quarters of the Japanese commandant and his staff, the offices of the internee-manned administration of the camp, and dormitories for both male and female adults and for girls 12 years of age and older; the concrete gymnasium, which housed male adults and boys 12 years of age and older; a one-story wood building in which children and their mothers were quartered; a one-story wood building which served as a hospital; a one-story concrete building which served as kitchen and dining room of the newly opened mess operated by the Red Cross and a small concrete building occupied by the Japanese guards. There was also a long, one-storey, wood building near the rear gate of the campus, which subsequently served as a warehouse for foodstuffs and other supplies used by the camp. But I do not recall whether or not it was occupied by the camp as early as January 1942.

The Japanese Commandant's office occupied a room on the ground floor of the main building. Two other rooms, adjoining the Commandant's office, were occupied as quarters by the Commandant and his staff. A small concrete building at the main gateway into the campus provided quarters for the Japanese guards stationed at the gate. A driveway, perhaps 500 feet in length, led from the gate to the main building. The entire campus was surrounded by a fence and the only entrance was the gate in front of the main building.

I was surprised upon my arrival to see so few Japanese about the internment camp. There was a guard of two Japanese soldiers and a Japanese civilian interpreter at the gate. In the lobby were two Japanese officers and a Japanese civilian interpreter to register the incoming internees and inspect their baggage. I was also told that the Japanese Assistant Commandant, and two or three Japanese clerks also occupied the Commandant's office. But I had no occasion upon my arrival to enter the Commandant's office and hence did not see the Commandant or members of his staff. I was also told that a Japanese guard made the round of the camp once or twice each night and that he called at the desk of the internee night monitor of the gymnasium but did not enter the building. The guards stationed at the gate to the campus appeared to be more concerned with keeping those who were not interned out of the camp than with keeping internees in.

This apparent laxity on the part of the Japanese was however merely evidence of their astuteness. They had announced in the daily newspaper, the *Tribune,* that all enemy nationals who failed to present themselves for internment before a specified date in January 1942, would be severely punished in accordance with Japanese military laws. And they shrewdly reasoned that, once interned, the internees were not likely to seek to escape as long as they were reasonably well cared for.

With the exception of registering internees and inspecting their baggage, issuing passes to those internees who for some reason were permitted to leave the camp, and inspection of packages sent to internees from outside the camp, the Commandant and his staff exercised no direct control over the great majority of the internees.

I was told that early in January 1942, shortly after the first group of internees arrived at the camp when they were lined up for inspection, a Japanese officer asked if any one of the internees was willing to represent the group. A man who said his name was Earl Carrol stepped forward and stated his willingness to represent the internees. No other internee volunteered for this job. The Japanese officer therefore made Mr. Carrol the representative of this first group of internees in their relations with the Commandant.

A central committee of five internees, with Mr. Carrol as chairman, was soon formed to represent the rapidly increasing number of internees. Exactly how this first central committee was chosen, I was unable to learn. Some of the internees said that Mr. Carrol chose them. Under the direction of this central committee, the internees were rapidly organized into a self-governing community. A monitor was placed in charge of each room which served as sleeping quarters. Each monitor was required to keep a roll of the internees quartered in his room, to check them into their quarters each evening, to see that the internees kept their room clean and took turns throughout the day as room guards. Each night they assigned sleeping space to new arrivals, and in general represented the internees of his group in their relations with the central committee.

The gymnasium, where more than 500 internees were quartered in a single room, was divided into sections of 20 to 30 internees each with a section monitor. Under him were several assistant monitors who took turns at this head monitor's desk.

The monitors were required to report daily to the central committee on the condition of their respective groups of internees. A corps of internee police under the direction of the central committee was charged with keeping the camp clean. A mess staff, composed of internees, cooked and served meals at the Red Cross mess operated for those internees who did not provide their own food. The internees' hospital was directed by an internee doctor and for the most part staffed by internees, although a few Filipino Red Cross workers were assigned to the hospital. Internee dentists provided a dental service. Another group of internees was placed in charge of the children in the children's quarters. A corps of carpenters and mechanics were in charge of installing additional plumbing and other construction work needed in order to make the camp more habitable. A central office, manned entirely by internees, looked after the registration and assignment to quarters of incoming internees and coordinated the activities of the various corps of workers. The central committee of internees maintained a liaison between the internees and the Commandant's office.

Every internee who was physically able was expected to do his share of the work of the camp. For most of the internees this meant not more than two hours of work each day. During my second day at the camp the monitor of the gymnasium called for two volunteers to work as orderlies at the hospital. There were half a dozen volunteers, including myself. The first two volunteers were chosen.

I heard considerable grumbling among the internees to the effect that the members of the central committee and others holding the more important administrative positions in the camp were self-appointed. I was told that elections had been held to choose the room monitors but that the other internee officials of the camp had not been elected. Later this grumbling resulted in the holding of new elections of room monitors, who, in turn, elected a new central committee. A change was thus effected in the membership of the central committee, although Mr. Carrol remained its head. I inferred that most of the grumbling had started at the camp after the central administrative organization had been set up and consequently had no part in the choice of the organization. Nevertheless, it seemed to me that the organization of the camp, as it existed when I arrived, was functioning quite efficiently, and that the internees, including the grumblers, were cooperating very efficiently to improve the conditions in the rapidly growing camp.

I had been suffering from hemorrhoids for several years. On the day of my arrival at Santo Tomas I had a hemorrhage which caused a large blood stain on the seat of my white trousers which I did not discover until I took off my clothes in the evening. Another hemorrhage occurred during the morning of the following day. I inquired of the head monitor at the gymnasium where I might find a doctor. He directed me to Dr. Fletcher, who was quartered in the gymnasium. Dr. Fletcher sent me with a note to the camp hospital. After I had been examined at the camp hospital I was told that, because the camp hospital was overcrowded, a recommendation would be made to the Commandant that I be sent for treatment to a Red Cross hospital located outside of the camp. Apparently securing the Commandant's approval for the transfer of patients to hospitals outside of the camp was largely a routine procedure. I was ordered to be ready to leave the camp at 5 am the following morning.

That afternoon, at 4 p.m., I went to the package-receiving line near the gate, where I learned that my wife had sent to me a narrow folding steel bed and several packages of food. With the help of an internee, I placed the food on the bed and then balanced the bed upon my head, in the oriental fashion. In this manner I carried my bed without further assistance to my quarters in the gymnasium nearly a quarter of a mile distant. I was rather exhausted upon my arrival.

At the gymnasium my monitor told me that my permanent meal ticket was ready for me. I said that I did not need a meal ticket because my wife had sent me ample food. But, at the monitors suggestion, I took the meal ticket for future use in case of need.

To obtain breakfast that morning I had used my temporary meal ticket. The breakfast consisted of an ample portion of boiled cracked wheat porridge with evaporated milk and sugar, a piece of *pan de sal*, and a cup of coffee with milk and sugar. I took a half dozen of my own bananas to the table and distributed all but one to my immediate neighbors.

The preceding afternoon, while waiting in line for dinner, I had encountered the vice president of one of Manila's larger mercantile enterprises. He was acting as a guard at one of the entrances to the dining room. He said that his wife and an unmarried daughter were also in the camp, that the entire stock of goods of his firm had been confiscated by the Japanese military authorities and that he had lost practically everything he owned. Then rather plaintively he said, "Right now I would give almost anything for a banana." "I think I can fix you up," I replied. Then I took him to the lobby of the main building, where my baggage was still deposited, and gave him a bunch of about a dozen bananas, which I took from my basket of food. He was very grateful, saying that he and his family ate at the Red Cross mess, where no fruit was served.

For lunch and dinner on my second day in camp, and for breakfast on the third day, the food which I had brought and additional food which my wife sent on the afternoon of the second day, was more than sufficient, so I did not need to use my permanent meal ticket.

On the morning of January 23, my third day in camp, I remained at the gymnasium awaiting a summons from the hospital. While waiting I joined three other internees in a four-hand game of pinochle. While we were playing, an orderly came from the hospital with a note, signed by the director of the hospital, which instructed me to report with my baggage at the hospital "for immediate release." I showed the note to my companions but told them that, as I understood it, I was not being released from internment but merely being sent to a hospital outside of the camp. They were filled with envy. One of the kibitzers took over my hand in a pinochle game.

I immediately carried my heavy suitcase to the camp hospital. There I was told that the ambulance was already waiting and that someone was required to help me carry the rest of my baggage to the camp hospital. The remainder of my baggage consisted of two baskets of food, an iron bed, and a mattress, pillows and blankets. Since one of the pinochle players was the secretary of a fraternal order of which I had been a member for ten years, I requested the pinochle players to assist me in carrying the rest of my baggage to the camp hospital. They refused. One of them impudently suggested that the Japanese officers stationed in the lobby of the main building would provide me with men to carry my baggage if I requested them to do so.

I then went to the head monitor of the gymnasium. He called for volunteers. Two men whom I had never before met stepped forward. Both of them were elderly men. They carried my bed and bed-roll while I carried the two baskets of food.

Upon our arrival at the hospital, the director of the hospital, himself an internee, said that there was no room in the ambulance for this additional baggage. But I was eventually permitted to load my bed and bed-roll into the ambulance. There was still ample space for the two baskets of food. Nevertheless, I was ordered to leave the food behind. One of the hospital orderlies, at my request, agreed to deliver the two baskets of food to a friend of mine, whose name and room number I wrote on the tags attached to the baskets.

On my unused meal ticket I wrote a note requesting my friend, Sam Deebel, to return the baskets to my wife with a note telling her that I had been transferred to Red Cross Hospital No. 8, located at the Ateneo University. The baskets had to pass inspection at the gate and the sending of any note, except a list of food needed or laundry being sent out, was prohibited. Sam had already told me how he succeeded in getting notes past the sentries. So I left that to his ingenuity.

Chapter 7,

I Am Interned at the Red Cross Hospital in the Ateneo University

I climbed into the ambulance. There were three other passengers. Two were destined for Saint Luke's Hospital and one, like myself, was being sent to Red Cross Hospital No. 8, which was located within the Ateneo University. Each of us was given a pass written in Japanese which we were instructed to be very careful not to lose. My pass had my name and "Red Cross Hospital No. 8" written in English in one corner. I was informed after my arrival at the hospital that my pass authorized my internment in the hospital for an indefinite period, there being no specified date on which the pass would expire.

Upon our arrival at the Ateneo University we exhibited our passes to the Japanese military guards stationed at the gate and were permitted to enter. A Filipino ambulance attendant helped us to carry our belongings into the hospital and then bid us good-bye with a sarcastic, "I wish you luck." I wondered if we had merely jumped out of the frying pan into the fire.

The Filipino doctor in charge of Red Cross Hospital No. 8, when he came to examine my companion and myself, indicated by his manner that he did not believe either of us was sick enough to justify hospitalization.

"There is really nothing the matter with you, but we are glad to have you hide and you are welcome to stay if you wish," he told my companion at the conclusion of his examination.

In my case the doctor was slightly less harsh. I had come with a request from the director of the camp hospital that I be operated on for the removal of hemorrhoids if the director of the Red Cross hospital thought it advisable. The doctor assured me that he could cure the hemorrhoids with an operation but that he would decide later when to perform it. In the meantime I was welcome to remain at the hospital if I so desired.

"Are you in a position to supply a part of your own food?" He asked me. I assured him that my wife would bring food to me as soon as she learned where I was. He said that the Red Cross would notify her of my whereabouts.

I learned later that during the last ten days of January 1942, additional internees were arriving at Santo Tomas at the rate of 100 to 200 per day, and sleeping quarters were already systematically released to outside hospitals in order to relieve the terrible congestion at Santo Tomas. This was the reason for the dubious manner in which the doctor received us at the Ateneo Hospital.

Red Cross Hospital No. 8 was established as an emergency hospital for the care of victims of bombing raids shortly after the outbreak of the war in December 1941. All schools had been closed by order of President Quezon on December 8. This released the school buildings for use as hospitals and for other war purposes.

The hospital occupied six classrooms on the ground floor of the east wing of the main building of the Ateneo University. These rooms opened on to a veranda facing a square courtyard at the rear of the building. The courtyard, paved with concrete and shaded by four huge acacia trees, was located in the angle formed by two wings of the building. It was bounded by the gymnasium on the side opposite the hospital and by the observatory on the remaining side. Access to the hospital was via a hallway through the adjoining wing to the veranda of an interior court. A lobby, which constituted the main entrance to the building was three stories in height. It was set back from the street by about fifty feet. The intervening space was occupied by a lawn. Windows of the wing occupied by the hospital opened on to the narrow lawn between the building and the street. Bordering the lawn next to the street was an iron grill fence backed by a tall hedge of hibiscus bushes, which screened the lawn from the street.

The campus itself occupied a square area of about six hectares (15 acres). It was bounded on three sides by streets. The fourth side adjoined the campus of the University of the Philippines. The entire campus was surrounded by a fence. Except immediately in front of the main building, this fence was a stone wall about eight feet high. At the rear of the main building were about a dozen smaller buildings and an athletics field. Among the smaller buildings were the afore mentioned observatory, the auditorium, the library and an industrial chemistry laboratory.

Almost directly across the street from the main building of the Ateneo was one of the buildings of the University of the Philippines. It was occupied by Japanese soldiers. Sentries stood in front of it day and night. From its window sills dangled clothing which Japanese soldiers had hung out to dry. Occasionally a Japanese soldier leaned out of a window and gazed idly across the street at the Ateneo.

When I arrived at the Ateneo Hospital three wards were in use—a men's ward, a women's ward and an isolation ward. For a lower garment the men wore pajamas which they, themselves, provided. Later some of the male patients were provided with pajamas furnished by the hospital. But there were never enough hospital pajamas to supply all the male patients. The women were permitted to wear dresses or pajamas which they, themselves, provided. On our feet most of us wore slippers, which we provided. Shoes were permitted, however.

Those patients who were able to walk about had free access to the veranda and to the courtyard upon which the veranda opened. This court was about 140 feet square.

We were permitted to draw books from the Ateneo University Library, which was located about 100 yards from the hospital. We were required, however, to secure permission from the doctor in charge of the hospital before going to the library. We were also permitted to attend religious services in the Ateneo Chapel, located in another wing of the main building, but we had to obtain permission from the chief doctor each time we attended. Having first obtained permission, we could also visit other parts of the campus. In general, we were required to obtain special permission to visit any part of the campus, except the court upon which the hospital faced.

The lights were turned on in the wards at 6.30 a.m., Tokyo time (5.30 a.m., standard time). Breakfast was at 7.00 a.m. We were required to remain in the ward until after the daily examination by the doctor, which occurred between 9.00 a.m. and 10.00 a.m. We were required to remain in our beds and to observe absolute quiet in the ward during the siesta period from 12.30 to 2.30 p.m. We were also required to be in bed when the lights were turned out at 9.00 p.m.

Chapter 8

Concerning Some of the Patients in the Men's Ward

When I arrived at the Ateneo Hospital five of the thirteen beds in the men's ward were unoccupied. Within three days internees arriving from Santo Tomas were assigned to all of the vacant beds. Soon the number of beds in the men's ward was increased to 18. It was seldom that more than one of the 18 beds was unoccupied. As rapidly as patients were discharged from the men's ward other patients, most of whom were internees, were admitted.

The Ateneo Red Cross Hospital was not exclusively a hospital for internees although internees always constituted the majority of its patients. The total number of patients was usually about 35. Of these about 30 were internees.

When Mr. Koontze and I arrived on January 24 there were already in the men's wards eight patients who had preceded us. Six of these were internees and two were non-internees. Of the six internees, four were Spanish-American War veterans over 60 years of age who were released to their homes within a week of my arrival.

One of the Spanish-American War veterans, whom I will call Mr. Smith, was paralyzed in both legs. He had a Filipino servant whom he called Pio who was expected to attend him at night. Pio, however, was often sleep when he was needed. Mr. Smith was a rather cantankerous individual who never allowed a day to pass without telling Pio what a worthless servant he was. One night we were awakened by Mr. Smith's frantic calls for his servant. "Pio, Pio, bring the urinal!," shouts Mr. Smith. 'Pio, Pio, you worthless servant, are you asleep again? Pio, Pio, bring the urinal!. Pio, Pio, don't you hear me? Pio, Pio—too late! Damn your worthless hide! I've pissed in the bed!" A few days later Mr. Smith was released. His son came and took him home.

Another of the internees who preceded me at the Ateneo Hospital was Mr. A., an American who was over 87 years of age. He was very feeble and it was evident that he had not long to live. The end came one night about ten days after my arrival. At about 10 p.m. Mr. A. awoke and called for the nurse. She came to his bedside and realized at once that he was dying. "Shall I call the priest?" said the nurse. "That's all I'm waiting for," answered Mr. A. clearly. No one was permitted to die in our ward. Four attendants were called. They carried Mr. A in his bed to a room in the isolation ward. A Jesuit priest was called in and after he had administered the last sacrament Mr. A. quietly relaxed and died. I was informed that Mr. A., during the greater part of his long life, had not been a very admirable person but he died a good Catholic.

Mr. Sieman was the only young man among the six internees in the men's ward when I arrived. He was about 30 years of age and was born in the Philippines of Czechoslovakian parents. His father had become a naturalized citizen. He was an attorney and for several years prior to the Japanese occupation of Manila had been employed in the Manila office of the United States Bureau. He had a young Filipino wife and two children, the eldest about 6 years of age. Mr. Sieman was an alumnus of the Ateneo University and one of his former classmates and intimate friend was Father Lim, a young Filipino Jesuit priest. Father Lim came daily to visit Mr. Sieman. The wife and children of Mr. Sieman also came almost daily to visit him.

One morning Mr. Sieman removed his hospital gown and pajamas and put on his clothes.

"Where are you going?" we inquired.

"I am going to be married this morning," he replied.

We gasped and said, "But you already have a wife!"

He smiled and answered, "She is the woman whom I shall marry this morning. Seven years ago we were married by a Justice of the Peace. Now I have become a good Catholic. This morning in the Ateneo Chapel my wife and I are to be married again by a Jesuit priest. For seven years my wife has been begging me for a Catholic marriage. Now she is to have her wish."

He did not invite us to attend the wedding, but after the wedding he brought his wife to our ward. Her eyes were shining with happiness.

Mr. Sieman was suffering from an ulcer of the stomach and he required a special diet which the hospital could not supply. About the middle of February he was released from the hospital to be interned in his home.

One of the two non-internee patients in the ward when I arrived was a French-African negro who had been wounded in the arm by a bomb splinter. He was a member of the crew of a ship which had been bombed and sunk in Manila Bay during the last week of December 1941. He spoke French, which none of us understood. Two French-African Negroes, who were also members of his crew, often came to visit him. The long gash in his arm had become infected and was very slow in healing. He was released late February after being in the hospital for about two months.

The other non-internee patient, whom I found in the ward when I arrived, was Mr. Ramon, a young Filipino, not more than 20 years of age. He had been a soldier with the USAFE force in Tayabas, south of Manila. During the heavy fighting which occurred when the Japanese effected their landing at Antimonan, a machine-gun bullet had shattered the bone of his right arm just below the shoulder. He was brought to the hospital in

December before the Japanese occupation of Manila. The fact that he was a soldier was carefully concealed from the Japanese military authorities. His hospital chart stated that he was a victim of the bombing of Manila during the last week of December. His arm was still in a cast when I arrived on January 24. Some weeks later, when the cast was removed, it was found that the shattered bone had knitted perfectly. He was permitted, however, to remain in the hospital until May 27, long after his arm had healed. His home was in Zambales Province and the road to his province passed through both the Japanese and the USAFE lines in Bataan. Hence he was unable to return to his home after the surrender of the USAFE forces in Bataan. He had no money with which to support himself if he was discharged from the hospital. A few days after the cast was removed from his arm, while playing basket-ball with members of the hospital staff, he fell and broke his arm at the point where it had knitted. The broken arm was again placed in a cast and again it healed perfectly.

One morning, several weeks after I entered the Ateneo Hospital, a young Filipino also about 20 years of age was brought to our ward. That morning he had been so severely beaten that he was unable to stand. He said that he had gone to an office of the Japanese military administration to register his bicycle in accordance with a military decree. He parked his bicycle in a place where parking was prohibited, although no notice of the prohibition was posted. For this offence he was beaten by four Japanese soldiers when he returned to his bicycle after registering it. It was five days before he recovered sufficiently to leave the hospital.

Red, who was suffering from malaria, was sent from Santo Tomas to the Ateneo Hospital in February. He remained with us for about two weeks. As soon as his fever abated he was returned to Santo Tomas at his own request. He was a typical able seaman of the American Merchant Marine. He had very little education. He was an enthusiastic member of the Seaman's Union and had participated in shipping strikes on the Pacific coast of the United States. He was fully convinced that the American working man was a victim of the capitalists. More than 100 American seamen of the Merchant Marine were interned at Santo Tomas. Red missed the companionship of his fellow seamen and was ill at ease among us at the Ateneo Hospital.

The Canadian came from Santo Tomas to the Ateneo Hospital early in February. When his pass expired he was sent back to Santo Tomas. We learned very little about him during the month that he was with us. He was a tall slender fellow with wavy red hair, who appeared to be not more than 40 years of age, but who was probably older. He said he served in France with the Canadian Army during the First World War. He came to Manila as a seaman on an American merchant ship and was marooned in Manila by the war. Just two days before the Japanese occupied Manila he married a young Filipina girl. She came to visit him daily during his month at the Ateneo Hospital. Like Red, the Canadian did not find any pals at the Ateneo. But, unlike Red, he did not return to Santo Tomas at his own request. He wanted to remain at the Ateneo where his young wife could visit him.

A few days after the surrender of Bataan in April a young Filipino who was suffering from malaria was admitted to our ward. We learned that he was a cousin of one of the nurses of the hospital staff. He had been a lieutenant with the USAFE at Bataan, but immediately after the surrender he escaped to his home in Manila. On the roster of hospital patients he was listed as a civilian resident of Manila. During the two weeks that he remained in the hospital he had very little to say concerning his experience at Bataan. He spoke of it reluctantly and only when directly questioned.

Chapter 9.

Concerning Captain Winship

Captain Winship, who arrived from Santo Tomas on January 27, was one of those whose pass provided for internment at the Ateneo Hospital for an unlimited period of time. He had suffered from sprue and feared the return of that disease if he continued to eat the diet high in starch and low in protein provided by both the Santo Tomas Internment Camp and the Ateneo Hospital.

The Captain was still a comparatively young man, being only 49 years old and appeared even younger. He came to the Philippines when he was about 24 years of age as an officer in the Coast and Geodetic Survey Service (CGSS). Within a few months he was promoted to the post of captain of the steamship operated by the CGSS. After holding this position for about three years he resigned from the service with the intention of going into business for himself. He was a civil engineer and proposed to become a building contractor. However, he was offered and accepted a temporary position as manager of a young and struggling embroidery export business and was still the manager more than 20 years later when war burst upon the Philippines in December 1941.

Captain Winship, who was born and reared in Maine, had proved to be a very shrewd and careful business man. When he took over the management of the embroidery business it was not prosperous. His employer, after instructing him to liquidate the business as soon as possible, returned to the United States. The firm made a business of purchasing cloth on credit in the United States, shipping it to the Philippines to be embroidered, and finally exporting the embroidered product back to the United States. The cloth upon its arrival in the Philippines was cut into pieces of suitable length, stamped with the designs to be embroidered and then distributed to embroiderers who did the embroidery by hand in their homes. When a piece of embroidery was completed the worker brought it to the office of the firm and received payment for her work. A careful record had to be kept of the names and address of the workers to whom the cloth was delivered. Often several months would elapse between the delivery of the cloth to the worker and the return of the finished product to the office of the embroidery firm.

At the time Captain Winship took over the management of the business a shipment of 60,000 yards of cloth was en route from the United States. The Captain's employer departed before the cloth arrived in Manila. There developed at this time a scarcity of cotton cloth in Manila and the price of such cloth as the Captain's firm imported rose rapidly. By the time the 60,000 yards of cloth reached Manila the captain had received several offers to purchase it at a handsome profit to his firm. The captain cabled his employer for instructions but received no reply. The price of cloth continued to rise in Manila and when the price reached one peso per yard the Captain sold the entire 60,000 yards for cash and deposited the 60,000 pesos in his firm's bank account. He then cabled his employer for instructions as to what he should do with the money. The Captain's employer had gone on a hunting trip immediately after his arrival in the United States, so it was several weeks before Captain Winship received a reply to his cables. In the meantime he urged his workers to hasten the completion of the embroidery which was outstanding and still in the homes of the workers when he had taken over the management of the firm. As a result he had been able to make a shipment of finished embroidery to his employer in the United States.

When the Captain eventually received a reply from his employer, he was congratulated for his shrewd sale of the cloth, was informed that the money obtained from the sale of the cloth was to become the working capital of the business, and was offered a partnership in the business and a permanent position as the manager of its Manila office. Captain Winship accepted this offer and the business prospered under his careful management. The volume of the firm's business increased until it exported from the Philippines about 1,500,000 pesos worth of embroidery each year.

When the Second World War began in Europe in 1939 Captain Winship, who was suffering from sprue, was in the United States on vacation. While in the United States he urged his business partner to liquidate their embroidery business. The Captain feared that the Philippines would eventually become involved in the war, with disastrous effect upon their business. His partner was unwilling to liquidate the business, but agreed to purchase the Captain's interest in the business provided the Captain would agree to continue as manager of the Manila office for two further years and train another man to take his place as manager when he retired. This proposal the Captain accepted.

By September 1941, the Captain had received as partial payment for his interest in the embroidery business the sum of 100,000 pesos, which had been deposited to his credit in a bank in the United States. When war broke out in the Philippines in December 1941, the Captain was still due a balance of about 20,000 pesos. Collection of this final sum had been delayed in order not to embarrass the embroidery business by drawing too heavily on its working capital. He was planning to return to the United States as soon as the receipts from the embroidery business permitted him to collect the final sum which was due to him.

The war, of course, completely paralyzed the embroidery exporting business. Fifteen tons of finished embroidery were in the warehouse awaiting transportation to the United States and about 100,000 yards of cloth were in the hands of embroidery workers when the war began.

The man whom Captain Winship had trained to become his successor was a young German who had become a naturalized Philippine citizen. As a result of a representation which this young German made at the office of the Japanese Consul-General of Manila, Captain Winship, after being questioned concerning his illness by the Commandant of the Santo Tomas Internment Camp, was released to his home late in February.

All of us were glad that the Captain won his release, but we were sorry to have him leave us. He had been a very pleasant companion. I, in particular, missed him. For a month he had been my opponent in our daily game of cribbage. He was an excellent player. I considered myself fortunate, after a month of play, to have won a total of two games more than he had won. We played two or three games each day.

Chapter 10.

Concerning the Miner and Planter

Among those who arrived at the Ateneo Hospital from Santo Tomas late in January was Paul Gulcik. He was 76 years old. If he had so desired he would have been released to his home because of his age. He was a bachelor without a home, however, and was without funds with which to support himself.

Paul was suffering from senile decay. His memory was failing. Events long past, he recalled with remarkable clarity. Often he could not recall the name of a friend, or the event of yesterday, or even the event of an hour past, but he was always cheerful. When he had them, he smoked some 20 cigars a day. Having no money he had to depend upon his friends for cigars. Fortunately there were several friends who sent him cigars at irregular intervals. When he had received a box of cigars he would smoke almost continuously until the box was exhausted. Then he would be without cigars for several days until another box arrived. During his periods of enforced abstinence he would "borrow" one or two cigars a day from other internees. Because he did not remember having borrowed them, he seldom replaced the cigars which he had borrowed.

For a dozen years prior to the war Paul had been a wealthy man and had given generously to both individuals and charitable institutions. I was informed that when he entered the Santo Tomas Internment Camp he had in his possession about 1,000 pesos in Philippine currency, but that he had given it all away to other internees. When he entered the Ateneo Hospital he had only two pesos in his possession. Almost immediately he offered a part of his last two pesos to other internees. The bank in which his money was deposited had been closed and was not permitted by the Japanese military authorities to reopen.

Paul was born in Hawaii. His parents were American missionaries. When he was still a child his parents went to Japan, where Paul lived for several years prior to 1880. He learned to speak Japanese but had since forgotten most of it. During the Spanish-American war he came to the Philippines as a soldier in the American Army. After being discharged he remained in the Philippines. For a number of years he was employed in the Philippine Customs Service. For several years thereafter he was employed in Manila by a large American firm of importers. Prior to 1920 he went to Baguio, in the mountain province, where for several years he was the manager of a small sawmill.

Very soon after his arrival in Baguio, Paul acquired an interest in a mining association which was prospecting for gold on a group of mineral claims located about ten miles from Baguio. The prospecting was continued for many years without success. But Paul never lost faith in the property. It was Paul more often than any of his associates who begged or borrowed the money to enable them to continue their prospecting. On one occasion, Paul persuaded an American physician to invest 10,000 pesos in the mining association. This physician later said that he gave the money only because Paul was his friend and had begged for it with tears in his eyes. That 10,000 pesos, so reluctantly invested in a dubious mining venture, eventually made the physician a millionaire and he retired from the practice of his profession to live in California.

By 1927 Paul and his associates had proven the existence on their property of a sufficient quantity of high grade gold-bearing ore to justify the erection of a mill to extract the gold. During that year he persuaded the Benguet Consolidated Mining Company, which at that time operated the only mine producing gold in the Baguio district, to provide the funds for the erection of the milling plant. The Balatoc Mining Company was then incorporated with a paid-up capital of 1,000,000 pesos. The Benguet Consolidated Mining Company purchased 60 percent of the capital stock of the Balatoc Mining Company for 600,000 pesos in cash, which provided the new corporation with funds to begin erecting the milling plant. The remaining 400,000 pesos in capital stock of the Balatoc Mining Company was delivered to Paul and his associates in exchange for a deed of title to their mineral claims. Each of the associates received six pesos, par value, in capital stock for each one peso which he had invested in the mining association.

The milling plant was erected in 1929. Thereafter the Balatoc Mining Company developed rapidly. It paid its first dividend in 1929 and continued to pay dividends regularly each year thereafter. The capacity of the milling plant was increased year by year from an initial capacity of 100 tons of ore per day to a final capacity of 2,000 tons of ore per day. The Balatoc Mining Company within the span of a dozen years became one of the largest and most profitable of the mining and milling plants. The capital stock was increased from 1,000,000 pesos to 6,000,000 pesos, par value. Thus Paul and his associates eventually received 36 pesos, par value, in stock of the Balatoc Mining Company which by 1937 had reached a market value of more than 360 pesos. In addition the mine had paid in cash dividends of more than 60 pesos for each 1 peso invested prior to 1927. Needless to say, the success of the Balatoc Mining Company made Paul a very wealthy man.

As soon as the Balatoc Mining Company became a success, Paul began to sell portions of his stock in order to reinvest the money in a large coconut plantation and cattle ranch which he and several associates were developing in Mindanao. By 1941 this plantation had become the largest coconut plantation in the world. It was owned by a corporation of which Paul was the majority stockholder.

Now, the war had forced both the Balatoc Mining Company and the coconut plantation to suspend operations and Paul's bank account was impounded. Although he was a wealthy man when the war broke out, he was now dependent upon the Philippine Red Cross for his food and lodging.

Paul was a small man and he had lost weight during his internment until he weighed only about 130 pounds. His shoulders were bent with the burden of age and his skin was mottled with the large irregular brown spots which not infrequently appear upon the skin of old men. He allowed his white beard to grow for a time and this beard, trimmed to a neat Van Dyck, gave Paul a more distinguished appearance than he possessed when his face was smooth shaven. A Filipino barber must have agreed to wait for his pay until the end of the war, for Paul seldom had any money.

All through the long hot season, when the rest of us were suffering from the heat, Paul apparently felt chilly. He insisted upon wearing a vest over his hospital gown and frequently wore a long thick bathrobe in addition to his other garments. Often he wore a cap upon his head.

During the first few weeks of Paul's internment at the Ateneo my wife washed his pajamas and bathrobe. Later he apparently requested the Jesuit Fathers who visited us to look after his laundry. At any rate two elderly Filipino nuns began to visit Paul regularly, once or twice a week. They brought him gifts of fruit which was more than he could eat. So he gave it to me with the request that it be divided among the patients in our ward.

One side of Paul's bed was against the concrete wall of our ward. One night Paul had a nightmare during the course of which, dreaming that he was struggling with some opponent, he violently kicked the wall. This resulted in painful injury to his foot and this confined him to bed for about a week.

Paul did not talk a great deal, but he was cheerful and seemingly content with his thoughts. His eyesight was remarkably keen and he was far more observant of his fellow internees than he appeared to be. Sitting in a chair beside his bed, he would watch the progress of a cribbage game 20 feet distant. He kept track of the score as it was pegged upon the cribbage board, knew which cards had been dealt to the players and observed the play of the cards upon the table. Occasionally his interest became so keen that he made some pertinent remark upon the play, but he never expressed a desire to play himself.

Paul was intensely loyal to his country. Occasionally he expressed with considerable spirit his abiding faith in the ultimate victory of the United

States and her allies. In the face of one defeat after another Paul's faith never wavered. It was this quality of profound faith, and his consequent steadfastness of purpose, which had enabled Paul to bring the Balatoc Mine to its ultimate success in spite of many years of apparent failure.

Sometimes, Paul expressed concern regarding the fate of Dave Walstrom and the latter's family. For many years Dave was the paying teller of one of Manila's leading banks. He had made a small fortune from his investment in gold mines and had resigned from his position with the bank. He built himself a fine house in Baguio, where he lived in retirement upon the income from his investment in the mines. He had also invested in Paul's coconut plantation. Shortly before the outbreak of the war the manager of the coconut plantation died. Paul had persuaded Dave to take over the management of the plantation until a new manager could be found. Dave left his family in Baguio and went to Mindanao to take charge of the plantation only a few months before the outbreak of war. Since the outbreak Paul had not heard from Dave. Reports reached us, however, that the plantation had been overrun by the Japanese. Paul feared that Dave had been killed. Much later we learned that Dave had been shot by the Japanese. A few days after the outbreak of the war Paul had sent money to Dave's family in Baguio, but he did not know whether it had been received by them.

When he learned one day that I was a stamp collector, Paul told me how as a boy he had acquired and sold for a few dollars a collection of postage stamps which would today be worth a fortune. His father, he said, was a very methodical man. During the decade between 1870 and 1886, when he had resided in Japan, his father had corresponded regularly with friends in Hawaii. The letters from Hawaii, bearing postage stamps which are now exceedingly rare, were carefully preserved by his father. When Paul was between 12 and 14 years of age he received the Hawaiian stamps from these letters and mounted them in an album. He also acquired a fine collection of the earliest Japanese stamps, which were given to him by friends in Japan. He took his stamp collection to the United States when he was sent there to finish high school. One day, having exhausted his allowance, and being temporarily without funds, he sold his collection for ten dollars. He said that he did not know at that time what its value really was. "I have thought many times since what a fool I was," he concluded. "I believe there were several Hawaiian stamps in that collection which today are worth ten thousand dollars each."

Paul remained at the Ateneo Hospital until it was closed on June 6, 1942. He was then transferred to Red Cross Hospital No. 4, where he remained until that hospital was closed at the end of June. Arrangements were then made for his internment again at the Ateneo where food and lodging were provided for him by the Jesuit Fathers. I visited him at Ateneo early in July 1942.

The war in the Philippines had already lasted longer than Paul, in the beginning, had anticipated and there was still no evidence that the end would come in the near future. Paul, however, was patient and serene. He did not doubt the ultimate victory of the allied nations.

Chapter 11

Concerning the Manner in Which Internees Were Permitted to Receive Visitors

At the Santo Tomas Internment Camp no visitors were admitted and internees were not permitted to speak to those who brought packages for them to the package-receiving line near the gate.

These restrictions were not applied to those interned in hospitals outside of the Santo Tomas Internment Camp. The internee patients in the hospitals were not only permitted to receive visitors but also permitted to talk with them in such privacy as the hospital premises afforded. Visiting hours were from 10–11 a.m. and from 3–4 p.m.

This privilege was a boon to all internee patients, but especially those whose wives and children, by reason of the wife's nationality, were not interned. Several of the men in my ward, like myself, had Filipino wives. Several had Spanish wives. Two had Russian wives. The privilege of having our wives and children visit us more than compensated for the short rations which the hospital provided and for the hospital regulations to which we were subject. It was for this reason that many internees whose ailments really did not warrant hospitalization sought to stay there and the director who was a Japanese civilian of the diplomatic corps was disposed to be lenient in this matter.

On the second day of my internment at the Ateneo Hospital my wife came to visit me. She had found a note hidden in the pocket of a pair of dirty white duck trousers, placed with other clothes to be laundered, inside one of the food baskets which was returned to her through the package-receiving line when she had gone to Santo Tomas to deliver a package of food for me the preceding afternoon. The note was from Sam Deebel, the friend to whom I had sent the two baskets of food with a request for him to get word to my wife that I had been transferred to the Ateneo Hospital. Sam's note informed her of my transfer and requested her to have his laundry done for him. Not knowing until later when she found Sam's note that I was no longer at Santo Tomas, she had left a box of food addressed to me at the package-receiving line. Included with the food was a fried chicken. Later, when she collected Sam's laundry from Santo Tomas she found a note hidden within stating that he had taken delivery of the chicken in my name and enjoyed eating it.

My wife was delighted to find that she could visit me at the Ateneo Hospital. "I prayed for you to be released from Santo Tomas and now it has come true!" She promised to bring our nine-year-old son, Leonard, when next she came to visit me. Thereafter my wife came to visit three times each week. Once a week our son came with her.

When I arrived at the hospital there were no restrictions on visitors except that they must come at the specified visiting hours. About two months later (March 21 1942) instructions governing the admission of visitors to see internee patients were received from the Japanese government by the Santo Tomas Internment Camp. These instructions prohibited the admission of visitors to see internees without prior approval of the Commandant. A mimeographed form was provided by means of which the Commandant's prior approval might be obtained. In this form were entered the visitor's name, age, sex, nationality, relationship to the internee, the name of the internee to be visited, whether the visits were to be casual or upon a specified day of each week and the name of the hospital. Application might be made for as many visitors as the internee desired, but each visitor was only permitted one visit per week. In view of this latter restriction, our chief doctor increased the visiting hours to a two-hour period from 10 to 12 a.m. and another two hours from 3 to 5 p.m. each day. All of the internees filled out applications covering the visitors who they wished to see. In a few days these applications were returned bearing the Commandant's approval. I secured permission for my wife and son to visit me each Sunday.

At our hospital the regulation restricting each visitor to one visit per week was never very rigidly enforced. With the chief doctor's approval, the male internees who were able to walk about formed a corps of gate-keepers. A gatekeeper's table was placed in the hallway giving access to the hospital premises. Each gatekeeper took a one-hour or two-hour shift, and a gate-keeper was always on duty from 7 a.m. to 7 p.m.

In actual practice visitors were handled in the following manner. Those for whom an authorization had been obtained from the Commandant were permitted to enter the hospital premises once a week on the day specified in the authorization. When visitors came on unauthorized days—to bring food, or for any other purpose—they were *not* permitted to enter the hospital premises. But the gate-keeper would either carry a message to the internee or call the internee to the gate, where a few words with the visitor were permitted. For the use of visitors who were not permitted to enter, a few chairs were placed in the hallway near the gate. A similar procedure was followed for visitors with no authorization from the Commandant. If the unauthorized visitor indicated a desire to repeat the visit, the gate-keeper, having first assured himself that the visitor would be welcomed by the internee, would fill out the necessary application for the Commandant's approval. The gate-keeper would also frequently surrender his seat to another gate-keeper in order to permit the latter to converse with a visitor who was not authorized to enter the premises. As a gate-keeper we might have the same visitor come several times a week during the hours when that gate-keeper was on duty. In this way he and his visitor could converse at the gate for a half hour or more without interruption. In addition to coming on Sunday, her authorized visiting day, my wife therefore came to visit me two or three times a week during the hours I was on duty at the gate.

Some of the women who were interned at the hospital grumbled that the gate- keepers took advantage of their turn at the gate to receive visitors at unauthorized hours. We assured them that if they were willing to take a turn at the gate they might enjoy the same privilege. None of the women, however, were willing to do gate duty. Perhaps this was in part because none of them had visitors who would, or could, visit them more often than once a week. Most of them were middle-aged or elderly American women whose relatives and many of whose friends were interned at Santo Tomas. Several of them were widows. The husbands of two were interned at Santo Tomas and were able to obtain passes to visit their wives only once a month. The husband of another was a captain with General MacArthur's forces in Bataan. On those rare occasions when an authorized casual visitor did call to see one of the women, the gate-keeper would call the woman to the gate and give her as much opportunity as circumstances would permit to converse with her visitor.

Chapter 12.

Concerning "Honest Abe"

Mr. Workman, like others who entered the Ateneo Hospital with passes for internment there for an unlimited period, arrived late in January. Soon after his arrival he read a biography of Abraham Lincoln and amused himself, and us, by growing an oddly trimmed moustache and sideburns, supposedly in the style once worn by Lincoln. Thereafter Mr. Workman was called Honest Abe, or, more often, simply Abe.

Abe must have been between 50 and 55 years of age. His wife was a Spanish woman born in the Philippines. They had four beautiful daughters, the youngest being about 15 years of age. Abe's wife and daughters could have been exempted from internment by reason of his wife's Spanish parentage. But when Abe entered the Santo Tomas Internment Camp early in January his wife and daughters chose to be interned with him, in order to protect the girls from possible violation by Japanese soldiers and because the boy friends of the girls were interned at Santo Tomas.

The birthday of one of Abe's daughters was to occur about three weeks after Abe entered the Ateneo Hospital. Abe busied himself with hand sewing a leather money belt as a birthday gift for his daughter. One of the hospital attendants went to Abe's house to secure materials for the belt. The leather was cut from a beautifully tanned brown goatskin which had been looted from the waterfront on January 1. Abe said that he purchased about 40 of these goatskins from the looter. He said that his wife and daughters were keeping their money concealed in the hair of their heads. He was afraid that the money might be lost, so he was making a money belt. We inferred from this that Abe's wife and daughters were carrying a considerable amount of cash in paper bills.

Although he seldom mentioned his illness, Abe really was a sick man. He suffered from anaemia and had what he said his doctor called a "blocked" heart. Abe's pulse was sometimes as low as 35 and was never higher than 42. Whenever his pulse was unusually weak he was given a heart stimulant injection. Our chief doctor, I was informed, predicted that Abe probably had not more than a year to live.

Usually Abe was a very cheerful person, but at times he was inclined to be bellicose and argumentative, particularly when he felt that the rights and perogatives of himself or his friends were being infringed. A German lady who, of course, was not interned, and who was a frequent visitor at the

Ateneo Hospital, donated a *rataan* table and four chairs for the use of the internees. A middle-aged British woman, who was one of the internees in the women's ward, soon appropriated one of the chairs and claimed it for her own exclusive use. If anyone was sitting in this chair when she appeared on the hospital veranda she demanded that the occupant vacate "her" chair. In the men's wards Abe waxed eloquent in his denunciation of this British woman's selfishness and one afternoon he decided to do something about it. The British woman emerged from the women's ward regularly at 2.30 each afternoon. On this particular afternoon Abe was occupying the *rataan* chair when she appeared.

"You are sitting in my chair," she said severely.

"Your chair!" replied Abe in apparent astonishment. "This chair was given to the hospital for the use of all of us. You have no right to claim it for your exclusive use. You have been imposing on us for some time and I have decided that it is time to put a stop to it."

The British woman retired in confusion and never again claimed exclusive right to any chair. The rest of us silently cheered Abe's outspoken defense of our communal rights.

Upon another occasion, however, Abe's lack of tact worked to our disadvantage. Abe was on duty at the gate from 7 to 9 a.m. each day. Persons desiring to visit the patients were not admitted during these hours. But persons desiring to visit the doctors and nurses were admitted at all hours. One morning late in May, Abe admitted a young man who said he wished to visit one of the nurses. However, our chief doctor discovered that this young man was in fact visiting a Filipino patient. He instructed Abe not to admit anyone to visit a nurse without first securing the chief doctor's permission. One Sunday morning, a few days later, a young woman called to visit one of the nurses. Because our chief doctor was absent Abe refused to admit her. The nurse whom the young woman desired to visit came to the gate and insisted that the young woman should be admitted. Abe lost his temper and voiced his refusal in a very tactless manner. The chief doctor returned at this moment. He found the nurse in tears and discovered that the young woman who had been refused admission was herself a Red Cross nurse and was the daughter of one of the most senior Red Cross physicians. Our chief doctor became exceedingly angry and immediately removed all internee gatekeepers, replacing them with members of hospital staff. As a result, the rules governing the admission of internees' visitors were thereafter enforced much more rigidly than they had been hitherto by the internee gate-keepers.

Soon after Abe entered the Ateneo he secured permission to visit his home in order to obtain some much needed clothing. A Red Cross attendant accompanied him. He found his servant had fled and had deposited the key to the house with a next-door neighbor. Most of Abe's supply of canned foods had been stolen but apparently nothing else was taken. A box of canned goods which his wife had hidden above the ceiling of the kitchen was still there. Abe took possession of the key to his house.

Thereafter Abe, on four different occasions, sent a messenger to obtain various articles from his house. A different member was sent on each occasion. Thus five different persons, besides Abe himself, at one time or another had possession of the key to Abe's house. These persons were his immediate neighbors, two different hospital attendants, and the wives of two other internees. The last messenger to enter the house was one of the hospital attendants, who reported that the back door of the house was open and that he could not find the items which he was instructed to bring to Abe at the hospital. The missing items were a roll of about 40 tanned goatskins and a case of Kotex. Abe claimed that the missing items were worth more than 500 pesos. He suspected that these goods had been stolen by the hospital attendant whom he sent to get them. A neighbor at first claimed to have seen the stolen goods being loaded into a cart by a person whose description was similar to that of the hospital attendant. One of our doctors, accompanied by the suspected hospital attendant, subsequently questioned the neighbor, who then denied that she had seen the missing goods being loaded aboard the cart, although she identified the hospital attendant as the person whom she had seen enter the house and remove certain articles. An official from the central office of the Red Cross conducted an investigation but could not determine who had stolen the missing goods and the matter was dropped.

About two months after Abe entered the Ateneo Hospital his youngest daughter, a beautiful girl of sixteen, obtained a pass from the Santo Tomas Internment Camp to visit her father at the Ateneo for two hours. She was Abe's first visitor and he proudly introduced her to his fellow internees. Thereafter she visited Abe once each month.

Although Abe was a rather small, slender man, he had a voracious appetite and ate more than any other patient in the ward. He supplemented his hospital ration with food which he purchased from a Filipino food vendor who visited the hospital several times each week. Abe also purchased food for his wife and daughters at Santo Tomas which he sent to them by the Red Cross station wagon.

About two months after his arrival at the Ateneo Hospital Abe obtained a small short-wave radio receiver from his home. Each evening we gathered around the radio to hear the news from San Francisco. But we were careful to keep the receiver tuned so low that it could not be heard outside the hospital premises. In the morning and at noon Abe alone would put his ear against the receiver and tune it to the news, which he later reported to us.

When the Ateneo Hospital was closed and other internees were transferred to Red Cross Hospital No. 4 on June 6, Abe was released to his home. At the same time Abe's wife and eldest daughter obtained their release from the Santo Tomas Internment Camp in order to care for Abe. Abe took his radio receiver back to his home when he was released. But once each week he visited us at Red Cross Hospital No. 4 and gave us an account of the news. There was no radio at Red Cross Hospital No. 4. Abe's weekly visit was therefore greatly appreciated.

Chapter 13.

Concerning Our Food at the Ateneo Hospital

The hospital operated its own kitchen. Most of the foodstuffs were supplied by a central Red Cross purchasing agency, but the cook was given a small daily allocation of cash for the purchase of fresh meat, fruit and vegetables from the public market. This cash amounted to only five pesos (US$2.50) per day. Since there were usually about 30 patients and 20 members of the hospital staff to be fed, this daily allocation amounted only to about five centavos (US$0.025) per person. As a result the diet supplied by the hospital did not include fresh meat, fruit and vegetables. I was informed that the total cost of the food provided by the hospital for its patients was 26 centavos (US$0.13) per person per day. This was a much smaller ration than was being provided at that time for the internees eating at the Red Cross mess in the Santo Tomas Internment Camp. Perhaps this was one of the reasons for the sarcastic manner in which the Red Cross ambulance attendant said, "I wish you luck," when we first entered the hospital.

The hospital ration was not sufficient to maintain the weight of even those patients who remained constantly in bed. Almost all the patients received additional food which they purchased or which was sent in to them by relatives and friends outside. One of the first questions which the chief doctor had asked me on my arrival was whether I was in a position to supply part of my own food.

The usual ration supplied by the hospital was as follows. For breakfast, a teacupful of cracked wheat porridge, a slice of bread, a very small banana or a small slice of papaya and a cup of coffee. For lunch, a very small piece of meat, a teacupful of boiled rice, a small portion of vegetable and a very small portion of sweetened dessert. For dinner, the same ration as for lunch. Half a cup of milk, or a milk substitute made from fresh coconuts, was usually served mid-afternoon.

To supplement the hospital ration, my wife provided me with four or five very small bananas per day and about once every two days with an egg, a glass of milk and a generous portion of boiled greens. Occasionally she brought a small loaf of bread, which provided an extra slice of bread each day. When the price of bread became prohibitive, due to the scarcity of flour, she made out of cracked wheat a kind of dry cracker about the size of a slice of bread. I ate one of these crackers each day. The additional food which my wife brought me was always sufficient to provide me with all the food which

I cared to eat. Often there was a small surplus which I distributed among less fortunate patients.

Until her supply of flour became exhausted, each Sunday for about two months, my wife brought two three layer cakes, which she donated—one to the hospital staff and the other to the patients. There were usually 25 to 30 of the latter. It was my task to cut the cake so as to provide a piece for each patient. About twice a week my wife brought a jar of lemonade sufficient to provide a cupful for each of the 12 to 15 patients in my ward. For making the lemonade she used small limes locally known as *calamansi*. Their juice is very rich in vitamin C. Occasionally my wife added to the lemonade the juice of a small, purple, plum-like fruit called *duhat*. This gave the lemonade added flavor and colored it pale purple. There was a chunk of ice in the jar when the lemonade arrived, which made it very refreshing on those hot days in what was the hottest season in the recorded history of Manila.

The internees were permitted to place eggs and fruit, which they purchased for themselves, in the hospital refrigerator, but we soon discovered that when we placed our food in the refrigerator a portion of it unaccountably disappeared. Ten out of a dozen eggs which one internee placed in the refrigerator disappeared. Another internee placed a large *papaya* (a melon-like fruit) in the refrigerator. One slice—about one-fifth of the *papaya*—was served to him at breakfast the following morning, the rest had disappeared. Milk was stolen from other internees. Although we complained to the chief doctor the thefts continued. As a result we were compelled to place our food beneath our beds in order to prevent it being stolen. I was informed by one of my fellow internees—although I was unable to verify the allegation—that the chief doctor permitted the members of the hospital staff to help themselves to any food which they found in the refrigerator. At any rate, we were convinced that the food was stolen by hospital staff—probably at night.

During March, because the Red Cross' supply of coffee became exhausted, the hospital kitchen was unable to provide coffee for our breakfast. We decided to provide our own coffee.

My wife's mother had about 20 kilograms (44 pounds) of green coffee beans which had been grown near Baguio in the mountains of the Philippines. The purchasing agent of the Red Cross gave me the address of a woman who did the roasting and grinding of coffee for the Red Cross. My wife delivered our green coffee beans to this woman. A few days later the ground roasted coffee was delivered to me at the Ateneo.

At that time the ceiling price, fixed by the Japanese-sponsored government for coffee grown in the Philippines, was 1.20 pesos per kilogram (US$0.27 per pound) of the roasted product. But it could not be bought for less than three times the ceiling price. Nevertheless, I packed our coffee in paper bags and sold it to my fellow internees at the ceiling price of 1.20 pesos. Each purchaser was limited to one kilogram and I retained one kilogram for myself. My wife delivered the proceeds of the sale to her mother.

The wife of one of the internees in my ward supplied an electric percolator in which to prepare the coffee. Whenever coffee was prepared, each internee who desired coffee contributed a spoonful of coffee to the pot. There were two internees in my ward who had no money. A kilogram of coffee was purchased for each of these two by other internees in the ward. We made our own coffee each afternoon thereafter. The hospital supplied milk and sugar for those who desired it.

Chapter 14.

Concerning the Retired Navy Cook

Mr. Gildow arrived about the middle of February, with a pass authorizing his internment at the Ateneo Hospital for one month. We called him Gil because that was the first syllable of his name. Gil served for many years as a cook in the United States Navy. He was a retired chief petty officer. For some time immediately prior to the Japanese occupation of Manila he had been a civilian employee of the United States Navy in Manila. He was in charge of the purchase and storage of foodstuffs for the navy.

When the US Army and Navy evacuated Manila late in December, Gil was left behind with instructions to continue dispatching supplies to Corregidor and Bataan. On December 31, when it became evident that he would be unable to dispatch all the Navy stores before the Japanese entered Manila, Gil turned over twenty truck-loads of the Navy stores to representatives of the Red Cross in Manila. He continued loading stores aboard barges for shipment to Corregidor and Bataan until after midnight of December 31. Then he opened the doors of the government-owned cold storage unit and permitted the public to take what was left. Hundreds of people came and received a gift of all that they could carry. Within a few hours many tons of fine food were thus distributed. Hams, bacon, chickens, turkeys, butter, oranges, apples, cheese, canned milk and many other foodstuffs were taken with amazing speed. Gil said that the last thing he did before leaving the place on January 1 was to spray kerosene over a huge quantity of butter which still remained in one of the cold storage rooms. All other foodstuffs had been carried away. Gil did not say that he set the butter afire after spraying it with kerosene. But whether he or someone else started the fire, the government cold storage plant burned down on January 1.

Gil was a massive, broad-shouldered man of medium height. When he entered the Ateneo he still weighed more than 220 pounds. But he said that when he entered Santo Tomas a month earlier he weighed about 250 pounds. He was less than 50 years of age. But he had ruined his health by intemperate eating and drinking. For several years he had been a total abstainer from alcohol but he was still intemperate in his eating. His heart and kidneys were in bad shape and he was suffering from arthritis. When he entered the Ateneo Hospital one foot was so much inflamed with gout that he was unable to walk except with the aid of a crutch.

Our chief doctor immediately placed Gil upon a very limited diet. Gil refused to adhere rigidly to it although he did eat more sparingly. As a result his health slowly improved. After a month at the Ateneo he was able to hobble about without the aid of a crutch. He still required hospitalization and his pass for internment at the Ateneo was renewed. At the end of two months he was able to walk without limping. Each evening for fifteen or twenty minutes he walked back and forth across the court upon which the hospital faced. In this manner he walked a mile each day. He did not wish to return to Santo Tomas, and when his pass again expired in April he obtained another extension of his internment in the Ateneo hospital.

Gil's wife was a Portuguese woman who had two grown children by a former husband. She was devoted to Gil and brought him much more good food than he ate. He distributed the greater portion of this food among his fellow internees.

Gil was a splendid cook and took great pleasure in preparing fine foods. But there was little opportunity for him to exercise his craft at the Ateneo hospital. Occasionally, however, he prepared a delicious fruit salad from materials which he and the other internees contributed. On these festive occasions several of us assisted him in peeling and dicing the fruit.

Prior to the war, Gil and a business partner owned and operated a sausage factory. They sold most of their product to the United States Navy. For the manufacture of sausage they imported frozen meats. When the Japanese occupation of Manila forced them to close their factory they had about 7,000 pesos worth of frozen meat in cold storage. When Gil and his partner were interned they left a Filipino employee in charge of the frozen meat. "Now I won't have to worry any longer about that seven thousand pesos worth of meat," was Gil's only comment.

Doctor Garcia, a Portuguese lady physician, was in Manila, en route from the Portuguese colony of Macao to Portugal, when the war caught up with her. Unable to obtain transportation out of Manila, she offered her services to the Philippine Red Cross and was placed in charge of an emergency hospital established in the building occupied by the University Club. When the Japanese forces occupied Manila the University Club was made the headquarters of one of the Japanese generals. He ordered the closing of the Red Cross Hospital, but graciously permitted Dr. Garcia to continue her residence in the building. He reserved the entire fourth floor for her exclusive use, and even paid the wages of her servants.

Because of her frequent and friendly contact with several Japanese officers of high rank, including the Commandant of the Santo Tomas Internment Camp, her requests, as a physician, for the release of internees to return to their own homes were invariably granted. She made several visits to the Ateneo Hospital and during these visits assured Gil that as soon as his condition would permit, she would obtain his release to go home.

When, by order of the Commandant of the Santo Tomas camp, a Japanese physician examined the internees at the Ateneo Hospital on April 22, he recommended that Gil and another internee, whom we called Tommy, be sent back to Santo Tomas. Gil got in touch with Dr. Garcia the following morning. She immediately went to the Commandant of the Santo Tomas Internment Camp and secured the release of both Gil and Tommy to their homes on the afternoon of that same day, April 23.

Thereafter, until the Ateneo Hospital was closed on June 6, Gil came once each week to consult our chief doctor. He never failed on these occasions to visit our ward. He said that he was continuing at home to eat sparingly and that he sometimes walked the entire distance of more than two miles from his home to Ateneo. He weighed himself each week at the Ateneo Hospital and found that he was holding his weight down to about 220 pounds. Later, when food became more scare his weight fell to about 180 pounds.

After our transfer to Red Cross Hospital No. 4 Gil visited us only once. He said that his heart was giving him trouble and his doctor had advised him to remain at home. When his pass expired Dr. Garcia secured for him an extension of 60 days, so that he would not have to report at Santo Tomas until sometime in August.

Chapter 15.

Concerning Tommy, The Club Manager

Tommy was sent from Santo Tomas to the Ateneo Hospital about the middle of February. He came with Gil. I never learned Tommy's age, but I do not believe he was over 40. He had a wife and six young children who were interned at Santo Tomas. His wife was a beautiful young woman, perhaps 30 years of age. She was born in Manila, the daughter of an American father and a Spanish mother. Tommy was a small slim man who weighed not more than 130 pounds. He had a deep, powerful voice and the enthusiasm of a good cheer leader.

At one time Tommy was partner in a successful Manila firm of opticians. He sold his interest in this business and for several years immediately prior to the outbreak of the war he was the secretary and manager of one of Manila's leading clubs.

During the last week of December, Tommy received instructions from the US military authorities to destroy the club's large stock of fine wines and liquors. The club was located on the shore of Manila Bay. A day or two before the Japanese forces entered Manila Tommy and his staff carried the club's stock of wines and liquors to the wall which separated the club's premises from the beach. One by one, bottles of champagne, burgundy, and other fine wines and liquors were tossed over the wall to crash and break upon the rocks below. The members of the club came and joined in the work of destroying more than 10,000 pesos worth of wines and liquors. Not one bottle was left to fall into the hands of the Japanese.

The club's cook was a German. On the day before the Japanese entered Manila the cook left and encouraged most of the kitchen and dining room staff to leave also. Tommy managed, however, to provide the residents of the club with food.

On January 2 Tommy and the residents of the club gathered on the roof and watched the Japanese soldiers enter Manila. They marched north on Dewey Boulevard until they reached the club. An automobile belonging to one of the residents of the club was the first automobile seized by the Japanese forces. A Japanese officer entered the club, inquired who owned the automobile and demanded the key. It was given to him and he drove away in the car.

The residents of the club were interned there for several days. On the morning of January 6 they were transferred to Santo Tomas. They took with them, as instructed by the Japanese military authorities, a supply of food to last three days. Later they regretted that they had not taken the club's entire foodstuffs. The Japanese failed to provide any food for the internees. It was not until the middle of January, ten days after the first internees entered the camp, that the Philippine Red Cross, with the assistance of the internees themselves, set up a kitchen to provide food for those internees who had no means of feeding themselves. Some of the internees went hungry during those first ten days in the Santo Tomas Internment Camp. The members of Tommy's club organized themselves into a mess and had sufficient food sent in to them. The Japanese permitted those internees who had money to purchase food and have it sent into the camp. Friends and relatives of internees were also permitted to bring food to the camp, but no food was provided by the Japanese.

During the first month of Tommy's stay at the Ateneo Hospital his only visitor was his wife's sister, who came regularly once or twice each week. She was employed in the Central Telephone Exchange of Manila. The Japanese military authorities had assumed control of the telephone system and had reduced her salary to about one-fifth of the wage she had received prior to the Occupation. She was thankful, however, that she still had a job.

Tommy's wife came to visit him about a month after he entered the Ateneo Hospital. She obtained a special pass for this visit and was brought to the Ateneo in the Red Cross station wagon. She informed Tommy that women with small children were being released from the Santo Tomas Internment Camp, provided they had a home and a means of supporting themselves outside of the camp. A few days later Tommy's wife and children were released and went to live in the house of his wife's sister. Thereafter they visited Tommy each week.

Tommy was suffering from a stomach ulcer and required a diet which the hospital was unable to supply. He made no complaint, however, and got along as best he could with the aid of a little food brought to him by his sister-in-law and, after her release, by his wife. He ate very sparingly.

On April 22, the Japanese physician sent by the Commandant of the Santo Tomas Internment Camp to examine the internee patients of the Ateneo Hospital ordered Tommy and Gil back to Santo Tomas, as already recounted in the preceding chapter. They immediately appealed to Doctor Garcia, the Portuguese lady physician, who went to the Commandant of the Santo Tomas Internment Camp and secured passes which released both Tommy and Gil to their homes on April 23. When Tommy's pass expired in May he was able to obtain its renewal for another month. But in June, when his pass again expired, he was ordered back to Santo Tomas.

At that time about 1,500 internees—one-third of the total number of internees—had passes permitting them to live outside of Santo Tomas Internment Camp. It was reported that the Commandant had decided that the number of passes permitting internees to live outside the camp should be reduced to 500. At any rate, very few of the passes which expired during June and July were renewed. Tommy was one of the many ordered back to the Santo Tomas Internment Camp.

Chapter 16.

Concerning the Banker

Mr. Nikkols arrived at the Ateneo Hospital about the middle of March. He was some 45 years of age, of medium height and weight, with a tendency to baldness, an enormous nose and a very vivacious manner. He was a native of Holland and for several years prior to the war had been the manager of the Manila branch of a Dutch bank. He informed us that he was a widower, that he had a 20-year-old son in Holland and that he was suffering from kidney stones. We promptly nicknamed him The Banker.

Mr. Nikkols was picked up by the Japanese military police early in January. For two months thereafter he was interned in Villamor Hall of the University of the Philippines, almost directly across the street from the Ateneo. Most of those interned at Villamor Hall were prominent members of the Chinese community, but there were also several Americans, including the publisher of a daily newspaper and the publisher of a weekly magazine, both of whom had caustically condemned Japan in their publications. It appeared that those interned at Villamor Hall were for the most part well-to-do persons who were suspected of having been active in disseminating anti-Japanese propaganda during the period immediately preceding the outbreak of the war between Japan and the United States. Apparently Mr. Nikkols was interned at Villamor Hall because the Japanese found the vault of his bank empty when they forced him to open it shortly after the Japanese entered Manila.

We were informed by Mr. Nikkols that the internees at Villamor Hall were constantly under a strong guard of Japanese soldiers, who frequently slapped and otherwise maltreated their prisoners. No food was provided for the prisoners, but their relatives and friends were permitted to bring them food.

It appeared that Mr. Nikkols was a shrewd and far-sighted banker. Prior to the outbreak of the war he transferred to banks in the United States a sum which was more than twice the total amount of the deposits in his bank. Like all other banks, his bank suspended operations five days before the Japanese occupation of Manila. During these five days all of his bank's remaining cash and all of its securities were deposited with the Philippine Treasury and transferred to Corregidor. His bank had not been permitted, of course, to resume operation after the Japanese occupation of Manila.

After Mr. Nikkols entered the Ateneo Hospital he called the Filipino employees of his bank to the hospital and paid them a quarter of their annual salary for the first three months of 1942. He hoped to continue paying his employees a portion of their salaries. To himself he allotted a sufficient monthly sum to cover his personal expenses and the cost of maintaining his household. He had persuaded several well-to-do Chinese to loan his bank sufficient cash for this purpose.

A comely young Russian woman was in charge of his house and servants. She visited him frequently and each day a servant brought him food and ice for his drinking water. There was almost always more food than he could eat and he was very generous in sharing it with his fellow internees. Occasionally his cook baked a cake which Mr. Nikkols divided among us. Each day he also provided several of the internees with sufficient ice to cool their drinking water. He assured us that in reality he was a very selfish person, that he gave away only the surplus after he made ample provisions for his own needs.

Mr. Nikkols was almost always gay. When any of us complained about the tedium of our internment he assured us that after being interned for two months at Villamor Hall he thought internment at the Ateneo Hospital was paradise. He went about among us full of jokes and laughter and little kindnesses.

A short time after Mr. Nikkols arrived at the Ateneo Hospital he learned that the Chinese with whom he had been interned at Villamor Hall had been transferred to a military prison at Fort Santiago. Sometime later Chinese friends who called on Mr. Nikkols at the Ateneo Hospital reported that it was believed that seventeen prominent Chinese confined at Fort Santiago has been executed. Their families had been instructed to cease bringing food for them to the prison.

The execution was not announced by the Japanese military authorities, however, until about two months later. Mr. Nikkols, who in the meantime had been released to his home, then requested his Chineses friends not to call on him anymore. He feared that if he continued to receive Chinese visitors he might be interned at Santo Tomas, or might even meet the same fate as the seventeen prominent Chinese who had been executed.

Mr. Nikkols was released to his home on May 22. His release was obtained by the Russian lady who cared for his home. She made a personal appeal to the Commandant of the Santo Tomas Internment Camp. But when Mr. Nikkols' pass expired in July he was interned at Santo Tomas again where he remained until all of us were released by the arrival of General MacArthur's first cavalry in February 1945.

Chapter 17.

Concerning the Women at the Ateneo Hospital

When I arrived at the Ateneo Hospital on January 23 there were nine women interned in the women's ward. There was remarkably little change in the internee population of the women's ward thereafter. The two youngest women were sent back to the Santo Tomas Internment Camp about the end of February. The seven other women, all of whom were middle-aged or elderly remained at the Ateneo hospital until it was closed in June. Two of these women were bedridden invalids who at rare intervals appeared in wheeled chairs for an hour or two upon the hospital veranda. There was only one addition to the internee population of the women's ward after my arrival at the Ateneo. This was a young Dutch woman who entered the Ateneo Hospital in February and remained with us until the hospital closed.

There were perhaps a half-dozen European women and a dozen Filipino women who, at various times, occupied beds in the women's ward even though they were not internees. One of these was an attractive young Filipino woman whose leg was broken and mangled by a Japanese bomb late in December. She was still unable to walk without the aid of crutches when she was discharged from the hospital in May. It was doubtful that she would ever recover the use of her injured leg.

Mrs. Ell was a massively built Russian woman, about 30 years of age, with broad hips and a very handsome face. She had a child about two years of age which was being cared for, together with about 30 other internee children, at what had formerly been a Catholic girls' school. Mrs. Ell's husband was an American who had returned to the United States about a month before the war began. Mrs. Ell had planned to accompany him, but for some reason she had been unable to obtain a passport before her husband's steamer sailed. Eventually she obtained a passport and was awaiting transportation when the war marooned her in Manila.

I did not learn the nature of Mrs. Ell's illness. Certainly she appeared to be a very robust young woman. At the end of February she was sent back to the Santo Tomas Internment Camp, after an unsuccessful attempt to secure internment at the former catholic school where her child was being cared for. When we were transferred to the Red Cross Hospital No. 4 early in June, we again met Mrs. Ell. She had obtained internment at that hospital some time before our arrival.

In preparation for her voyage to the United States Mrs. Ell had secured traveler's checks to the amount of US$1,000. When she was interned in

January she had very little money aside from these traveler's checks and the Japanese military administration had issued a decree prohibiting the cashing of such checks. During her internment at Red Cross Hospital No. 4 a steamer called at Manila to pick up members of the consular staffs of the Allied Nations who were to be exchanged for Japanese consular officials at Lorenzo Marques in Africa. While this ship was in port a European Jew of Mrs. Ell's acquaintance transferred her traveler's checks to members of the departing Manila consular corps in exchange for Japanese war notes. She said that the Jew gave her 2,000 pesos in Japanese war notes. Later she was informed that he obtained for her traveler's checks at least 3,000 pesos, and possibly 4,000 pesos, in this Japanese paper currency. Traveler's checks were in demand among the members of the consular corps, who desired to get rid of all their Japanese war notes before they left the Philippines.

Early in July Mrs. Ell, who now had funds with which to support herself, secured a pass releasing her to the home of a friend.

Mrs. Warrington was a middle-aged American woman who was suffering from sprue. Her husband, who was interned at Santo Tomas, obtained a pass to visit her at the Ateneo Hospital for two hours once each month They owned a fine home in Manila which they had rented to a Spanish family for 25 pesos a month in order to prevent it being looted. Mrs. Warrington for many years had been the proprietor of a prosperous embroidery business, which had been completely ruined by the war. The business was not permitted to reopen after the Japanese occupation of Manila. When the Ateneo hospital closed early in June Mrs. Warrington obtained a pass releasing her to the house of a friend.

Mrs. Trevor was an attractive Dutch girl, not over 30 years of age, who had formerly lived in Java. Her young American husband was interned at Santo Tomas. At the outbreak of the war Mrs. Trevor was the secretary of the Netherlands Consul in Manila and a short time before the outbreak of the war she suffered a broken hip.

When the Japanese occupied Manila, Mrs. Trevor was still bedridden in her home. The Japanese immediately interned Mr. Trevor, but permitted Mrs. Trevor to continue residing in her home. There she remained until her slender store of cash was exhausted and she no longer had money with which to purchase foods for herself and her Javanese servants. She then consigned her most cherished household furnishings to the care of various friends and sought refuge at the Ateneo Hospital. She had seen compelled to leave behind her Javanese servants in her house, to look after themselves in this strange land as best they might.

When Mrs. Trevor arrived at the Ateneo Hospital she walked with such a pronounced limp that one leg appeared to be at least an inch shorter than the other. We feared that she would be permanently crippled. Each day, however, with the aid of her cane she limped resolutely back and forth across the courtyard. As day followed day, her limp slowly, almost imperceptibly at first, became less and less pronounced. At the end of three months she scarcely limped at all.

Mrs. Trevor had attained a special pass which authorized her to reside at the Ateneo Hospital but which also permitted her to go out upon the street whenever she so desired. She contended that she was not an internee. However, our chief doctor considered Mrs. Trevor to be an internee and subject to the same restrictions as any other internee concerning her visitors. When Mrs. Trevor refused to request the Commandant of Santo Tomas Internment Camp to authorize her visitors to enter the Ateneo Hospital our chief doctor instructed the internee gate-keepers that Mrs. Trevor's visitors were not to be admitted. The gate-keepers compromised by calling Mrs. Trevor to the gate and permitting her to converse with her visitors in the hallway at the entrance of the hospital. Our chief doctor chose to ignore this evasion of the rules.

One of Mrs. Trevor's visitors was her Javanese cook. On his first visit he requested her to give him some money. This she was unable to do. On his next visit he reported that the Japanese had confiscated her automobile. When he called a third time she refused to come to the gate to talk to him. The cook continued to reside in her home, however, and to protect her property as best he could. I did not learn how he managed to support himself.

Mrs. Trevor's desperate need of money caused her to make contact with a young European who made a living by buying and selling the household effects of internees. She instructed him to sell her electrical refrigerator, which she had placed for safe keeping in the house of a friend. This friend at first refused to surrender the refrigerator, but eventually the sale was completed and the young European who sold it delivered the proceeds of the sale to Mrs. Trevor. Mrs. Trevor was then able to purchase additional food to supplement the very meager hospital rations.

The business of the young European who sold Mrs. Trevor's refrigerator appeared to be of an illicit nature. He informed Mrs. Trevor that he would get into trouble with the Japanese military authorities if they learned that he was selling internee property and delivering the proceeds to the internee. He expected that the United States would win the war and feared that he might be prosecuted by the American authorities after the war was over. I inferred that some of the property which he bought and sold was looted from the homes of internees.

When the Ateneo Hospital was closed early in June, Mrs. Trevor obtained a pass permitting her to continue to reside at the Ateneo. She joined a group of British women who were refugees from Shanghai and who were interned in one of the Ateneo dormitories. The British women, whom she joined, purchased and cooked their own food.

Chapter 18.

Concerning Jack, the Sailor

Jack Howard arrived at the Ateneo Hospital during the early part of February. He was a large stout man in his late forties whose rubicund countenance made him appear younger than he actually was. Jack was a retired chief petty officer of the United States Navy.

At the outbreak of the war Jack was employed by the Northern Luzon Transportation Company, which operated a fleet of passenger buses in the province of Northern Luzon. The headquarters of the transportation company was at San Fernando, the capital of La Union Province and the Northern terminus of the railroad to the provinces of Ilocos Sur, Ilocos Norte and Abra, North of San Fernando.

The colleges and universities of Manila were closed immediately after the outbreak of the war on December 6. During the next few days the buses leaving San Fernando for the Northern provinces were crowded with students returning to their homes. On the day before the Japanese landed in Vigan, Ilocos Sur Province, Jack's firm dispatched about one hundred buses from San Fernando to the Northern provinces. Most of these buses were unable to return before the Japanese occupied Vigan and the USAFE forces destroyed the bridges into Vigan and San Fernando. The buses thus marooned north of Sand Fernando were seized by the Japanese providing them with a means of transportation for their subsequent push southward.

Jack witnessed the heavy fighting in the vicinity of San Fernando, La Union Province, on December 21. It was evident by nightfall of the 21st that the USAFE troops at San Fernando would not be able to hold up the Japanese advance much longer. Jack and the president of his firm fled southward to Manila by automobile on the night of December 21. Mr. Minie, the manager of the bus company, remained and took refuge in the mountains east of San Fernando when the Japanese entered the town. Several months later Jack received word at the Ateneo Hospital that Mr. Minie was still hiding in one of the outlying mountain regions of San Fernando and vowed he would never surrender to the Japanese. He was being concealed and supplied with food by friendly Filipinos.

Jack's wife was a Russian woman whom he met and married in China while he was stationed there as an enlisted man of the United States Navy. Jack and his wife had two children, a boy of fourteen and a girl ten years of age. Jack's wife and children were not interned and they visited him frequently at the Ateneo Hospital. Jack's wife, who was an excellent cook and occasionally brought doughnuts, or a prune cake, which Jack divided among the residents of our ward. Jack, himself, who suffered from diabetes, ate very sparingly.

About the end of February, when wheat flour became very difficult to obtain, a brother of Jack's wife purchased a quantity of cracked wheat, which he ground in a corn mill and sold as whole-wheat flour at 10 pesos ($5.00) per sack of 49 pounds. As a friendly gesture, Jack offered my wife a sack of this whole-wheat flour at 6 pesos ($4.00). But my wife refused the offer because she had very little cash available. Four months later, when white flour was selling at 43 pesos ($1.50) per 49-pound sack and whole-wheat flour was not obtainable at any price, my wife regretted that she had declined Jack's offer.

Jack delighted in recounting a repertory of vulgar but humorous stories which was apparently inexhaustible. In the evening, just after dinner, a majority of the inmates of the men's ward gathered for the "dirty story hour" in a remote corner of the courtyard where they were not likely to be overheard by the ladies. Jack's high-pitched treble giggle was heard after each coarse joke, whether told by himself or someone else.

Although Jack was usually a very cheerful person, he occasionally had the blues. On such occasions he pessimistically opined that we would probably be internees for at least a year and perhaps longer. At that time most of us believed that the Japanese would be driven out of Manila by the end of June 1942!

When Jack's pass for internment at the Ateneo Hospital expired in March it was extended until March 31. But on March 28 Jack was released on a pass which was secured for him by Doctor Garcia, the Portuguese lady physician who was successful in obtaining release to their homes for several of the Ateneo internees. Jack's pass for internment in his home was renewed for a further month when it expired in May. But in June Jack after being examined by a Japanese physician, was sent back to the Santo Tomas Internment Camp.

Chapter 19.

Concerning the Automotive Mechanic

Mr. Loggey was a ruddy-faced enlistment who arrived at the Ateneo Hospital just a day later than I did. Like myself, he had been sent to the Ateneo Hospital after being interned at Santo Tomas for only two days. We learned that he was 56 years old; that he suffered from high blood pressure; that he owned a home in Mandaluyong, one of the most remote suburbs of Manila; that by his first wife, who had died, he had a daughter 20 years of age and a son 18 years of age and that his present wife was a fine-looking Filipino woman, about 35 years of age, with whom he had been living for about fifteen years.

Because Mr. Loggey's home was a considerable distance from the Ateneo Hospital and because, due to the war, transportation was costly, his wife visited him only once each week. Saturday was her visiting day. In order to avoid any possibility of their being interned, his son and his daughter were living with Filipino friends in Manila. I do not recall that his son ever visited him, but his daughter, who lived near the Ateneo, came quite frequently and sometimes brought him food. She was living at the home of a former colonel of the Philippine constabulary.

During March and April Mr. Loggey was on duty as gate-keeper at the entrance of the Ateneo Hospital from noon until 2 p.m. each day. At that time of the day there were almost no visitors. Hence Mr. Loggey and his daughter were able to enjoy their daily visit at the gate with little interruption. These daily visits were, of course, a violation of the rule limiting each visitor to one visit per week. But that rule was never rigidly enforced at the Ateneo Hospital. This laxity was facilitated by the fact that there were no restrictions on visitors to any part of the Ateneo premises except the hospital.

Mr. Loggey ate very little and he was very fussy about what he did eat. He refused to eat about one-half of the food which the hospital provided. Sometimes he gave the food which he rejected to a fellow internee. Quite frequently he sent the rejected food back to the hospital kitchen with some caustic comment. Occasionally, in exchange for hospital food which he rejected, I gave him some of the food which my wife brought to me. Fortunately though, his wife and daughter brought him some food which *was* to his taste.

Aside from his caustic comments about the food served at the hospital, Mr. Loggey was very cheerful. He almost always had a whimsical joke of some sort which brought smiles to the faces of doctors and nurses when they visited him each morning.

Mr. Loggey was an expert automobile and tractor mechanic. When the war began he was employed in Manila by a large mercantile firm which dealt in machinery. During the bombing of the river front, Mr. Loggey had been working in a warehouse near the south of the Pasig River. One bomb burst in the street in front of the warehouse. The front wall of the warehouse had been pierced by some splinters so that it looked like a sieve. Fortunately, Mr. Loggey had been working at the rear of the warehouse where the damage occurred. The area in which he worked had been bombed several times. He said when this happened he did not leave his work and that he did not feel particularly nervous while the bombing was in progress. But after he reached his home in the evening he would find himself trembling and the following morning he always felt a profound reluctance to return to his work.

Mr. Loggey's home was located near the Wack Wack Golf Club, which was occupied by Japanese soldiers. Not far away was Camp Murchy, which was also occupied by Japanese soldiers. On January 26, Camp Murchy was bombed by USAFE planes. Mr. Loogey's wife reported that the Japanese soldiers at the golf club had climbed into trucks and had driven out to the road in front of her house, where they parked their trucks beneath the trees and hastily took refuge in the ditch beside the road. This air raid occurred between 5 and 9 o'clock on a clear moonlight night when the sky was overcast with scattered low-hanging clouds.

Early in February Mrs. Loggey brought a leaflet which she had picked up on the yard of her home and which she said had been dropped by an airplane. Printed on the leaflet was a message from President Roosevelt in which he urged the Filipinos to continue their resistance, assured them that American aid was coming, and concluded by saying, "Filipinos, your day is coming." The message was dated, as I recall it, February 1, 1942, but the leaflet had been found a week later.

The Japanese military authorities confiscated all field glasses which they discovered. It was a serious offense to be caught with a field glass in one's possession. Mr. Loggey possessed a pair of binoculars. Fearing his house might be searched by the Japanese military authorities, he instructed his wife, early in February, to bring the binoculars to the Ateneo hospital. When they arrived he gave them to the chief doctor who promptly secreted them.

In February Mrs. Loggey reported that the Japanese were stationed at the bridge across the San Juan River, which formed the boundary between Mandaluyong and Manila. She said that the drivers of horse drawn vehicles seeking to cross the bridge from Mandaluyong to Manila had been slapped and otherwise maltreated by Japanese soldiers.

The Japanese military authorities, in an announcement published in the *Daily Tribune*, advised every resident of Manila and its suburbs to obtain a residence certificate from the Japanese military authorities. No fee was charged for the issuance of this certificate, but each person to whom the certificate was issued was required to exhibit a residence tax receipt showing that the residence tax for 1942 had been paid to the Philippine government. In this announcement, the Japanese military authorities called attention to the fact that most of the Japanese sentries neither spoke nor read English. Therefore a residence certificate issued by the Japanese military authorities would serve as a pass which would avoid unpleasant encounters with Japanese sentries.

Because Mrs. Loggey had to pass a Japanese sentry at the San Juan Bridge every time she came to Manila to visit her husband she was, I believe, the first wife of an Ateneo internee to obtain a residence certificate from the Japanese military authorities. The wives of the other internees soon followed suit.

At that time, the only office issuing Japanese residence certificates was located in the former Army and Navy Y.M.C.A. building in the Walled City (*Intramuros*). Each day there was a long line of people waiting outside of this building to obtain residence certification from the Japanese military authorities. Most of the people waited in line for several hours before obtaining their residence certificates. My wife reported that the people were kept in line by the Japanese guards who were quite brutal in maintaining order. The wife of one Ateneo internee reported that a Japanese guard slapped a Filipino woman who attempted to crowd ahead of someone else in the line. My wife was very courteously treated. She appealed to a Filipino policeman of her acquaintance who was acting as one of the guards. He personally conducted her into the building and assisted her in securing a residence certificate.

For several weeks there was only this one office from which Japanese residence certificates were issued. But after the newspapers announced that 120,000 residence certificates had already been issued, several other issuing offices were established in various parts of Manila and the surrounding area, in order to speed up the issuance of residence certificates to the remainder of the population. By the end of February, residence certificates had been issued by the Japanese military authorities to practically all of the residents of Manila and its surrounds. No statement of the total number of residence certificates issued was ever published, but it must have been in the region of 400,000. This was a very effective method of collecting residence tax, which many people were reluctant to pay to the Japanese-controlled puppet government of the Philippines.

After he had been interned for about two months at the Ateneo Hospital, Mr. Loggey began to feel a powerful biological urge to cohabit with his wife.

"It is the lack of nooky that's been getting me down," he observed with an impish grin on several occasions. Our chief doctor offered to recommend Mr. Loggey internment at his home. But Mr. Loggey was one of the few internees whose pass provided for internment at the Ateneo Hospital for an unlimited period of time. It was certain that if his pass was sent back to Santo Tomas with an application for internment at his home such internment, if granted, would be for a limited period of time at the end of which he might be ordered back to Santo Tomas and not the hospital. Therefore, Mr. Loggey preferred to remain at Ateneo as long as his pass for such internment was unlimited.

In April, when our passes were sent back to the Commandant of the Santo Tomas Internment Camp to be renewed, we were informed for only limited periods of time, Mr. Loggey requested internment at his home. On May 2, when our passes were returned, Mr. Loggey learned to his delight that his request had been granted. He was released to his home on May 3. A couple of weeks later he paid us a visit looking as chipper as a cock sparrow. Internment at his home very evidently had improved his health. Or perhaps it was the "nooky" that put a new spring in his stride and a cheerful grin on his ruddy face!

Chapter 20.

Concerning the Jesuits and the Manner in Which They Ministered to Us

The war disturbed the lives of the Jesuits no less than it disturbed the lives of other residents of the Philippines. The Ateneo University and the seminary for theological students which the Jesuits operated for the Philippine government and which was located on the campus of the Ateneo University was closed by the Japanese occupation of Manila. The American Jesuits engaged in missionary work were forced to leave their missions. The business enterprises in which the funds of the Jesuits were invested and which were the sources of their income were either destroyed or confiscated by the Japanese. Their cash resources were impounded in banks which were closed when the Japanese occupation of Manila began.

Conditions brought about by the war forced a concentration at the Ateneo of all Jesuits in the Philippines. Even before the war, a large majority of them resided at the Ateneo where quarters were provided for all Jesuits employed in the Weather Bureau and for all Jesuits employed as professors and administrators of the Ateneo University. The Jesuits who conducted a seminary for theological students were transferred to the Ateneo when the seminary was closed immediately after the outbreak of the war. When the Japanese occupied Manila the only Jesuits not already concentrated at the Ateneo were six American Jesuit missionaries whom the Japanese had interned in the residence of the Roman Catholic Bishop in the town of Naga in Southern Luzon. Two young Filipino Jesuits dispatched to Naga by the Father Superior succeeded in persuading the Japanese military authorities to permit the transfer to the Ateneo of the six American Jesuits interned at Naga. Their arrival in March completed the concentration, at the Ateneo, of all Jesuits in the Philippines.

Although a majority of the Jesuits concentrated at the Ateneo were Americans, there were several Spaniards and a considerable number of Filipinos. No restrictions were imposed by the Japanese upon the Spanish and Filipino Jesuits. But the American Jesuits were interned at the Ateneo.

For about a month Japanese sentries were stationed at the entrance to the Ateneo. The sentries were withdrawn early in February. Thereafter the conditions of internment at the Ateneo were considerably less arduous than those were imposed upon those interned at Santo Tomas. Within the Ateneo premises the American Jesuits were free to do as they chose. They were permitted to receive visitors without restriction of any sort. The Ateneo Chapel was open to the public and the American Jesuits were permitted to celebrate mass in the chapel. The American Jesuits were even provided with papers which permitted them to leave the Ateneo premises during the hours of daylight. However, they must return before sunset, and not more than five American Jesuits were permitted to be absent from the Ateneo at the same time.

Notwithstanding the passes which had been issued to them, the American Jesuits very rarely left the Ateneo premises. They shrewdly surmised that their frequent appearance outside of the Ateneo would result in the cancellation of their passes and might result in their internment elsewhere in less comfortable quarters. Several officers of the Japanese military administration had already suggested that the Ateneo University should be vacated by the Jesuits so that it might be used for Japanese military purposes.

In March the Father Superior obtained from the Japanese military administration permission to reopen the Jesuit seminary for theological students. The seminary was reopened at the Ateneo. This added about 25 Filipino students to the Jesuit community. Although they were not interned, these Filipino students resided in quarters provided for them on the Ateneo campus and ate at the Jesuit mess.

The violent typhoons which frequent Philippine waters during about six months of each year and the consequent heavy loss of ships and lives prompted the Spanish government of the Philippines, during the latter half of the nineteenth century, to construct and operate a meteorological service. The Jesuit meteorologists made such an outstanding success of this work that the administration of the Weather Bureau created after the American occupation of the Philippines was placed in their hands. The Jesuits continued to administer the Weather Bureau until it was forced to cease functioning by the Japanese occupation of Manila. From the date of its creation, the director of the Weather Bureau was always a priest of the Jesuit order. Its offices and equipment were located on the campus of the Jesuits' Ateneo University and much of the equipment used by the Weather Bureau and the building which it occupied were the property of the Jesuits.

Although the Weather Bureau had ceased to function, the Jesuit meteorologists continued to record such meteorological data as they were able to observe from the Ateneo premises. During the month of May 1942, the temperature in Manila rose to 106° F, which exceeded any temperature previously recorded for the Philippines. Because of the high humidity which accompanied it, we suffered terribly from the heat. In the Ateneo Observatory were housed several seismographs. During our internment at the Ateneo there occurred at about eleven o'clock one night an exceptionally prolonged and violent earthquake. We rushed from our beds to the courtyard in front of the hospital. The pavement heaved beneath our feet. Seeing several of the Jesuit Fathers hurrying across the campus to the Observatory, we joined them. In the Observatory we discovered that the recording needles of the seismograph had been thrown from their pivots by the violence of the earthquake. But from the record so abruptly terminated the Jesuit Fathers estimated that it had exceeded intensity seven.

Food was the most serious problem which confronted the Jesuits. Including the students of the seminary, there were more than 150 persons to be fed at the Jesuit mess. The Jesuit's income had practically ceased and their bank account was impounded. The Father Superior remarked one day that they had lots of credit but very little money. The cost of flour, canned goods and other foodstuffs which could no longer be imported became prohibitive immediately after the start of the Japanese occupation of Manila. Even rice, the chief food produced in the Philippines, was difficult to obtain because the Japanese military administration had taken over its distribution. The sale of rice to consumers except by the military government, was prohibited. The price of the rice sold to consumers by the Japanese military administration was not that high. It was fixed by military decree at 34 centavos per ganta (about US$0.032 per pound). But the maximum amount of rice which could be purchased from the military government was rationed to 200 grams (two-thirds of a pound) per person per day and there were many days when the military government was either able to supply only a part of the ration or unable to supply *any* rice at all. Fresh meat, fish, fruit, vegetables, and corn were not rationed and were usually obtainable at the public markets, but frequently not in quantities sufficient for so large a mess as that operated by the Jesuits. Before the end of January 1942, the Jesuits found it expedient to limit themselves to two meals per day. Only by so doing could they preserve their small reserve of foodstuffs for use at a future time when it was anticipated that food would be even more difficult to obtain.

Prior to the Japanese occupation of Manila the Jesuits had managed to accumulate a reserve supply of foodstuffs sufficient, in case all other sources of food were cut off, to last them about three months. In one corner of the campus were housed about 200 hens, which supplied the Jesuit mess with eggs. Six sheep and three cows grazing upon the Ateneo campus constituted their reserve supply of fresh meat.

A portion of the campus was divided up and planted as a vegetable garden. For several hours each day of the long hot dry season, younger members of the Jesuit community toiled in the garden. Their reward was a substantial, but nevertheless insufficient, supply of green vegetables. Additional vegetables were purchased in the public market.

The Industrial Chemistry Laboratory at the Ateneo was well equipped for the manufacture on a small scale of a variety of commercial products. In charge of the laboratory was Father Guigi, a very competent chemist. The revenue obtained from the sale of products which Father Guigi manufactured in the laboratory was not large, but it constituted almost the only income of the Jesuits after the Japanese occupation of Manila. The soft drinks which Father Guigi manufactured were retailed by a restaurant located on Manila's principal retail business street. The truck from the restaurant visited the Ateneo several times each week to return empty bottles and pick up the soft drinks which were ready for delivery.

The laboratory was also equipped for the manufacture of reconstituted milk from powdered skimmed milk, butter and water. The limited supply of milk powder and butter on hand prevented the sale of this product. But each day Father Guigi manufactured several gallons of reconstructed milk for the use of the Jesuit mess. Milk was provided only for the weaker members of the Jesuit community.

Several of the Jesuit Fathers were assigned by the Father Superior to minister to those interned at the Ateneo Hospital, but in addition to the Fathers specifically assigned to this duty, numerous other members of the Jesuit community often visited us. By their unfailing cheerfulness and friendly interest in our personal problems they did much to maintain our morale. We thirsted for news of the war undistorted by Japanese propaganda. Invariably they brought us such news. Some of this news they picked up by short wave radio receiver from allied sources overseas. But much local news was brought to them by Filipino visitors who came, not only from Manila and its suburbs, but also from more distant parts of the Philippines. They were better informed concerning many occurrences throughout the Philippines than were the Japanese. News came to the Jesuit Fathers which was carefully concealed from the Japanese. We longed for allied victory. Their profound faith that the war would be won by the Allies comforted us and enabled us with greater fortitude to bear the disaster which had engulfed us. Many of them were Irish Americans who expressed their patriotic devotion to America and their wholehearted detestation of the Japanese with a forthrightness which warmed our hearts. The Jesuit Fathers never embarrassed those of us who were not Catholics by discussing religion unless we ourselves expressed a desire to discuss that subject. The masses celebrated each day at the Ateneo Chapel were open to the public and were attended by many persons who did not reside at the Ateneo. Those who were interned at the Ateneo, Catholics and non-Catholics alike, were invited to attend these masses. Often those of us who were not Catholics did attend mass. I believe that we derived as much comfort from them as we could have derived from religious services conducted by clergymen of our own faiths. The disaster of the war had increased our desire for religious communion and had broadened our tolerance for religious creeds which differed from our own. It was enough that the Jesuits communed with our God and by so doing brought us comfort.

The reopening of the Jesuit seminary for theological students restored to the Ateneo campus something of the cheerfulness and carefree enthusiasm of college life. A majority of the students were Filipinos, but there were also about a dozen young American Jesuit brothers who had served as instructors at the Ateneo University but who had not yet completed their training for the priesthood. Late each afternoon the students performed a rite which never failed to fill our hearts with a warm glow of admiration and approval. Standing in a close massed group before a shrine upon the Ateneo campus they first intoned a brief prayer. Then they sang "God Bless America." As they sang their voices swelled in a determined and defiant surge of sound which must have carried to the Japanese soldiers billeted across the street from the Ateneo Campus.

Chapter 21

Concerning Certain Persons Who Sought and Were Granted Refuge at the Ateneo University

The Jesuits provided quarters for about 25 persons who had sought refuge at the Ateneo and whose internment there was subsequently authorized by the Japanese military authorities. These internees were provided with passes which authorized them to leave the Ateneo premises for the purpose of purchasing food, clothing and medicines, but they were not permitted to remain away from the Ateneo overnight. In most cases no food was provided for them. But they were provided with facilities for cooking the food which they purchased for themselves. Among these internees were Americans, British and Jews. A majority of them were women who had small children to care for and whom the war had separated from their husbands.

One of these women was the young wife of an American lieutenant. When she learned that her husband had been killed during the siege of Corregidor she gave birth to a stillborn child.

Three of the four pregnant women at the Ateneo delivered stillborn infants. The doctors believed that this was due in large measure, to grief and brooding over the violent disruptions of their lives which the war had caused.

The American husband of another young women interned at the Ateneo was killed during the bombing of the U. S. Navy yard at Cavite. With her three small children she fled from Cavite to Manila and sought refuge with the Jesuits.

There were several British women from Shanghai. The ship on which they were being evacuated to Australia was at sea near Manila when the Captain was informed by radio of the attack on Pearl Harbor. Fearing that his ship might be bombed at sea by Japanese planes, he sought refuge at Manila. Informed that the ship would not be allowed to continue its voyage to Australia, he set sail from Manila without waiting for his passengers to return to the ship and without discharging their baggage. The ship reached Australia safely. Among the passengers who were left stranded in Manila without baggage were the British women and their children who came to be interned at the Ateneo. Their husbands, because sufficient transportation was not available, had remained at Shanghai, where they too were later interned by the Japanese.

Among the Americans interned at the Ateneo was Dr. Beyer, who for many years prior to the war, was professor of anthropology at the University of the Philippines. He enjoyed an international reputation as an authority on the anthropology of Southeastern Asia and the Pacific Islands. For several days after the Japanese occupied Manila, Dr. Beyer was interned at Villamor Hall on the campus of the University of the Philippines, directly across the street from the Ateneo. Because he was recognized by the Japanese as a distinguished anthropologist who had shown a deep and friendly interest in the early development of the Japanese race he was soon released to his home. When he found that during his few days of internment his quarters had been completely looted he sought and was granted a refuge with the Jesuits at the Ateneo University. He was lodged in one of the dressing rooms beneath the stage of the auditorium and was provided with food at the Jesuit mess.

The Japanese military authorities had provided Dr. Beyer with a pass which permitted him to move freely about the city. He made frequent use of this pass and upon his return from expeditions to various parts of the city entertained us with an account of his observations of the effect the Japanese occupation was having upon the lives of the people of Manila.

Dr. Beyer had occupied two rooms at Villamor Hall One of these rooms served as his classroom, the other as his office and study. In the course of many years spent exploring sites of the early inhabitants of the Philippines and other Asiatic countries, Dr. Beyer had acquired many specimens of pottery, tools and weapons of wood, stone and metal; utensils of stone, bronze and iron; coins of bronze, silver and gold; ornaments of bronze, silver and gold which early peoples had worn for personal adornment and as evidence of their tribal rank. This priceless personal collection of anthropological specimens was housed in the two rooms which Dr. Beyer had occupied at Villamor Hall. In his office were also housed his library of books on anthropology and related subjects, his files, of correspondence with students of anthropology in many parts of the world, the manuscripts of his lectures on anthropology, the notes recording the results of his many years of research and the completed manuscript of a book which he had written, but which was still unpublished, upon the anthropology of the peoples of Southeast Asia and the Pacific Islands.

About a month after he took up residence at the Ateneo Dr. Beyer obtained from the Japanese military authorities who occupied Villamor Hall permission to visit the rooms which he occupied. He found that his valuable collection of gold coins has been stolen, but that nothing else was missing. He was granted permission to visit his rooms whenever he so desired. Thereafter he spent considerable time reading and studying at Villamor Hall.

Dr. Beyer had received letters from students of anthropology in many different countries. After he had read each letter he returned it to its envelope and placed the envelope in his files. Each letter, of course, bore postage stamps of the country from which it came, when he visited his office one morning after several days of absence he found the floor littered with hundreds of envelopes taken from his files. Someone, without bothering to remove the letter which it contained, had cut out from each envelope the corner on which the stamps were affixed. The thief had taken only those fragments of each envelope, leaving the floor strewn with the mutilated letters. Dr. Beyer was furious. Upon his return to the Ateneo he informed us indignantly, "I did not mind the loss of my gold coins. I cared nothing for the stamps and would have gladly given them to the thief if only he had left my letters unmutilated." He spent several days laboriously sorting out the severed fragments of letters and joining them with paste and narrow strips of paper.

The Japanese military administration issued a decree prohibiting the publication of any book or pamphlet which had not been examined and approved by the Japanese board of censors prior to its publication. Learning of Dr. Beyer's unpublished manuscript on the anthropology of the peoples of southeast Asia and the Pacific Islands, the board of censors required Dr. Beyer to submit his manuscript for examination and approval. When Dr. Beyer told us about it, he did not appear to be greatly concerned. He said that he did not believe the Japanese would do very much with his book. I never learned whether or not the manuscript was returned to him. I was informed that valuable books and manuscripts in the Philippines were confiscated by the Japanese and sent to Japan to enrich their own libraries.

Chapter 22.

Concerning Charlie, the Policeman

Charlie Welch arrived at the Ateneo Hospital from Santo Tomas late in January. We called him the policeman because he had served at one time on the Manila Police Force. Charlie was a husky fellow, six feet tall and weighing about 180 pounds. He was 56 years old, but appeared younger. A large hooked nose dominated his face. He complained of rheumatism in his back, but appeared to be otherwise in good health. The electric massage and heat treatment which was given to his back each morning did not, Charlie said, relieve his rheumatic pains. Nevertheless he seemed quite content to remain at the Ateneo Hospital.

Charlie came to the Philippines in 1903, arriving just a little too late to be rated a Spanish-American War Veteran. After leaving the army he was for several years a member of the Manila Police Force. Later he worked for seven years in the largest sawmill in the Philippines, eventually becoming its night mill superintendent. The gold boom of 1933 found him in Baguio working in the repair shop of a large truck transportation company. For several years immediately prior to the outbreak of the war he had been employed in the Cavite Navy yard.

Fortunately for him, Charlie left the yard to go home for lunch a few minutes before the Cavite Navy yard was bombed with such heavy loss of life early in December.

At the time the Navy evacuated Cavite, late in December, Charlie was given a quantity of foodstuffs from the Naval stores. He immediately rented a furnished apartment in Manila and made four trips with his car to transport this foodstuff from his home in Cavite to the apartment in Manila. His furniture he left behind in Cavite.

Charlie's wife was a middle-aged Spanish woman, to whom he had been married for only five years. She was a widow with several children when they married. They were devoted to each other and she visited him at the Ateneo Hospital almost daily. After she was limited to one authorized visit per week, their unauthorized visits were carried on at the gate during the two hour period each day when Charlie was gate-keeper.

Charlie's wife was a Catholic and I believe that Charlie became a convert during his internment at the Ateneo Hospital. One of the Jesuit Fathers visited Charlie each morning. They always sought a secluded corner of the courtyard and inferred that Charlie was receiving instruction in the tenets of the Catholic faith.

Charlie's wife brought him a greater quantity and variety of food than was received by any other internee, but he rarely shared any of it with his fellow internees. He was a big man and a heavy eater. He ate all of the food which the hospital supplied as well as that brought by his wife. He neither gained nor lost weight, so what he ate was probably what he required.

Although they were well supplied with foodstuff, Charlie and his wife had very little cash. He refused to contribute toward the purchase each day of a daily newspaper for our ward. He did purchase a kilogram of coffee and joined the group of internees who each contributed a spoonful of coffee to the communal coffee pot.

Although Charlie was unwilling to contribute either money or food for the benefit of his fellows, he was more ready than anyone else to render personal service. Each afternoon it was Charlie who carried a cup of milk from the kitchen to each patient's bedside. It was Charlie who usually prepared and served the communal coffee. It was Charlie whom the nurses usually called upon to perform any little chore which needed to be done. He was always cheerfully ready to render any service of this sort.

And his service was not entirely without compensation. For serving the milk the nurses usually rewarded him with an extra cup of milk. His ration of food from the hospital kitchen was also frequently a little larger than that served to the rest of us.

He was suspected for a time of petty theft in the preparation of the communal pot of coffee. It was alleged that he did not contribute any of his own coffee to the communal pot but actually added to his own can of coffee a small portion of the coffee which he collected from other internees. I noted, however, that about the end of June Charlie's own supply of coffee was smaller than that of the rest of us.

Each evening, Charlie would plod back and forth around the court in front of the hospital. He walked just as a policeman walks when leisurely pacing his beat, his right arm swinging to and from as though a night stick were suspended by a strap around his wrist and loosely clasped in his hand.

We expected that Charlie would be sent back to Santo Tomas when the Japanese doctor inspected us late in April. But Charlie was lucky. His pass was extended until June 10 and, after we were transferred from the Ateneo to Red Cross Hospital No 4, his pass was extended again until June 25.

Toward the end of June, when it was planned to close Red Hospital No. 4, Charlie's doctor recommended him for internment at his home. The Commandant of the Santo Tomas Internment Camp ordered Charlie to present himself for examination at the Commandant's office on June 29. When he presented himself on June 29 he was given a provisional pass for internment in his home for ten days and was ordered to report for examination on July 9. On the latter date the Japanese doctor decided that Charlie was entirely too healthy to be interned at home. He was reinterned at Santo Tomas on July 10.

I went to Santo Tomas on July 10 for my own examination by the Japanese doctor. Charlie was waiting for me when I came out of the Commandant's office. He inquired what the doctor's verdict was in my case. When I reported that I had been granted a pass for internment in my mother-in-law's home until August 10, Charlie requested me to carry a message to his wife.

Chapter 23.

Concerning the Marine Chief Engineer

Tom Hanking arrived at the Ateneo Hospital from the Santo Tomas Internment Camp during the second week of February. His pass provided for internment at the hospital for one month. I did not learn the nature of his illness. On some subjects Tom was very reticent.

Tom was a native of Kentucky. He was a tall, lean man, over 60 years of age. His head was long and very narrow. His nose was long. His mouth was large and his chin was square. His eyes were a pale blue. His sparse and close-cropped hair, neatly parted in the middle was the color of a wheat straw. His face was deeply tanned and when he beamed innumerable tiny wrinkles appeared.

We called Tom The Chief, because he was a licensed Marine chief engineer. He served in the Philippines for many years as a civil employee in the U.S. Naval Transport Service, from which he was eventually retired with a pension. For several years there after he operated a small sawmill.

Tom was reputed to be well-to-do. He owned his home, which was located on the same street as the home of my mother-in-law. His much younger wife was Spanish and they had no children. Tom, however, had a son, long since grown to manhood, by an earlier wife.

At the time war came to the Philippines in December 1941, Tom was the engineer in charge of the private yacht of a wealthy mining executive of the Philippines. During that hectic period in December immediately preceding the Japanese occupation of Manila, Tom's employer was in Hong Kong and Tom had a lot of leisure time on his hands. He took advantage of his leisure to lay in a large stock of foodstuffs, which he stored in his house. Although Tom did not say so, I surmised that a part of his ample supply of foodstuffs may have been ship's stores which he salvaged from his employer's yacht immediately before the Japanese occupation of Manila.

Tom was a convivial soul. He had a great store of coarse barroom jokes and his discourse—in the company of his own sex—was interspersed with the lusty vernacular of a seaman. But he was also something of a lady's man. His bluff good humor made him an agreeable companion for men and women alike. Yet one sensed an underlying hardness and obstinacy in his nature which could upon occasion make him a difficult person to deal with.

On the day that Tom arrived at the Ateneo Hospital my wife visited me. By her, Tom sent a message to his home requesting that food be brought to him at the Ateneo. Tom's wife was at that time absent from her home and did not return until about ten days later. When she finally came to visit him, he learned that she had left Manila with a truck loaded with canned foodstuffs and other merchandise which she expected to sell in one of the provinces adjacent to Manila. It was her intension, when she had sold this merchandise, to purchase rice which she would sell in Manila. Her merchandise and the truck which transported it were confiscated by the Japanese army in a provincial town not far from Manila. She was marooned in this town for several days before she was able to obtain transportation back to Manila.

Each internee upon entering the Santo Tomas Internment Camp, was required to make a written statement describing, and indicating the exact location of, any automobile that he owned. Tom had an old, but still serviceable, Packard automobile of 1925 vintage. One day, late in February, Tom's wife reported that the Japanese, accompanied by a Filipino policeman, had taken possession of Tom's automobile and had driven it way.

A couple of days later my wife reported that the Japanese had taken possession of our Ford car. The battery was dead and they towed it away with a truck We learned that the Japanese had inspected all the internee's automobiles and had taken possession of most of them. Tom had stored in his garage together with about 10,000 pesos worth of machinery. The Japanese inspected this but did not take it.

Early in March, a few days before his pass for internment at the Ateneo was to expire, Tom applied for internment at his home. Chiefly because he was over 60 years of age he was released to his home on March 14.

Chapter 24.

Concerning the Professor

The professor arrived at the Ateneo Hospital about the end of February. He was a short stout man about 65 years of age, whose snow-white hair and beard made him appear even more venerable than he actually was. When the war began he was a professor of history at the Santo Tomas University. After the Japanese occupied Manila he was interned at the university where he had so recently taught. He contracted influenza at the internment camp and was sent to the Ateneo Hospital to recuperate.

The professor came to the Philippines as a soldier during the Spanish-American War. After his discharge from the army he became a teacher in the Philippine Bureau of Education. He soon married a woman of Spanish-Filipino ancestry. This first wife died after bearing him a son and two daughters. For many years thereafter the professor was a widower but eventually he remarried a Filipino woman. He had no children with his second wife.

The Professor was a supervising teacher when I first met him in 1914. He was ambitious, however. He studied law and was admitted to the bar while still serving as a supervising teacher In 1916 he resigned from the Philippine Bureau of Education and returned to the United States where he obtained a position in the Federal Civil Service. He was also a reserve officer in the United States Army. When the United States entered the First World War he was called up to active duty and was given a captain's commission. He resigned his commission at the end of the war and for seven years thereafter was an attorney for the Standard Oil Company in Cuba. In 1925 he returned to the Philippines and became a civilian employee in the Quartermaster's Service of the United States Army in Manila. When he retired with a pension in 1938, he secured employment as a professor of history at Santo Tomas University.

The professor's second wife and the three children by his first wife avoided internment by claiming Philippine citizenship. They visited the professor soon after his internment at the Ateneo Hospital.

All the professor's children were married and had children of their own. One of his daughters was married to an American, who was interned at Santo Tomas. The other daughter, who was married to a Spaniard, was a professor of English Literature at Santo Tomas University. His son, at the time the war began, was a civilian employee of the U.S. Army in Manila.

The professor's second wife was a middle-aged Filipino woman whom he married after his return to the Philippines in 1925. She operated a small store and a meat stall in the public market, both located in Pasay, a suburb of Manila. The professor and his wife lived on the second floor of the building occupied by their store. On January 1 most of the stores in Pasay were looted. But the professor and his wife prevented the looting of their store with the aid of four Filipino guards armed with bolos. The professor, himself, was armed with a shotgun. Bands of looters came several times appearing in front of the store, but moved on to easier pickings when they encountered the embattled professor and his Filipino guards.

The professor and his three children jointly owned a rice farm in Pampanga Province which they had inherited from the professor's first wife. It was cultivated by tenant farmers who paid, as rent to the professor and his children, one-half of the annual crop of 2,000 *cavanes* (sacks) of *palay* (unhulled rice). The rice was ready to harvest when the Japanese forces arrived. About 500 sacks of *palay* belonging to the professor and his children were still stored on the farm when the professor entered the Ateneo Hospital. He said that any attempt to transport it to Manila for sale would result in its confiscation by the Japanese military authorities.

The professor's own bank account was impounded by the Japanese military authorities. But his wife had an account in the Philippine National Bank, from which she was able to withdraw 400 pesos when the bank reopened in February. She owned a small parcel of land in which she planted *camotes* (sweet potatoes). Her daily net income from the meat-stall in the public market was about 2 pesos. Fearing that it might be looted, she disposed of most of the small stock of goods in her store soon after the professor entered the Santo Tomas Internment Camp in January.

As a result throughout the war the professor's children were without income and their savings were impounded in banks which had not been permitted to reopen. So the professor's wife was supporting his children and grandchildren. There were, altogether, seventeen in the family.

The professor was a great talker. He arose at daylight and immediately began talking in whispers to avoid awaking those who were still asleep. His whisper, however, could be heard across the room.

Doctor Garcia, the Portuguese lady physician who had been marooned in Manila by the war and was connected with the Philippine Red Cross, became interested in the professor's case when he was confined with influenza in the Santo Tomas Hospital. She visited him soon after his arrival at the Ateneo Hospital to let him know that she was working for his release. She obtained a pass which released the professor to his home on March 24.

Chapter 25

Concerning the Manner in Which We Obtained News of the War

The Jesuits possessed excellent radio receivers. Although they had removed the outdoor aerials and had carefully concealed the receivers in order to avoid possible confiscation of the equipment by the Japanese, the Jesuits were able, nevertheless, to pick up broadcasts from London, San Francisco and Australia, as well as the "Voice of Freedom" which broadcast from General MacArthur's headquarters on Corregidor.

A group of Jesuit priests and brothers was assigned to listening to those broadcasts and preparing daily a typewritten statement of the news received from each broadcasting station. For several weeks a summary of each day's radio news was given to us verbally by one of the Jesuit Fathers who visited the men's ward in the hospital each evening. Often the Father Superior, himself, came and told us the news. Beginning late in February, either the Father Superior or one of his subordinates brought us a typewritten copy of each day's news. We were required to return each day's typewritten sheets when the typewritten sheets of the succeeding day's radio news were delivered to us. In order to avoid the discovery of these typewritten sheets by possible Japanese visitors, we concealed the news sheets in an old magazine which was passed from internee to internee, and to the members of the hospital staff, until all had read the news.

Early in March an American internee, whom we called Honest Abe, obtained from his home a small but powerful radio receiver. Since Abe's family was interned at Santo Tomas and Abe himself was not permitted to visit his home, the radio receiver was brought to the hospital by one of the Filipino hospital attendants, whom Abe sent to his house for that purpose. Abe installed the radio in one of the compartments of the linen closet in our ward. But, at our chief doctor's suggestion, it was later installed upon a table on the hospital veranda. The doctor said that the Japanese authorities had not prohibited the use of a radio receiver but that the use of a concealed receiver might get us into trouble.

We were discreet in our use of the radio, however. When not in use it was kept covered with a cloth so that the nature of the object upon the table would not be evident to a visitor who did not lift the cloth. To make it still less obvious, various items of hospital equipment were usually stacked upon the table beside the receiver. The doctor's contention was that, placed in this conspicuous place, the radio was less likely to be discovered than if it had been hidden in a closet. Furthermore, if it was discovered, we could say we had not concealed it, that we put the cloth over it to keep out the dust, and that we were not aware that the use of a radio receiver was forbidden. The receiver was connected by means of a dummy electric light cord and socket suspended above the table. This was connected to an aerial which was suspended beneath the roof of the room above which housed the shower baths. Power was obtained from a genuine electric light cord and socket which was also suspended above the table. When not in use the receiver was disconnected from both the aerial and the electric light socket.

With this receiver, we were able to pick up short wave broadcasts from all over the world. Each evening we gathered around the radio to hear the news from San Francisco. We were careful to keep the receiver tuned so low that we, ourselves, sitting at the table upon which it rested, had difficulty in hearing the news. The doctors used their stethoscopes very efficiently for this purpose—one end of the stethoscope being placed in contact with the receiver. Each morning and again at noon Abe alone put his ear against the receiver and tuned in to the news which he later reported to us.

Although Japanese army officers and other Japanese officials visited the hospital on several occasions, they paid no attention to the radio receiver. A Jesuit brother stationed at the main entrance to the Ateneo always warned us by electric buzzer when the Japanese entered the building. Hence the radio was never in use when the Japanese visitors reached the hospital.

During our internment at the Ateneo the Japanese had not yet prohibited the use of short wave radio receivers nor had they forbidden listening to overseas broadcasts. They had already issued, however, a military decree which prohibited the dissemination of news, by word of mouth, by typewritten or mimeographed sheets, or any other manner. News could only be published in newspapers subject to Japanese military censorship. The penalties for violation of this decree were very severe. This was the reason for the care taken by the Jesuit Fathers to secure the return to them of every typewritten news sheet which they delivered to us.

As time went on the Jesuit Fathers became so preoccupied with other matters that the typewritten news sheets were delivered to us at irregular intervals, instead of daily. But by that time we had our own radio and were able to pick up overseas radio news for ourselves.

Much local news was brought to us by Filipino visitors, both those who visited the Jesuit Fathers and those who visited patients in the hospital. These visitors supplied us with news which could not be published by the Japanese censored newspapers. Some of the news which we obtained from Filipino visitors is recorded in subsequent chapters.

We subscribed to one of the Japanese-controlled daily newspapers—a four-page tabloid which was devoted to publishing the decrees issued by the Japanese military administration and by the puppet government. Such news as it did contain was filled with Japanese propaganda.

Chapter 26.

Concerning Ford, the Editor

Ford came from Santo Tomas to join us at the Ateneo Hospital in February. He was a small quiet man who appeared to be between 35 and 40 years of age. Prior to the war he was the city editor of one of Manila's daily newspapers. The last issue of this daily appeared on the morning of January 1, 1942. Its publication was suspended by the Japanese occupation of Manila on January 2. It had enjoyed an uninterrupted publication of more than 41 years.

Although Ford was able to walk when he arrived in February his muscular control was imperfect—like that of a child just learning to walk. Like a child, he occasionally fell and hurt himself, although never seriously. I never learned the exact nature of his malady. But whatever it was he slowly gained control over the movement of his lower limbs. At the end of three months he was so much improved that he walked with a nearly normal stride, although he had the appearance of concentrating his mind upon his walking to a greater degree than the normal adult finds necessary.

Ford occupied his time with reading and writing. He had a small folding stool with a canvas seat. For two or three hours each day he might be seen, either upon the veranda or beneath a tree in the courtyard, perched upon his stool and absorbed in a book. Each day he put in about two hours filling loose sheets of typewritten paper with his neat script. I never inquired as to what he wrote, but a fellow internee informed me that Ford copied into his notes considerable portions of the news items contained in the *Manila Daily Tribune*. This was a Japanese-sponsored newspaper which we received each day at the hospital. I gained the impression that Ford either was keeping a very detailed newsman's diary or was writing a book about the war.

There were perhaps a half dozen Filipino friends who visited Ford regularly and brought him books and food. They also brought him considerable news of events taking place in Manila and elsewhere in the Philippines. Most of this news was of such a nature that it was not recorded in the pages of the Japanese-controlled *Daily Tribune*. Ford gave very close attention to these reports and I suspect it was recorded in the voluminous notes which he wrote each day. I also surmised that his work was delivered to one of his frequent visitors for safe keeping.

For several months Ford neither invited nor repelled friendly overtures. He always replied courteously when spoken to but never sought to prolong a conversation. But after he had been with us for about three months he began to take a greater interest in his fellow internees. He accepted an invitation to join us in a game of cards after dinner each evening. We played either rummy or pitch. The players usually included Charlie, Ford, myself, and two or three others.

When the Ateneo Hospital was closed early in June, Ford was one of those transferred to Red Cross Hospital No. 4. Early in July, when Red Cross Hospital No. 4 was closed to internees, Ford and several others secured passes interning them once more at the Ateneo, where they were provided with food and quarters by the Jesuit Fathers. Their passes gave them the same privileges as the passes of those who were interned at home. Ford frequently left the premises to visit various parts of the city. His pass authorized him to make such excursions only for the purpose of obtaining food, clothing and medical attention. But no one ever questioned him as to his reason for being out upon the street.

Chapter 27.

Concerning Ira, the Surveyor

Ira arrived at the Ateneo Hospital about the middle of March. He came from Santo Tomas Internment Camp, where he had been interned for only about a week before being sent to the Ateneo. He was about 65 years of age, a lean man of medium height with blue eyes, white hair and beard. We often called him the Kentucky Colonel because he wore his beard trimmed to a goatee.

Ira was a surveyor and geologist by profession. During the early years of the American regime in the Philippines he was a surveyor in the Bureau of Lands. Later for many years he was engaged in private practice as a mineral lands surveyor. He married a Filipino woman and reared nine children—four daughters and five sons. Eventually his wife died and most of the children married. He had retired from the his profession and at the outbreak of war was living with one of his daughters in San Juan, a suburb of Manila.

In December, Ira with two of his daughters—each with a baby—and their husbands, fled to his cattle ranch and coffee plantation, located in the mountains of Nueva Viscaya Province in North Central Luzon. Ira remained on the ranch for two months after the Japanese occupation of Manila. A Japanese force had occupied Nueva Viscaya late in December. Occasionally Japanese scouting parties passed close to Ira's ranch and Ira went into hiding until the Japanese departed. The Japanese drove off and slaughtered a number of Ira's cattle. He reached the conclusion that sooner or later he would be discovered and captured by the Japanese and that he would fare better if he surrendered voluntarily. So toward the end of February he sent word to the Japanese Commandant at Bayambong, Nueva Viscaya, that he was ready to surrender when called upon to do so, but was prevented by a game leg from walking to Bayambong to report in person. He was instructed to remain at the ranch until a Japanese patrol called for him. The patrol arrived a few days later. Ira, his two daughters and their babies were transported to Bayambong. The husbands of the two daughters were absent from the ranch. At Bayambong the two daughters were given refuge in a convent occupied by Catholic nuns. Ira was quartered temporarily with the parish priest of Bayambong.

Early in March, Ira and four other old men, two of whom were American Negros, were put aboard a truck and were dispatched to Manila for internment at Santo Tomas. A guard of Japanese soldiers accompanied them. The journey took five days. At one of the Japanese outposts Ira and his companions were subjected to rough treatment in an unsuccessful attempt to extract from them information concerning the hiding place of USAFE guerrillas who were then operating in the mountains of Nueva Viscaya.

Ira informed me that, up to the time he left Bayambong, USAFE guerrillas were very active both in Nueva Viscaya and in the adjoining mountain province. Late in February Major Warner and several other American officers, with a detachment of Filipino soldiers, came to the vicinity of the cattle ranch where Ira was then living. A Filipino soldier brought a message from Major Warner to Ira offering him the privilege of joining the guerrillas. Ira declined because his game leg would make him an encumbrance to the guerrillas and because he had already notified the Japanese of his whereabouts. He sent a message to Major Warner letting him know that a Japanese patrol had passed within a half mile of the ranch house that very morning and giving Major Warner permission to drive off some of the cattle to feed his soldiers.

The headquarters of three guerrillas, according to Ira, was a cave located somewhere in the mountains of Nueva Viscaya. An American civilian, who was an executive of a motor transportation company, became convinced that war with Japan was inevitable. About a year before the actual outbreak of hostilities, this executive began preparations to retire with his family into the mountains as soon as the Japanese invaded the Philippines. While hunting bear he had found a cave, which he chose as his place of refuge. In this cave he stored essential camping equipment and a supply of foodstuffs sufficient to last a year. A guard was stationed at the cave to avoid the possibility of it being looted. When the Japanese began their advance south from Aparri, this American and his family retired to their cave as they had planned. Later, they were joined by several other American civilians and by Major Warner and his detachment of soldiers. Ira did not know where the cave was located and he said that up to the time he left Bayambong the Japanese had not discovered its location.

At Bayambong Ira was told of an encounter between a Japanese detachment and USAFE guerrillas under Colonel Horan which had occurred in the Mountain Province. The Japanese boarded several trucks and went in pursuit of Colonel Horan's guerrillas. At one point the road was cut into the face of an almost perpendicular cliff. The guerrillas ambushed the Japanese at this point by placing an obstruction across the road forcing the Japanese to stop their trucks. The guerrillas posted on the cliff above then set off a blast of dynamite. This precipitated a landslide which engulfed the trucks. Two of the trucks were pushed off the road and fell several hundred feet. About fifty soldiers were killed. The few Japanese who survived fled. Ira said that the account of this engagement came from the Japanese Commandant at

Bayambong who expressed his admiration of the cleverness of the guerrillas in trapping their Japanese pursuers.

It was about two weeks after his arrival at the Ateneo that Ira was at last able to send a messenger to his home in San Juan. None of the members of his family were in the house. It was being occupied by a Filipino tenant who, although unable to pay rent, was caring for the personal effects of Ira's family. The tenant came to visit Ira.

One of Ira's sons-in-law had left Bayambong for Manila about a week before Ira himself departed from Bayambong. Ira now learned that his son-in-law had not reached Manila and his whereabouts were unknown. It was not until several months later that Ira received word from his daughters in Bayambong that his son-in-law, unable to secure a pass through the Japanese lines, had returned to Bayambong and that all of the members of Ira's family in Bayambong were safe.

Ira arrived in Manila with no money in his pocket. Since there were no members of his family in Manila to provide him with either money or food, he was forced to get along as best he could upon the meager ration provided by the hospital. For a time, his bed was next to mine and I shared with him some of the food which my wife brought. Other internees provided him with cigarettes and with a kilogram of coffee so that he might contribute his share to the communal pot.

Ira was transferred with the rest of us to Red Cross Hospital No. 4 when the Ateneo Hospital was closed early in June. When Red Cross Hospital No. 4 was closed to internees and was converted into a hospital for Filipino war prisoners early in July, Ira was one of the eight old men who were permitted to remain in the hospital until some other place could be found for them.

The public dispensary which the Red Cross had maintained at Red Cross Hospital No. 4 continued to function after the hospital was closed to internees. After my release to my home on June 30, I went to this dispensary once each week to receive an injection of liver extract. On these occasions I always visited Ira.

When I visited Ira on August 1, he told me that a Spaniard who owned a cattle ranch on the island of Palawan had brought very disturbing news concerning two of Ira's sons.

A penal colony was located at Iwahig in Palawan. Following the Japanese occupation of the Philippines there was an almost complete breakdown of the enforcement of the law and order in Palawan. Many of the prisoners escaped from the Iwahig penal colony and became roving bands of robbers who pillaged farms scattered along the coast of the island. The major in command of the Philippine constabulary soldiers stationed on the island did nothing to check the depredations of these robbers. It was said that many of his soldiers had deserted and that some of them had become robbers too. Japanese forces had not yet occupied Palawan. Meanwhile a state of anarchy prevailed on the island.

When the Japanese eventually occupied Puerto Princesa, the capital of Palawan, the major in command of the constabulary became a Japanese collaborator and was made the puppet governor of the province.

Two of Ira's sons were operating a cattle ranch which Ira owned on the island of Palawan. One of these sons, Alfred, was engaged to the daughter of a Spaniard who owned an adjoining ranch. When conditions became chaotic on the island, Alfred persuaded the Spaniard to leave his ranch in Alfred's care and seek refuge with his family in Manila. The Spaniard left his eighteen-year-old son on the ranch with Alfred, but moved with the rest of his family to a village on the seacoast to await the arrival of his motor boat to transport them to Manila.

The day after the Spaniard's departure the major, who had become the puppet governor of the province, visited the Spaniard's ranch. Alfred accused the major of dereliction of duty in failing to protect the ranchers from the depredation of robbers. The major became furiously angry, drew his gun and shot Alfred, wounding him, though not seriously. Alfred in self-defense then shot the major, killing him instantly.

The Spaniard's motor boat called at the ranch the following day. The Spaniard's son, who had witnessed the encounter between the Major and Alfred, boarded the motor boat and rejoined his father. The motor boat then brought the Spaniard and his entire family to Manila. When they left Palawan Alfred was still at the Spaniard's ranch and no attempt had been made to arrest him. Later, news reached Ira that Alfred and his brother had joined the USAFE guerrillas operating in Palawan.

Chapter 28.

Concerning the Mining Engineer

Victor, the mining engineer, was 70 years old, but he did not appear to be more than fifty. He was six feet two inches tall and weighed about 220 pounds. He carried himself erectly and walked with the light but vigorous step of youth. His high-brow and strong, well-formed features were remarkably free from wrinkles and his dark hair was only slightly frosted at his temples. His blue eyes, peering from beneath very dark and heavy eyebrows, were alert and kindly. Altogether, he was a handsome and forceful man.

Victor came to the Philippines during the mining boom of 1933-35. When the war began he was Dean of the Mining School at the University of the Philippines. His wife, son and daughters were in the United States and he lived at his club until he was interned at Santo Tomas.

He joined us early in April with a pass authorizing him to reside at the Ateneo Hospital for two weeks while his dentist was fitting him with a set of false teeth. His pass permitted him to visit the office of the dentist but he was usually accompanied by a Red Cross attendant. He returned to Santo Tomas when his pass expired on April 22.

Although he was with us only two weeks, Victor made a more lasting impression upon us than many with whom we were associated for several months. From the moment of his arrival, he entered quietly but zestfully into the communal life of our ward. Internment at Santo Tomas had neither impaired his glowing health nor dampened his spirit. He took life as it came and made the best of it. We shared our food with him. He shared his food with us.

We learned that he was one of the officials of the central governing committee of the Santo Tomas Internment Camp. It was his duty to receive the daily reports of the room monitors and prepare a digest of these reports for submission to the central committee. He said that the central committee had prepared a set of rules for governing the camp but had no means of enforcing these rules except by reporting infractions to the Japanese Commandant of the camp. Action would then be taken by the central internees to enforce voluntary obedience to the regulations.

Literary and musical programs for the entertainment of the internees were given each week at the Santo Tomas Internment Camp. Victor had agreed to deliver two lectures. He prepared the manuscripts of these lectures while he was with us at the Ateneo Hospital. He submitted the manuscripts to Ira and myself and requested us to make suggestions for their improvement. One of these manuscripts discussed the art of writing. It began with the earliest pictograms and traced the origin and evolution of several different alphabets. Ira had made a study of anthropology and was able to contribute several suggestions which Victor incorporated. I found the finished manuscript well written and the subject presented in such a manner as to interest and entertain the layman. We received a note from Victor after his return to Santo Tomas stating that his lectures had been well received and thanking us for our assistance in preparing his manuscript.

Unlike most of us, Victor evinced no desire to discuss the progress of the war. Apparently he considered such discussion to be a useless waste of time. There was nothing that we internees could do to affect the outcome. However he was confident in the victory of the allied nations. His son, we learned, was a commissioned officer in the United States Army.

Chapter 29.

Concerning Japanese Visitors at the Ateneo

Although after the end of January 1942 no Japanese guards were maintained at the Ateneo University, it was frequently visited by officers of the Japanese Army.

On one occasion a Japanese officer, accompanied by a squad of soldiers, appeared at the Ateneo and demanded instant admission to the room in which were stored the rifles which, prior to the war, had been used by the cadet corps of the Ateneo University. As the room was padlocked one of the Jesuit Fathers went to the office of the Father Superior to obtain the key. Unwilling to wait, the Japanese officer instructed his soldiers to break down the door and so the rifles were removed from the Ateneo by the squad of Japanese soldiers.

The Japanese had forced the Weather Bureau at the Ateneo to cease functioning immediately after they occupied Manila. In its stead they set up their own meteorological station on the roof of the Bay View Hotel. Nevertheless, the meteorologists of the Japanese Army made frequent, in fact almost daily, visits to the Weather Bureau at the Ateneo. The exact purpose of these visits was not clear but they may have suspected the existence of a short-wave radio transmitter on the premises. Alternatively, it may have been that they merely came to learn about the equipment and methods used by the distinguished Jesuit meteorologists who had made such an outstanding success of forecasting weather conditions in the Philippines.

The Japanese military officials who visited the Weather Bureau never concerned themselves with the Red Cross Hospital located at the Ateneo. There were other Japanese officers and officials, however, who occasionally visited the Ateneo University for reasons which they did not divulge. They merely insisted upon being shown about the premises of the University, sometimes including the hospital.

We referred to all Japanese visitors as the "Smith Brothers." Whenever we were warned that the "Smith Brothers" were anywhere about the Ateneo premises we quickly took to our beds. A moment before these warnings there might be a dozen or more internees upon the veranda and in the courtyard. A minute after the warning everyone had disappeared into their wards.

Father John Hurley, the Father Superior of the Jesuits, stationed several Filipino Jesuit brothers in the lobby of the main entrance to the Ateneo. It was the duty of these Filipino brothers to engage any Japanese visitors in conversation in order to delay them at the lobby until another brother had given a warning signal throughout the main building that Japanese visitors had arrived. The warning signal was given by touching the button of an electric buzzer. This button was located beneath the desk of a brother who served as receptionist in the lobby.

The Father Superior usually left his office on the second floor as soon as he received the signal that Japanese visitors had arrived. He would not reappear until one of his subordinates had met the Japanese visitors and determined the nature of their visit. Sometimes the Father Superior did not reappear until after the Japanese had departed. The primary reason for the Father Superior's inaccessibility to the Japanese visitors was the fact that officers of the Japanese Army had on several occasions attempted to induce the Father Superior to turn the Ateneo premises over to the Japanese Army for military use. The Father Superior, unable to give a flatly negative answer to this proposal, was doing a masterly job of stalling. Another reason for the Father Superior's inaccessibility to Japanese visitors was probably the fact that to a Japanese mind the importance of an official was reckoned by the difficulty in securing an audience with that official. Father Hurley was one of the highest dignitaries of the Catholic church in the Philippines, and he maintained in his attitude toward the Japanese a reserve commensurate with his high office in the church. The Japanese, on the other hand, were at this period still seeking to win the support of the Catholic church in the Philippines. Hence, in so far as possible, they avoided clashes with high officials of the church

Things came to a head late in March 1942. There came to the Ateneo a Japanese colonel who insisted upon seeing the Father Superior and demanded that the Ateneo premises be turned over to the Japanese Army for the use of Japanese soldiers upon their return from Bataan. The Japanese-controlled press had already announced that the fall of Bataan was imminent. The Father Superior did his usual job of stalling. But when he told us about it during his visit to our ward that evening, he was rather dubious about being able to avoid Japanese military occupation of the Ateneo. He said that a Japanese Catholic priest who was a colonel in the religious section of the Japanese Army had promised to intercede for him. But the Japanese priest feared that the matter had gone so far that the decision to occupy the Ateneo would not be rescinded. "However," concluded Father Hurley cheerfully, "Maybe we'll be lucky. We have been so far." Next morning there was affixed to the main entrance to the Ateneo a notice which read, "This building is reserved for the use of Japanese soldiers when they return from the capture of Bataan." It was several weeks later, however, when Bataan finally surrendered and in the meantime the Japanese military authorities decided not to occupy the Ateneo premises.

Chapter 30.

Concerning USAFE's Defeat and Surrender to the Japanese

When the Japanese occupied Manila early in January 1942 we knew, of course, that the position of the Philippine forces was desperate. But we still hoped that they would be able to hold out until aid arrived from America. During those early months of 1942 we still believed that aid would reach the Philippines before the end of June. How mistaken we were! We did not know how weak the United States was, how unprepared she was, how utterly unable she was to defend the Philippines at that time. We believed President Roosevelt when he announced that powerful aid from America was coming soon and urged the people of the Philippines to fight until aid arrived.

The supposedly impregnable British base at Singapore fell. The small American naval force which escaped from the Philippines was practically wiped out in a heroic but futile defense of Java. The Japanese penetrated Burma and overran Java and Sumatra.

But still USAFE fought doggedly on at Bataan and at Corregidor. And USAFE forces in other parts of the Philippines were still fighting, although they had been forced to retreat into the mountains and resort to guerrilla tactics.

Each day we hoped for news of an allied victory indicating that the tide of Japanese conquest had been stemmed. But we hoped in vain.

The "Voice of Freedom", broadcasting from the American fortress at Corregidor, shouted defiance at the Japanese. Filipinos who collaborated with the Japanese were branded as traitors and it was announced that they would be dealt with sternly when the Japanese had been driven out of the Philippines. Death will be the penalty of all traitors shouted the "Voice of Freedom."

In the midst of overwhelming disaster the heroic stand of the USAFE forces in Bataan and at Corregidor cheered us. And we needed cheering. The "Voice of Freedom" informed us that the USAFE lines in Bataan were holding and that the Japanese were taking terrific losses in their determined but futile attempt to crack those lines. As week followed week and the USAFE forces still held out in Bataan, the Japanese high command chose to publish an explanation of the apparent lack of Japanese success in the Bataan campaign. The Japanese Imperial Army has the USAFE forces bottled up in Bataan and Corregidor. They cannot escape. Their ultimate defeat is certain. Unless they surrender they will be completely terminated. When the auspicious moment arrives the Japanese Imperial Army will move against them with overwhelming force.

During this period we witnessed two brief attacks by USAFE planes upon the Japanese forces in Manila. USAFE had very few planes and such as they had were light planes capable of carrying only small bombs. But the attacks were well planned and successfully executed.

The first raid occurred at about 9 o'clock on the moonlit night of January 26, when the sky was overcast with scattered low-hanging clouds. A USAFE plane coming in at very low altitude from the direction of Manila Bay, flew directly over Ateneo Hospital. On the campus of the University of the Philippines across the street from the Ateneo, an anti-aircraft battery let go a brief and ineffective burst of shell-fire. We saw the shells exploding in the air. A moment later we head the boom of a bursting bomb. On the following day we learned that this bomb had fallen in the street in Paco, about 20 feet from the house of the Japanese consul-general. This was about a mile from the Ateneo, The Japanese consul-general was entertaining several Japanese officers of high rank at a dinner party when the bomb fell. The bomb was a small one and none of the Japanese were injured. But on the street a Filipino woman was killed and several other Filipinos were injured. We were informed that the Japanese consul-general moved to other quarters the following day. During that raid bombs were dropped at several points in Manila and its suburbs where there were concentrations of Japanese troops. It was reported to us that immediately after this raid the Japanese troops which had been concentrated in a few large buildings were dispersed to smaller buildings scattered throughout the city. The Bay View Hotel was one of the large buildings evacuated. It was also said that the Japanese commanding general had moved his headquarters to the Manila Hotel.

On the morning after this air raid the Japanese-controlled *Manila Daily Tribune* announced that the internment camp at Santo Tomas University had been bombed. But two internee patients who arrived at the Ateneo Hospital from Santo Tomas a day or two later reported that no bomb had fallen on the internment camp but we learned that a concentration of Japanese troops at the San Lazaro race track, about a mile from the internment camp, had been bombed.

This air-raid demonstrated that General MacArthur's secret service operating in Manila had furnished him with very precise information as to the disposition of the Japanese forces in Manila and its suburbs. It was also evident that the pilots who participated in the raid were very familiar with the city. Although anti-aircraft guns went into action in several parts of the city, their fire was ineffective and all of the USAFE planes returned safely to their base. The Japanese were caught napping and the raid was over before any Japanese planes got into the air.

We were greatly cheered by this air raid and hoped fervently that it would be followed in the immediate future by more of the same. In fact there was only one other USAFE air raid upon the Japanese forces in Manila, and again the Japanese were caught napping.

The Manila Polo Club was occupied by a group of Japanese officers. The clubhouse was located on the shore of Manila Bay in the southern outskirts of Manila, about two miles from the Ateneo Hospital. On a Sunday about a month after the first USAFE air raid on the Japanese in Manila, a large number of Japanese officers assembled at the Manila Polo Club for luncheon. At about midday, while the luncheon was in progress, USAFE planes appeared unexpectedly and bombed the clubhouse. Many of the Japanese officers were killed. Others were wounded. The USAFE planes dropped their bombs and escaped without a single Japanese shot being fired.

Several of us were sitting on the veranda of the Ateneo Hospital when this raid occurred. The veranda faced south, about two miles from the Polo Club. The clubhouse was hidden by intervening trees, but it was directly in line with a street which ended at the Ateneo campus. There was a row of tall trees on each side of this street. From where we sat on the veranda we looked southward between the trees which lined the street toward the Polo Club. A moment after we heard the explosion of the first bomb we saw a plane rise above the trees which formed the horizon at the southern end of the street. The plane turned to the west and disappeared behind intervening trees. Immediately after the first plane disappeared we saw a second plane dive and disappear below the treetops at the end of the street. A moment later it rose above the tree tops, turned west and also disappeared behind the intervening trees, exactly as the first plane had done. No sooner had the second plane disappeared than a third plane appeared, dived swiftly below the treetops, reappeared above the treetops and disappeared to the west. One after another, in swift succession, seven or eight planes appeared upon the horizon, dived below the tree tops, reappeared above the tree tops and disappeared to the west. A moment after each plane disappeared we heard a bomb explode. Not more than ten or fifteen minutes elapsed between the appearance of the first plane and the disappearance of the last plane.

There was no objective in that direction which Japanese planes might bomb hence we concluded that the planes which we saw must be USAFE planes and that they had made another raid upon the Japanese. We knew that the Polo Club was occupied by the Japanese but we also knew that in the same direction, about a mile beyond the Polo Club, was a Japanese occupied airport. So we were not certain whether it was the Polo Club or the airport which had been bombed. But it did seem certain that USAFE planes had again bombed the Japanese and had again got away safely. We were highly elated.

The next morning several visitors who came to the Ateneo Hospital informed us that the Polo Club had been bombed by USAFE planes and that many Japanese officers had been killed or wounded. Among the casualties were several Filipinos employed as servants by the Japanese officers who resided in the Polo Club.

Again the efficiency of General MacArthur's spies in Manila had been demonstrated. They learned that a large number of Japanese officers were to assemble for luncheon at the Polo Club and had informed General MacArthur of both the day and hour at which the luncheon was to occur.

The siege of Bataan dragged on. The USAFE lines held steadfast against the constant pressure of an enormously superior Japanese force. Each evening the "Voice of Freedom", broadcasting from Corregidor, brought us details of the siege. Japanese casualties were enormous. USAFE casualties were much smaller.

Could USAFE hold out until help arrived? We all hoped, and some of us prayed, that they might. But one day late in March, Father Hurley said he had received a report that the USAFE troops were suffering from a lack of sufficient food and from an epidemic of malaria and dysentery. Would starvation and disease force them to yield? Dear God in heaven, care for them and give them strength!

The news that General MacArthur had left Bataan and had gone to Australia came to us as a profound shock. Was Bataan about to surrender? The "Voice of Freedom" announced that General MacArthur had been ordered to Australia to take supreme command of the war in the Western Pacific. The Japanese-controlled press jeered that General MacArthur had deserted his army in the face of inevitable defeat and that he had fled to Australia to escape capture. We did not question General MacArthur's courage. We did not doubt that he left Bataan because he had been commanded to do so. But what about the USAFE troops in Bataan. Would they, could they, still fight on? General Wainwright, who succeeded General MacArthur in command, announced resolutely that they would continue to fight.

But the Japanese-controlled press was jubilant. The end of the Bataan campaign was near, it proclaimed. Soon the USAFE Army must either surrender or be completely exterminated. A few days later the Japanese military authorities posted on the door at the main entrance to the Ateneo a notice which read, "This building is reserved for the use of Japanese soldiers when they return from the capture of Bataan." We were informed that there was rivalry between the Japanese Army and the Japanese Navy for the use of certain buildings and that the Japanese Army had posted the notice reserving the Ateneo building in order to prevent the Navy from taking it over.

The USAFE Army in Bataan surrendered about three weeks later. Major General King, who was in command at Bataan, effected the surrender to General Homma, the Japanese commander-in-chief. The announcement of the surrender of Bataan did not surprise us. Events of the preceding three weeks had indicated quite clearly that the surrender of Bataan was imminent.

General Wainwright announced grimly that his forces in Corregidor would continue to fight. But how long could Corregidor hold out after the surrender of Bataan? Interned in my ward were two men who had been retired from the United States Navy. It was their opinion that Corregidor could not hold out for more than two weeks after the surrender of Bataan. How fervently we hoped that they were wrong!

The island of Corregidor is separated from the southern coast of Bataan by a narrow channel not more than half a mile in width. Prior to the surrender of Bataan, Corregidor had been subjected only to attack by air. But now the Japanese not only bombed Corregidor from the air but also shelled it with heavy artillery set up on the southern tip of the Bataan Peninsula. They also assembled barges in preparation for an attempt to effect a landing on Corregidor by moving troops across the narrow channel which separated Corregidor from Bataan.

Each night throughout the first week of May the Jesuit Fathers sat on the roof of Ateneo and watched the artillery duel between the guns of Corregidor and the Japanese guns on the Bataan Peninsula. Corregidor was ten miles distant across Manila Bay. But they saw the flashes of bursting shells and heard the dull booms of distant heavy artillery.

The end came on May 6. That night there was no flash of shells bursting over Corregidor and no sound of artillery could be heard. The "Voice of Freedom", which each evening throughout the siege had broadcast its message from Corregidor, was silent.

On the morning of May 8 the Japanese-controlled newspapers of Manila announced that Japanese troops had effected a landing on Corregidor, that the USAFE force on the island had surrendered and that General Wainwright would that evening broadcast an important message concerning his surrender.

On the evening of May 8 we gathered around the radio receiver on the veranda of the Ateneo Hospital to listen to General Wainwright's message. Speaking from the Japanese-controlled radio station in Manila, General Wainwright announced his surrender. He stated that the conditions imposed upon him required the surrender, not only of the force at Corregidor, but also of all other USAFE forces still active in the Philippines. Calling by name each of his subordinate commanders—the general in command in the Visayan islands, the general in command in Mindanao, and the colonel in command in the mountains of Northern Luzon—General Wainwright ordered them all to surrender to the commander of the nearest Japanese force. Failure to do so, he declared solemnly, would have a most disastrous consequence. He implied, although he did not directly state, that the entire force which had surrendered at Corregidor would be executed if any of the subordinate commanders whom he named failed to surrender. He concluded by saying that a message bearing his order to surrender was being dispatched to each of the commanders whom he named.

As they listened to General Wainwright's message, several of the women wept. Sadness and foreboding filled the hearts of us all. Already we had learned of the cruel and inhuman treatment accorded to those who surrendered at Bataan. Now the conquest of the Philippines by a ruthless invader was complete. What did the future hold—for the USAFE forces which surrendered, for the people of the Philippines and for us who were held as civilian internees? We did not know. But we were filled with misgivings.

The final surrender of the USAFE forces in the Philippines produced no immediate change in the treatment accorded by the Japanese military authorities to civilian internees. It was several months later, when General MacArthur began his push northward from Australia and the Japanese Navy and Army in the Southwest Pacific began to taste defeat, that our Japanese jailers began to impose greater restrictions upon us and to make our lot as civilian internees more difficult to bear.

Early in 1943, when the Japanese had already begun to impose greater restrictions upon us, we were addressed at Santo Tomas by the Japanese diplomat who up to that time had been the civilian Commandant of the Santo Tomas Internment Camp. Very accurately he expressed the Japanese attitude toward civilian internees when he declared, "Now that we are victorious we can afford to be magnanimous." He admitted that more onerous conditions of internment had already been imposed upon us. In justification of this change in treatment he said that his countrymen were suffering in New Guinea.

We pondered the Commandant's address with misgiving and rightly so. At each new victory won by General MacArthur's forces the Japanese expressed their resentment by making our lot harder to bear. In the end many of us died. By February 3, 1945, we were released by the arrival of General MacArthur's first cavalry division. Our situation had become so desperate that if we had not been released all of us would have died within a month or two. If the Japanese were ruthless in victory, they were even more ruthless in defeat.

Chapter 31.

Concerning Slim and His Family

Mr. Meukow, his wife and their two young sons arrived at the Ateneo Hospital on May 8. All of them were suffering from malaria. Mr. Meukow, who was infected with the malignant type of malaria, was in a serious condition. His blood showed a count of only about one-seventh of the normal number of red corpuscles. His face was a ghastly white and he was scarcely able to stand on his feet. He was given two blood transfusions within forty-eight hours of his arrival. For several days it was doubtful that he would survive. But he clung tenaciously to life and when the quinine had broken his fever he began to recover slowly.

Mr. Meukow was more than six feet tall and was so lean that we called him Slim. He said that his normal weight was about 180 pounds but that he now weighed not more than 130 pounds.

Slim had served for twelve years in the United States Navy, where he attained the rank of chief petty officer. He was retired from the Navy because of impaired hearing. While stationed with the United Sates Navy in China he married a Russian widow. His wife's first husband was a German, with whom she had one child, a son. She had also borne Slim a son. The two boys were about 12 and 9 years old, respectively. Slim appeared to be about 45 years old and his wife perhaps ten years younger.

At the outbreak of the war Slim was a civilian employee in the United States Navy yard at Cavite, across the bay from Manila. He and his family escaped injury during the bombing of Cavite early in December. When the Navy evacuated Cavite Slim took his family to Bataan, where he secured employment as a civilian mechanic in the transport service of the USAFE forces under General MacArthur.

Slim and his family were with the USAFE force in Bataan throughout the entire period of the siege. They suffered from a lack of sufficient food and when they eventually contracted malaria their malady was aggravated by a lack of quinine for treating it.

The shortage of food was made more serious by the large number of civilian Filipinos who fled to the Bataan Peninsula ahead of the Japanese advance. These civilians arrived with practically no food and USAFE was compelled to feed them out of its own meager stores. Slim believed that the number of civilian refugees exceeded the number of USAFE soldiers. This large population of civilian refugees aggravated the epidemic of malaria and dysentery which decimated civilians and soldiers alike. The streams of Bataan had long been notorious for breeding deadly anopheles mosquitos which transmit malaria. With the influx of a large population of civilian refugees these streams, which were the principal source of drinking water, also became contaminated with the organisms which cause dysentery.

Several days after the surrender of Bataan, Slim's Russian wife succeeded in securing a pass to Manila for herself, her husband and her two sons. Slim then loaded his family and their baggage upon an abandoned U.S. Army truck and took the road to Manila. At the town or Orani in Bataan they were stopped by a Japanese lieutenant who confiscated their pass, took possession of their baggage and truck, and placed them in a temporary war prisoners' camp. They remained there for about ten days, during which Slim was so ill with malaria that he was delirious a part of the time. Slim's wife eventually secured their release by appealing to the Japanese Commandant of the camp. They were able to recover the truck in which to continue their journey to Manila, but most of their baggage has been stolen. The Japanese lieutenant who had detained them and who was responsible for the loss of their baggage was reprimanded by the Commandant. The lieutenant apologized to Slim and gave him a one-pound tin of Granger smoking tobacco as a partial recompense for the loss of his baggage. Slim and his family were stopped and questioned by Japanese sentries several times during their journey to Manila. When they ran out of gasoline a Japanese sentry very obligingly provided them with a can.

Upon their arrival in Manila they reported to the military police, who interned them for about a week in the military prison at the former Fort Santiago. Slim's wife appealed to the Commandant of the military police for their release. When he learned that she was a Russian and that, because her first husband was a German, her oldest son was a German citizen, the Commandant suggested that her request for release should be transmitted through the German consul at Manila. The Commandant provided an automobile in which she was conducted to the Office of the German Consul. As a result, she, her husband and her two sons were sent to the Ateneo Hospital for the medical attention they so desperately needed. Slim, being an American citizen, was interned at the Ateneo Hospital. But his wife and her two sons were not interned and were free to leave the hospital as soon as their health was restored.

Slim and his family were ravenously hungry when they arrived at the Ateneo Hospital. The two boys expressed amazement and delight when they discovered that they were to receive three meals a day instead of only two. But the hospital did not provide sufficient food for the hungry family. They also ate an even greater quantity of food which Slim's wife purchased outside of the hospital. As she herself was ill with malaria, she arranged for food to be brought to the hospital by a Russian girl of her acquaintance.

Slim's wife and the two boys recovered rapidly and were discharged from the hospital within two weeks. They secured quarters in another part of the Ateneo building so that they might be near Slim. The two boys were gaunt and listless when they arrived at the Ateneo. But they soon began to put on weight and recovered the normal liveliness of healthy children.

Slim's own recovery was slow. He did not realize how ill he was and objected to taking the quinine which was so necessary to destroy the malarial parasites. He suffered two attacks of chills and fever during the first three days after his arrival. The quinine then began to take effect and he had no further fever as long as he continued to take the quinine. But a discontinuance of the quinine was followed by a relapse and it was necessary to renew the treatment. As a result of the blood transfusions, a multitude of small boils developed all over his body. It was two months before all of these boils were fully healed. He ate enormous quantities of food but did not put on any weight. At the end of two months his blood showed a count of 2,600,000 red corpuscles—still far below the normal count of 5,000,000 but much better than the 700,000 with which he had entered the hospital.

When the Ateneo Hospital was closed early in June, Slim was transferred to Red Cross Hospital No. 4. His family remained in the quarters which they had secured at the Ateneo. Early in July Slim secured a pass interning him at the Ateneo, where his family was living. He discontinued taking quinine when he left the hospital. About the middle of July he suffered a recurrence of malarial fever. On August 2, I was told by a friend who visited him that Slim was quite ill.

Chapter 32.

Concerning the Suffering and Death of USAFE War Prisoners from Bataan

One day, several weeks after the fall of Bataan, Antonio Escoda came to the Ateneo Hospital. Prior to the war he had been a member of the editorial staff of a daily newspaper published in Manila. The city editor of this newspaper was interned at the Ateneo Hospital. Antonio came to visit him quite frequently.

I had known Antonio for more than twenty-five years. I was one of his teachers when he was a senior in high school. When Antonio arrived I was on guard duty so we sat at the gate and talked a while before he went into the hospital to visit his friend. This is the story Antonio told me.

About a week after the surrender of Bataan reports began to filter into Manila concerning the terrible plight of the Filipino and American war prisoners who were being forced to march on foot from Bataan to the concentration camp at Camp O'Donnell, a distance of nearly 100 miles. Thousands of the war prisoners were suffering from malaria and dysentery contracted during the siege of Bataan. Many were wounded. All were weakened by months of semi-starvation during the siege. When they fell exhausted by the roadside during the terrible march many were cruelly beaten, bayoneted, or shot. When they arrived at Camp O'Donnell no hospital facilities and no medicines were provided for them. Hundreds of them were dying each day.

Antonio's wife, Josefa Llanes Escoda, was a trained nurse. Prior to the war she was prominent in Manila as a social worker. When she heard of the terrible plight of the war prisoners at Camp O'Donnell she gathered from various sources in Manila a truck load of medicines, surgical dressings and other hospital supplies. Accompanied by Antonio, who drove the truck, she set out for Camp O'Donnell. They were stopped at San Fernando in Pampanga Province, 45 miles north of Manila, by the Japanese military authorities. After some delay Antonio's wife obtained permission from the Japanese commander at San Fernando to take the truck to Camp O'Donnell.

At San Fernando there was a barbed-wire enclosure where a group of war prisoners were being held temporarily before being sent on to Camp O'Donnell. Antonio approached the barbed-wire fence and spoke to several of the Filipino war prisoners. One of them handed Antonio 700 pesos with instructions to deliver the money to his wife in Manila. Another handed Antonio 1,500 pesos with similar instructions. They said that during the siege of Bataan they received several month's pay. All of the war prisoners had considerable money in their possession when they surrendered but most of them had been robbed of their money by Japanese soldiers. These two had managed to conceal their money.

When Antonio and his wife reached Camp O'Donnell they were horrified by what they saw. War prisoners were still marching into the camp. Some of them reached the camp only to lie down beside the road and die. American and Filipino army doctors, themselves prisoners of war, had reserved several barracks for use as a hospital but there were no beds or cots. There were not even blankets. The suffering prisoners lay upon the bare floor. There were no medicines, no surgical dressings, nothing to relieve the suffering of the sick and wounded. Toilet facilities were of the most primitive sort. Thousands of prisoners suffering from dysentery deposited their faeces in open pits. Millions of flies, which bred in the exposed faecal matter, swarmed over the prisoner's food and spread dysentery throughout the camp.

After delivering the first truckload of medicines and hospital supplies to Camp O'Donnell, Antonio and his wife obtained a truck load of hospital beds which they delivered to Camp O'Donnell a few days later. They were in Manila gathering a third truck load of hospital supplies when the Japanese military authorities issued a decree stating that civilians were forbidden from furnishing hospital supplies or any other form of aid to the war prisoners. Antonio and his wife were not permitted to deliver the third truck load of hospital supplies to Camp O'Donnell.

The hospital supplies which Antonio and his wife had succeeded in delivering to Camp O'Donnell doubtless saved the lives of many war prisoners but were, nevertheless, not sufficient to meet the tremendous need of the camp. Furthermore, many war prisoners were already so near death when the medicines arrived that their lives could not be saved. For several weeks four hundred or more war prisoners died at Camp O'Donnell each day.

Several months later the Japanese military authorities cynically erected at Camp O'Donnell a monument to the memory of the thousands of Filipino war prisoners who died there. No mention was made of the many American war prisoners who also died there. A group of prominent Filipinos were invited to participate in the dedication of this monument. Several of these Filipinos counted their own sons among those who died at Camp O'Donnell as the result of Japanese indifference and neglect.

Chapter 33.

Concerning the Auditor and His Wife

Mr. Demek was born in Czechoslovakia, the only son of a well-to-do father who owned a small glass factory. The same family had owned this glass factory for several hundred years. The factory specialized in the manufacture of colored glass. The secret of its manufacture was carefully guarded and was handed down from father to son. Mr. Demek's father sent his son to the United States to acquire a business education. The father hoped to increase the profit of his glass factory by the adoption of American business methods.

During his residence in the United States Mr. Demek became a naturalized American citizen. After his graduation from college, instead of returning to Czechoslovakia to enter his father's business, Mr. Demek came to the Philippines as a teacher in the Bureau of Education. He arrived in Manila in June 1914. After completing his two-year contract with the Bureau of Education, Mr. Demek secured a position as an accountant in the office of the Manila Electric Company, Manila's largest corporation. He remained with this firm for more than 25 years and eventually became its auditor. He prospered financially and became a director of one of Manila's leading banks.

Mr. Demek was in the Philippines when the United States entered the First World War. The draft was not extended to the Philippines and volunteers without previous military training were not desired by the small American force stationed in the Philippines. So Mr. Demek did not get into the army during that war. But he always regretted it. A few years after the end of the First World War he became a reserve officer in the United States Amy. A few months before the outbreak of the war with Japan he was called to active duty and was given a captain's commission. When General MacArthur evacuated Manila Mr. Demek went to Bataan with the USAFE forces.

A few years after he came to the Philippines Mr. Demek married an American girl who, prior to her marriage, was a teacher in the Bureau of Education. They had no children. Mrs. Demek remained in Manila when her husband went to Bataan. After the Japanese occupied Manila she was interned at the Ateneo Hospital. She was now gray-haired and suffered from arthritis.

Throughout the long siege of Bataan Mrs. Demek received no word from her husband. But late in April, after the surrender of the USAFE forces in Bataan, she received a note from Captain Demek stating that he was in good health and that he was a prisoner of war at Camp O'Donnell in Tarlac Province. He requested his wife to send him some clothing. The message was brought to Mrs. Demek by a Filipino electrician of the Manila Electric Company who had been sent to Camp O'Donnell to install electric wiring. Two or three weeks later Mrs. Demek received another note from her husband. He wrote that he was detained as an orderly of the Japanese Commandant of Camp O'Donnell, that he was still in good health, that it was rumored that all American prisoners of war would be sent to Japan within a week, and that if she did not receive any further message from him she was to go to San Francisco at the first opportunity and he would join her there after the war was over.

About a week later the American prisoners of war were removed from Camp O'Donnell. But instead of being sent to Japan they were transferred to Caganatuan in the Nueva Ecija Province, where another camp for American prisoners of war had been established.

When the Ateneo Hospital was closed early in June Mrs. Demek obtained a pass releasing her to the house of a friend. Her own home has been looted and occupied by Japanese. Most of us were transferred at that time to Red Cross Hospital No. 4.

Late in June a prominent Filipino attorney in Manila, who was a friend of Captain Demek, visited Red Cross Hospital No. 4. He told us that Captain Demek had died of dysentery in the war prisoner's camp at Cabanatuan and that he had that morning informed Mrs. Demek of the Captain's death.

During the afternoon of that day, while we sat on the veranda of the hospital, we saw Mrs. Demek. She walked slowly past the hospital, using a cane and limping from the pain of her arthritis. Her head was bowed in grief. She did not look up to greet us.

Chapter 34.

Concerning the Playboy

Mr. Bohannan arrived at the Ateneo Hospital from Santo Tomas on January 27. We called him Bo, because that was the first syllable of his name. His initials were "C.M.B.", but we never learned what the initials "C." and "M." stood for.

Bo was an Irish-American with a roguish face which revealed alert intelligence and a cynical but tolerant worldliness. He was a bachelor and was a little more than 60 years of age. He had come to the Philippines as a soldier during the Spanish-American war. After his discharge from the army he served for a time in the Philippine Bureau of Customs. On leaving the Bureau of Customs, he found employment as the representative in Manila of a British firm of underwriters which dealt in fire and marine insurance. For many years prior to his retirement he was the head of the Manila office of this firm. When he retired in 1938 his firm paid him an accumulated bonus of more than 100,000 pesos. He had then taken a trip across the world and had spent several weeks in Germany in 1939, a few months before the war began in Europe.

For many years prior to his retirement from the insurance business Bo had owned an interest in several mineral claims which adjoined the property of the Benguet Consolidated Mining Company near Baguio in the Mountain Province of the Philippines. His business partner in this mining venture was another Irish-American, who had staked the claims and who, for a number of years, was the assayer of the Benguet Consolidated Mining Company. Eventually gold-bearing ore of a mineable grade was found on the claims of Bo and his partner. A contract was entered into with the Benguet Consolidated Mining Company whereby the latter agreed to mine and mill the ore on a profit-sharing basis up to the end of November, 1941. The mineral claims of Bo and his partner had produced a total of more than one million pesos worth of gold.

For many years the commissions on Bo's insurance sales had netted him a considerable income. He had invested a portion of his savings in several Philippine mines which yielded him a substantial income in dividends. Thus Bo, when he retired from the insurance business, was a wealthy man.

At various times over a period of many years Bo's health had been very poor. Both his kidneys had been operated upon for the removal of kidney stones and one of his kidneys was eventually removed. His gall bladder had also been removed. By being careful as to what he ate and drank Bo's health gradually improved and at the time of his retirement he was apparently in good health. He was about six feet tall and at that time weighed about 220 pounds.

On his return to the Philippines after his trip around the world he found himself with an income much larger than he needed. He had no family to claim his attention and no business to occupy his time. As a result, he devoted himself far too assiduously to eating and drinking and spent too many nights at the gambling tables of Manila's night clubs. He told me that he had lost 100,000 pesos at the gambling tables of Manila's nightclubs. The effect upon his health was disastrous. He developed diabetes and his one remaining kidney began to rebel at the excessive burden put upon it.

When Bo arrived at the Ateneo Hospital he was carried into our ward upon a stretcher. When I had last seen him before the war he had weighed over 220 pounds. He now weighed less than 150 pounds and was so emaciated that I did not at first recognize him. One foot was swollen and so sensitive that he was unable to walk.

Our chief doctor immediately placed Bo upon a very restricted diet and discontinued the daily injections of insulin which Bo had been taking. The doctor said that his laboratory examinations of Bo's blood and urine did not indicate a diabetic condition. Bo rebelled at this and the doctor gave him his choice of either obeying his orders or going back to Santo Tomas. Bo said he would obey orders but almost at once he began to evade his dietary restrictions.

A Filipino food vendor was permitted to enter our ward and sell food to the internees. From him Bo purchased bread, eggs and fruit, which he concealed beneath his bed. Being forbidden to eat eggs, Bo had a fellow internee send the eggs to the kitchen to be cooked. Thus, although the doctor had placed him upon a liquid diet, Bo managed each day to eat a certain amount of bread, eggs and fruit. To give the devil his due, however, it must be admitted that, although he ate some forbidden food, he ate sparingly. And in spite of several relapses, his health slowly improved. Eventually the swelling in his foot subsided and he was able to walk about.

Our chief doctor once told me that he was aware that Bo was surreptitiously purchasing and eating food in addition to the liquid diet provided by the hospital. The doctor said that he took this fact into account when he gave instructions that Bo should receive only liquid food from the hospital kitchen. On one occasion, when Bo had a relapse, the doctor came to his bedside and gravely said, "Don't eat yourself to death."

Until he got well enough to walk about once more Bo was rather cantankerous. He often made very caustic comments concerning the food and service of the hospital. At times, however, Bo was a very agreeable person indeed. By alternately scolding and praising the attendants and nurses, he managed to wrest from them better service and more favors than any other internee received. Members of the hospital staff were very patient with him. On one occasion, when Bo had severely tried his doctor's patience, the doctor remarked to me with exasperation, "See how he acts! Yet we continue to try to cure him and work for his release from the hospital."

Bo's chief grievances were the doctor's refusal to administer insulin and the rigid dietary restrictions to which he was subjected. He complained that if he ate only the food which the hospital provided he would slowly starve to death. Bo had brought to the hospital his own supply of insulin. The doctor placed this in the hospital's refrigerator. But only once did the doctor give Bo an insulin injection and that was during one of Bo's relapses, when a test of his urine indicated the presence of sugar. Eventually the fact that Bo's health slowly improved without the use of insulin indicated that the doctor had made the correct diagnosis and had prescribed the proper treatment. Thereafter Bo no longer complained.

Several years before the outbreak of the war Bo had built himself a home in Mandaluyong, one of the outlying suburbs of Manila. The house was a substantial concrete structure and was splendidly furnished. It was located upon a tract of land covering 25 hectares (62.5 acres). He had several servants and a tenant farmer who cultivated the land on a crop-sharing basis. The principal crop was rice. But the land also produced peanuts and fruit, which included bananas and the delicious Philippine mango. Bo employed a chauffeur and owned both a sedan and a station wagon.

Bo's home was located near Camp Murphy, which was repeatedly bombed by Japanese planes during the first three weeks of the war. One day, while Bo stood outside of his home watching an air raid, a Japanese plane dived low and machine-gunned his house. Bo hastily took refuge behind his garage, with machine-gun bullets striking all about him.

During the last week of December, after the USAFE forces had evacuated Camp Murphy, Bo left his home in the charge of his servants and took quarters in the Elks Club in Manila. From the roof of the Elks Club, during that last week of December, Bo witnessed the bombing and burning of the port area and the nearby Walled City. On the night of December 31, he witnessed the burning of warehouses and army barracks along the banks of the Pasig River. On January 1, he saw the looting of nearby shops by mobs of Filipinos whom the police made no effort to restrain. And finally, on the afternoon of January 2, from the same vantage point on the roof of the Elks Club, he watched the Japanese troops enter the city of Manila. They came from the south, marched north along the Dewey Boulevard until they reached the Elks Club, and then deployed on the Luneta Plaza facing the Elks Club. The editor of the *Manila Daily Bulletin* stood beside Bo and murmured sadly, "I watched a city die."

On January 6 the Japanese military authorities took the residents of the Elks Club, including Bo, to the Santo Tomas Internment Camp. Prior to their departure from the Elks Club, they were instructed by the Japanese to take to Santo Tomas sufficient food to last them for three days. This they did. Later they regretted that they had not taken to Santo Tomas the entire stock of foodstuffs which they left behind in the kitchen of the Elks Club.

A few days after Bo entered the Santo Tomas Internment Camp his chauffeur visited him and informed Bo that his home in Mandaluyong had been occupied by Japanese troops. The servants, including the chauffeur, after being maltreated by the Japanese soldiers, had been forced to leave the premises.

Soon after he arrived at the Ateneo Hospital Bo requested Mr. Loggey's wife, who lived in Mandaluyong, to call Bo's house by telephone and find out if it was still occupied by Japanese troops. Mrs. Loggey called Bo's house several times during February and each time the person who answered the telephone spoke Japanese. When she called again early in March no one answered.

A few days later Bo went in the Red Cross Station Wagon to the Santo Tomas Internment Camp to request permission to visit his house for the purpose of getting some clothing and medicine. At the office of the Japanese Commandant Bo was informed that there were no longer any Japanese soldiers in his house and that it was probable that everything had been removed from his house and placed in a warehouse for safe-keeping. Hence it would be useless for Bo to go there. He was informed that inquiries would be made and if it was found that Bo's belongings were still in his house a permit for him to visit would be sent to him at the Ateneo Hospital.

Bo had mentioned his desire to visit his home to the Portuguese lady physician who made occasional visits to the Ateneo Hospital. She was reputed to have some influence with the Commandant of the Santo Tomas Internment Camp and with several other Japanese officers of high rank. After waiting for about three weeks without hearing a word from Santo Tomas concerning his request to visit his home, Bo again took the matter up with the Portuguese lady physician. She promised to obtain a pass for him to visit his home the following morning. True to her promise, she appeared the next morning with an automobile and a pass which stated that she must accompany Bo to his home and bring him back to the Ateneo.

Bo was absent from the Ateneo Hospital for about two hours. When he returned from his visit to his home he brought a pasteboard box full of photographs, but no clothing. He reported that his house had been completely looted. The bottom had been drilled out of a steel safe. All he had been able to rescue were a few bottles of medicines and perhaps 50 unmounted photographs. The latter Bo salvaged from a pile of loose papers and other rubbish in one corner of his living room. Both his sedan and his station wagon had been taken. The wreckage of his station wagon was discovered beside the road about a mile from his home. The wheels, tires, engine, and the greater part of the wood body, had been removed. In fact, very little of the station wagon, except the chassis, was left.

Bo was a member of several different clubs and fraternal orders. And for many years he was charged with the duty of engaging professional vaudeville entertainers for luncheons and dinners given by these several organizations. Thus Bo had become intimately acquainted with all of the leading vaudeville artists of Manila. He had, in fact, become a patron from whom they obtained assistance during periods of financial distress. Many of the photographs which Bo had salvaged were pictures of these artists, taken at various social gatherings where they had performed under Bo's patronage.

I do not recall that any visitors came to call on Bo during the first two and a half months of his internment at the Ateneo Hospital. His American and English friends were interned at Santo Tomas and his Filipino friends did not know that he had been transferred to the Ateneo Hospital. Bo did not complain.

One day early in April a young Filipino inquired of the internee who was on duty at the gate whether Bo was one of the patients. Upon receiving an affirmative answer, this young Filipino stated that he was Bo's chauffeur. He could not be admitted because he was not an authorized visitor. But Bo was called to the gate and he talked with his chauffeur there. Bo's request that his chauffeur be permitted to visit him was approved within a few days. Thereafter the chauffeur visited Bo regularly once each week. The chauffeur notified the rest of Bo's servants and several of the vaudeville artists that Bo was permitted to receive visitors at the Ateneo Hospital. As a result Bo soon had more regular visitors than any other internee.

After he began to have visitors, Bo was much more cheerful. His health improved steadily, in spite of the fact that his visitors brought him considerable quantities of forbidden foods.

Bo learned that his chauffeur obtained 500 pesos from the sale of the 100 sacks of *palay* (unhulled rice) which was stored on the lower floor of the house of Bo's tenant farmer. The tenant fled on the day the Japanese occupied Bo's house. The tenant's house, located about a quarter of a mile from Bo's house, was not entered by the Japanese until several days later. In the meantime the chauffeur succeeded in removing at night, without the knowledge of the Japanese, 100 sacks of *palay*. The remaining 400 sacks of *palay* which were stored in the tenant's house were confiscated by the Japanese when they entered the house.

Bo's chauffeur had distributed a portion that he had received from the sale of the *palay* to Bo's servants, and another portion to several of Bo's vaudeville artist friends who were unemployed because of the war. The balance of the money had been retained by the chauffeur. Learning that Bo was almost out of money, the chauffeur gave him ten pesos. He also brought fruit which he gathered from the trees on Bo's estate.

From the chauffeur Bo learned that a twelve year old girl, the daughter of one of Bo's servants, had been raped by the Japanese on the day they entered Bo's house.

As might be expected, most of Bo's vaudeville friends were young women. There were, however, two or three young men who came to visit Bo. One of the latter was an Hawaiian who was an expert ukulele player. Two of the young women were living almost across the street from the Ateneo Hospital. Almost every day they sent Bo a luncheon which included such delicacies as hot chicken soup and boiled chicken. Bo's friends were soon bringing him more food than he could eat. They also occasionally brought him American cigarettes, which were difficult to obtain and sold for 1.50 pesos ($0.75) per packet of 20.

Bo owned a stock of fine wines and distilled liquors, which he had removed from his home and stored in the home of a Swiss friend before the Japanese entered Manila. It seemed that the Swiss friend was now absent, but had left a caretaker in charge of his home. A young man who visited Bo had formerly been a vaudeville artist but was now supporting himself by selling merchandise on a commission basis. This young man was commissioned by Bo to sell the stock of wines and liquors. The young man was to receive 50 percent of the proceeds as his commission, but was to bear all of the expense of selling and delivering the goods. Buyers were difficult to find at first. Bo's share of the first sale was only ten pesos. But he continued to receive varying sums as his share of the sales which the young man made from time to time. On one occasion he received 300 pesos.

Bo's bank account had been impounded by the Japanese military authorities. He had entered the Ateneo Hospital with very little cash. Hence, the sale of his wines and liquors provided him with a much needed source of ready money. Thereafter Bo no longer worried about where he would obtain sufficient money to carry himself through the war.

The fiancé of one of the young women who visited Bo was a young American soldier. After the surrender of Bataan, this American soldier, together with other soldiers from Bataan, was placed in a concentration camp at the former USAFE Camp O'Donnell, near the town of Capas in Tarlac Province, about 70 miles north of Manila. The young woman had a girlfriend whose fiancé was also an American soldier interned at Camp O'Donnell. Very alarming reports had reached Manila concerning the treatment accorded the war prisoners interned at there. The two young women, therefore, went to Capas to communicate with their fiancés.

After their return to Manila, the young women visited Bo and gave him an account of their visit to the Camp O'Donnell. They remained at Capas for a week, during which time they were not permitted to enter Camp O'Donnell or to communicate with their fiancés. There were a number of Filipino carpenters, however, who were employed on construction work within the camp and who lived in the town of Capas. These carpenters entered the war prisoners' camp each morning and returned to Capas each evening. Each carpenter carried food into the camp for his midday meal. By means of these carpenters, the girls sent food and messages to their fiancés in the camp. The latter, in turn, sent messages back to the girls.

Because there were not sufficient barracks at Camp O'Donnell to house all of the prisoners, many American prisoners were without shelter of any sort and were sleeping upon the bare earth. Whether for this or for some other reason, the Japanese decided to transfer the American prisoners to an internment camp located at Cabanatuan in the Nueva Ecija Province, about 60 miles by railroad from Camp O'Donnell, about a week after the two girls reached Capas.

Carrying a pot of hot coffee, the girls went to the railroad station in Capas. There they saw their fiancés waiting to board the train. The girls were not permitted to approach their fiancés. But the two young American soldiers soon obtained permission from a Japanese guard to speak to the girls. There was sufficient time before their train departed for the young men to drink the pot of coffee and to have a brief visit with their sweethearts. The girls returned to Manila on the following day. They informed Bo that their fiancés were in good health although many of their fellow prisoners were suffering from malaria and dysentery.

Bo was one of the internees transferred to Red Cross Hospital No. 4 when the Ateneo Hospital was closed on June 6. Several of Bo's friends had offered him a home and the doctor had offered to recommend Bo's release. But Bo preferred to remain at the hospital rather than become a burden upon his friends. When Red Cross Hospital No. 4 was closed at the end of June, Bo was one of several internees who returned to the Ateneo, where internees were provided with food and lodging by the Jesuit Fathers.

Chapter 35

Concerning the Activity of the Jesuits in the Underground Movement

Father John Hurley, the rector of the Ateneo University and the Father Superior of the Jesuit order in the Philippines, was a youthful-appearing Irish-American about 50 years of age. He had a cheerful and magnetic personality. His daily visits were always welcomed and were a considerable factor in maintaining the morale of the internees at the Ateneo. We regarded him as a friend and a fellow internee as well as a priest.

In Father Hurley's heart burned a fierce hatred of the Japanese invaders. In spite of the limitations of his internment, and with the adroitness characteristic of an Irish-American, he found opportunities to further the allied cause. He sought to keep alive the spirit of resistance to the Japanese conquerors.

As a result of more than 20 years' residence in the Philippines he enjoyed a wide acquaintance and exerted a profound influence. He had contacts with many parts of the Philippines through Filipino priests and through alumni of the Ateneo University. About a month after the Japanese occupation of Manila the Japanese guards were withdrawn from the Ateneo University. Thereafter no restrictions were imposed upon visitors. On Sundays a huge throng of worshippers attended the masses celebrated in the Ateneo Chapel. Alumni of the Ateneo who were fighting with General MacArthur's Army in Bataan slipped into Manila and brought Father Hurley first-hand reports of conditions at the fighting front. Filipino priests and other visitors brought him news from both the Japanese-occupied and the unoccupied portions of the Philippines. He was informed of the activities of guerrillas.

The only war news which the Japanese permitted to be published in the newspapers consisted of exaggerated and often entirely false reports of Japanese victories. But in their tortured hearts the people of the Philippines refused to believe that America was losing the war. The accounts of Japanese victories published in the newspapers must be false. "If you wish to learn the truth read the newspaper reports backward," said some. "When the Japanese report that they lost one warship while sinking ten American warships, the truth is that the Americans lost one warship while sinking ten Japanese warships."

But authentic news of the war was difficult to obtain. Most of the people either did not possess radios or possessed only radios which could not pick up radio news from the allied forces overseas. For four months the *Voice of Freedom* broadcast news from the USAFE headquarters at Corregidor. But when General Wainwright surrendered early in May the *Voice of Freedom* was stilled. For some time after a person who called himself "Juan de la Cruz" (John of the Cross) continued to broadcast news favoring America and her allies from a hidden radio station. But the Japanese caught Juan de la Cruz and shot him. A decree was issued by the Japanese military authorities forbidding the people to listen to overseas broadcasts. In order to enforce this decree the people were ordered to remove all outdoor aerials and to submit their radio receivers to the Japanese for alteration so that only local Japanese-controlled long-wave broadcasts could be received.

Manila was full of rumors of Allied victories. Rumors were passed eagerly from mouth to mouth with almost incredible rapidity. "Have you heard the latest war news?" was the usual greeting of acquaintances when they met. Many of these rumors were either grossly exaggerated or entirely false. Interspersed with such rumors was some authentic news but it was usually impossible to sift the true from the false.

One of Father Hurley's earliest activities was to satisfy the thirst of the people for authentic news. He reasoned accurately that this would bolster their morale. The Jesuits possessed an excellent short-wave radio receiver capable of picking up broadcasts from all parts of the world. Father Hurley assigned a group of Jesuit Fathers to the task of listening to and recording the radio news from Allied forces. Two of the fathers were constantly on duty at the radio. Most of the news came from San Francisco and London, although news from Australia and from other stations was also recorded. A typewritten transcript was prepared of the radio news received each day. Copies of these transcripts were delivered to carefully selected Filipinos who disseminated the news throughout the city of Manila and even beyond the boundaries of Manila.

Persons who had in their possession transcripts of news from Allied sources or who disseminated such news in any manner were severely punished when caught by the Japanese military police. Several persons were executed for this offense. But Father Hurley's agents were very discreet. They were not caught.

The constantly increasing number of visitors who came to see Father Hurley eventually took up so much of his time that he was unable to continue his daily visits to the hospital. Now and then, however, he found the time to pay us a visit and was doubly welcome when he did come.

The duty of bringing to us the daily typewritten news sheets was delegated by Father Hurley to his second in command. But the news sheets were received thereafter at irregular intervals. The second in command, like Father Hurley himself, was occupied with other matters.

We learned of Father Hurley's underground activities only gradually and indirectly. Some of his underground activities we doubtless did not learn about at all. Most of the information concerning these activities which we did acquire came to us by inference or from Filipino friends who visited us at the Ateneo Hospital. Father Hurley did not discuss his underground activities with us, but occasionally from his conversation with us we drew obvious inferences of such activity.

In time the Japanese military authorities began to suspect that Father Hurley was engaging in underground activities, although they had no proof. About a year after the Ateneo Hospital was closed and we were interned elsewhere the Japanese military authorities compelled the Jesuits to leave the Ateneo University and take quarters elsewhere. Three times Father Hurley and four other Irish-American Jesuits were imprisoned in the notorious Japanese military prison at Fort Santiago. After their third imprisonment at Fort Santiago they were interned at Santo Tomas. Four of them were in such a deplorable physical condition as a result of their incarceration in the military prison that they required hospitalization. But their spirits were undaunted.

Father Hurley became the chief orderly in the hospital at the Santo Tomas Internment Camp. Under his direction other Catholic priests also toiled as orderlies. Throughout the remainder of our internment they bathed patients, emptied bed pans and urinals, changed bed clothing filthy with the excreta of bedridden patients and performed all the other unpleasant tasks which are required of a hospital orderly. Not the least of their tasks was the preparation for burial of the bodies of the three or four patients who died each day in the camp hospital. Father Hurley and his fellow orderlies were not compelled to perform these tasks. They volunteered for this work because they wished to help their fellow internees.

Chapter 36.

Concerning a Secret Hospital for Guerrillas

Immediately after the surrender of Bataan, a few USAFE officers and several hundred USAFE soldiers slipped through the Japanese lines undetected and took refuge in the densely forested mountains north of the Bataan Peninsula. The officers and soldiers who thus escaped became organized bands of guerrillas which harassed Japanese outposts throughout Central Luzon.

These USAFE guerrillas included both Americans and Filipinos, although the majority of them were Filipino. They were soon joined by civilian Filipinos who fled into the mountains to escape the brutalities of the Japanese military government. Led by daring and resourceful officers, they soon became an exceedingly annoying, if not serious, threat to Japanese military authority.

Bill Fassoth was an American who operated a large sugar cane plantation near the village of Dinalupihan not far from the Bataan Peninsula. Bill was assisted in the management of his plantation by his twin brother, who was a bachelor and lived with Bill on the plantation. Bill's wife was a Filipina.

Bill's plantation was situated very closed to the Northern extremity of the line occupied by the Japanese forces when they besieged Bataan. When the Japanese forces approached his plantation Bill and his twin brother escaped to the Bataan Peninsula, where they remained with the USAFE throughout the siege of Bataan. Immediately after the surrender of Bataan, Bill and his brother slipped though the Japanese lines and took refuge with the USAFE guerrillas in the mountains north of the Bataan Peninsula. Bill's plantation and the nearby village of Dinalupihan were on the level plain at the foot of these mountains. The forest which covered the mountains skirted the village and ended at the boundary of Bill's plantation. During, and after, the siege of Bataan Bill's wife lived with friends in the village of Dinalupihan. Bill visited her after he took refuge with the guerrillas in the mountains near Dinalupihan.

One of Bill's friends was a Filipino sugar-planter named Bernia, who lived on his plantation near the village. Bernia, in whose heart burned a fierce hatred of the Japanese invaders, visited Bill at the guerrilla camp. Bernia undertook to obtain and deliver to Bill food, medicines and equipment for the hospital. Bill was to transport these supplies from Dinalupihan to the guerrilla camp. An American army assistant was put in charge of the administrative details.

Bernia returned to his plantation, climbed into his truck and drove to Manila, where he made contact with Father John Hurley, Rector of the Ateneo University and head of the Jesuit order in the Philippines. Bernia was an alumnus of the Ateneo University and he knew that Father Hurley, in spite of being interned, was active in the underground movement.

Father Hurley gave his enthusiastic approval to the plan to establish a hospital for guerrillas. With his assistance contributions of food, medicines and supplies for the hospital were obtained. Bernia loaded these supplies into his truck and delivered them to Bill at Dinalupihan. At Bill's command a group of guerrillas carried the supplies on their backs to the guerrilla camp. Bill persuaded Father Hurley to come to the guerrilla hospital and assist the doctor in caring for the patients.

At times there were as many as 70 patients in the guerrilla hospital. Often guerrillas admitted to the hospital were not ill or wounded, they were merely half starved. Any guerrilla who sought admission was received, cared for and fed for as long as he chose to remain at the hospital. Guerrillas worn out by a series of raids upon Japanese outposts would come to the hospital to rest and recuperate before undertaking another series of raids.

Detachments of Japanese soldiers were constantly ranging through the forest searching for guerrillas. Several times the hospital was hastily moved to a new location in order to prevent its discovery and capture by the Japanese.

It was Bernia, however, who performed the most dangerous task. There were detachments of Japanese soldiers in several of the towns through which Bernia passed in transporting supplies from Manila to Dinalupihan. Eventually the Japanese, becoming suspicious, halted Bernia and examined the contents of his truck. When he refused to state either the source or the destination of the supplies, the Japanese shot him.

Deprived of its source of supplies the guerrilla hospital was forced to suspend operations. About eighteen months after the surrender of Bataan, Bill and his brother, both desperately ill with malaria, surrendered to the Japanese. They were sent to the war prisoners' camp at Cabanatuan, where they remained until they were released by the arrival of General MacArthur's forces in January 1945.

It was while I was interned in the Ateneo Hospital that I learned that Bernia was transporting supplies from Manila to the guerrillas, but I do not recall the source of this information. Later I learned that Bernia had been executed by the Japanese. Still later the surrender of Bill and his brother was announced in a Japanese-controlled newspaper published in Manila. This announcement implied that Bill and his brother had been of important leaders among the guerrillas and that their voluntary surrender was a source of satisfaction to the Japanese military authorities. Bill and his brother were not executed and publicity was given to their surrender in the hope that other guerrillas might thereby be induced to surrender.

It was Bill however, who furnished me with some of the details of the foregoing account. By chance I met Bill in Manila about two months after his release from the war prisoners' camp at Cabanatuan. Each of us was delighted that the other had survived the war. I asked Bill to tell me about his activities as a guerrilla. Bill said that he and his brother were not guerrillas. They lived with guerrillas and operated a hospital for guerrillas, but they did not take any part in the guerrilla raids upon the Japanese.

There were, Bill informed me, two kinds of guerrillas. The USAFE guerrillas attacked small detachments of Japanese troops whenever an opportunity arose. These guerrillas sought to protect the civilian population from the brutalities of the Japanese. Not infrequently they captured and executed Japanese who raped Filipino women or committed other crimes against the Filipino people.

But there were other men who called themselves guerrillas too. However, they were actually roving bands of armed robbers preying upon their fellow countrymen. These so-called guerrillas avoided the Japanese instead of attacking them. They visited and robbed outlying farms. In order to satisfy their brutal lust they kidnapped and took to their hideouts Filipino women and young girls. Among these marauders were discontented farm laborers and tenants who attacked, robbed and murdered their former employers and landlords.

Bill said that one of his reasons for surrendering to the Japanese was his discovery that some of his guerrilla associates had become robbers. As food became more scarce even the USAFE guerrillas occasionally robbed the civilian population in order to obtain food.

Chapter 37.

I Obtain a Brief Glimpse of Manila During the Early Months of Japanese Occupation

Early in February the physician in charge of the hospital informed me that, because of the scarcity of surgical supplies, the Japanese military authorities had issued instructions that no operations except emergency operations were to be performed. Very heavy fighting was in progress in Bataan and it was desired to conserve surgical supplies for the wounded. For this reason the operation to remove my hemorrhoids would be postponed indefinitely. In the meantime I could continue to be a patient at the hospital.

On 24 February, however, the chief physician called me to his office and informed me that, since I was not very ill and since all the beds in my ward were occupied, he would have to send me back to the Santo Tomas Internment Camp. He desired to have at all times one vacant bed for emergency use. Furthermore, a Japanese physician might inspect the hospital and my chart did not indicate that I was a legitimate hospital patient.

I asked for a few days grace, until I could notify my wife and have her bring back my iron bed. She had taken the bed home because I was not permitted to use it at the hospital. The doctor readily consented to this.

My wife came the following day and begged the doctor, with tears in her eyes, to permit me to remain at the hospital. The doctor made no promise. But, the next day he sent me, accompanied by a Red Cross attendant, to Red Cross Hospital No. 4 for a fluoroscope x-ray examination.

Two other internee patients accompanied us—Mr. Koontze, a young American from my ward; and Mrs. McGuire, a middle-aged American widow who for many years had been a school teacher. Mr. Koontze was going for dental treatment and Mrs. McGuire for an x-ray examination of some sort. Mr. Koontze had made the trip for dental treatment on several previous occasions, but Mrs. McGuire and I had not been outside of the Ateneo campus since our internment began.

We came out of the main gate of the Ateneo. There had been Japanese guards stationed at the gate when I entered the Ateneo a month earlier, but there were no guards at the gate now. They had been withdrawn soon after my arrival. We walked westward for two blocks on Padre Faura and A. Mabini Street. Neither of the sentries we saw there paid any attention to us. The auto-repair shop, which occupied a large lot at the corner of Padre Faura and A. Mabini, was being used by the Japanese Army and doubtless this was the reason for the presence of the two sentries. We did not encounter any other sentries.

It was a bright sunny morning and warm enough to make us perspire a little. The street was lined with shady trees through which the sunlight filtered to form a mosaic of bright spots upon the pavement. A curious and death-like silence pervaded the street. There was no vehicular traffic. The few pedestrians whom we met moved silently, and it seemed to me furtively, about their business. On both sides of the street were residences interspersed between scattered retail shops. Many of the residences were vacant and at least half the shops were closed. We wondered if they had been looted on that turbulent New Year's Day just before the Japanese entered Manila. Here and there were shops open for business but the merchandise they offered was in most cases quite different from that proclaimed by the signs which hung above their doors. At the gateways to many of the vacant residences were tables on which were offered for sale small quantities of a great variety of merchandise. On the same table might be seen a few bottles of toilet preparations, a few bars of soap, cigars, cigarettes, rolls of toilet paper, tins of evaporated milk, baking powder, chewing gum and candy in glass jars, tins of corned beef, a bottle of pickles. The goods displayed upon these tables were undoubtedly, for the most part, loot which had been stolen from the shops on January 1.

In one shop two young Spaniards offered for sale American cigarettes and smoking tobacco. We were offered a one-pound can of Granger smoking tobacco at 7.50 pesos (US$3.75). Chesterfield cigarettes were offered at 80 centavos ($0.40) for a packet of twenty. These prices seemed exorbitant to us and we did not buy any. We could not know at that time, of course, that before the war ended American cigarettes would sell for ten dollars a packet and that American smoking tobacco would sell for $160 a pound!

We saw a large group of people waiting in front of the closed door of a shop. We were told that in this shop rice was sold under the rationing system enforced by the Japanese military authorities. The day's supply of rice had not yet been received from the warehouse of the government-owned National Rice and Corn Corporation. The shop would not open for business until a truck arrived with the rice. Sometimes the truck did not arrive until late in the afternoon. Sometimes it did not arrive at all. Meanwhile, the people with their ration cards waited outside the shop for hours.

The rice supplied by the government was retailed at 34 centavos ($0.17) per ganta. A ganta contains exactly three liters and a ganta of rice weighs approximately 2.4 kilograms (about 5.3 pounds). Rice obtained on the "black market" at that time cost 70 centavos ($0.35) per ganta. Before the war ended the price of "black market" rice was to rise to more than $50 per ganta (about $10 per pound)!

Each ration-card holder at that time was permitted to purchase one-half ganta (2.65 pounds) per day at the shops which the government supplied with rice. Later the ration of rice sold by the government was fixed at 300 grams (0.66 pound) per person per day. Eventually the ration was reduced to 200 grams per person per day. But the government was unable to supply even this reduced ration. Hence the price soared as the demand for black market rice increased.

After a leisurely walk we finally arrived at Red Cross Hospital No. 4, located at the corner of A. Mabini and San Andres Street. The hospital occupied a two-storey concrete building which formerly housed the parish school of Malate Catholic Church. The hospital was filled with internee patients. Many of them were old men. Most of them were strangers to me. I was greeted by a few acquaintances, however.

We reported to the physician in charge of the hospital. Mr. Koontze was sent to the office of the dentist, while Mrs. McGuire and I were turned over to the doctor in charge of the x-ray laboratory. The doctor informed me that the fluoroscope revealed calcified spots in my lungs, indicating that I had at one time suffered from tuberculosis but that the disease was no longer active. An x-ray photograph of my lungs was taken, but as the hospital had no chemicals for developing the negative it was uncertain when the image would be available. A written report of the fluoroscope examination was delivered to the Red Cross attendant who accompanied us.

We remained at the Red Cross Hospital for about an hour and then walked back to the Ateneo. We left the Ateneo at about 9 am. It was 11 am when we returned.

The physician in charge of the Ateneo Hospital, after examining the report of the fluoroscope examination of my lungs, informed me that he now had a sound reason for keeping me in the hospital and that he had decided not to send me back to Santo Tomas. Thus a dread weight lifted from my shoulders. It is true that in reality I was imprisoned in the hospital but it was so much less like a jail than Santo Tomas! Also, most importantly my wife and son could visit me in the hospital whereas at Santo Tomas they could not.

That afternoon a Filipino patient who was not an internee was released from my ward. This provided the vacant bed which our chief physician desired for emergency use.

The chief physician gave me a prescription for calcium gluconate and requested me to have my wife purchase this medicine. Two or three days later my wife brought the calcium gluconate which the doctor had ordered.

Thereafter, twice a week for about two months, I was given an intravenous injection of calcium gluconate to prevent a possible recurrence of tuberculosis.

The diagnosis of arrested tuberculosis was, I believe, merely a subterfuge for keeping me in the hospital. On several occasions prior to the outbreak of the war an X-ray examination of my lungs had been made. The physicians who made these examinations stated that there was no evidence of tuberculosis, past or present, and that the calcified areas in my bronchial tubes were a result of bronchitis.

Chapter 36.

Concerning Mr. Koontze

Mr. Koontze, who came with me from Santo Tomas to the Ateneo Hospital on January 24, was a tall young man about 35 years of age. At the outbreak of the war he was a civilian employee of the Quartermaster Corps of the United States Army in Manila. When the United States Army evacuated Manila on December 24, 1941, Mr. Koontze was given a gun and was left in Manila to supervise the loading of gasoline and crude petroleum into barges for shipment across the bay to the USAFE forces at Corregidor and Bataan. While the waterfront was being bombed on December 27 he was aboard a launch which was towing a barge loaded with crude petroleum down the Pasig River through the section of the waterfront which was being bombed. He said that he was forced to draw his gun on the crew of the launch to prevent them from pulling up to the shore and abandoning the launch. He continued loading barges until late on the night of December 31.

Mr. Koontze was picked up by the Japanese military authorities and interned in Santo Tomas early in January. Immediately prior to being sent to the Ateneo Hospital he had spent several days in the camp hospital at Santo Tomas suffering from a mild attack of influenza. When he reached the Ateneo Hospital he was so far recovered from the influenza that he could scarcely be said to be ill. It is probable that he was sent to the Ateneo Hospital primarily to relieve the congestion at Santo Tomas. In order to provide an excuse for keeping Mr. Koontze at the Ateneo Hospital, our chief doctor prescribed for him two intravenous injections of calcium gluconate per week. It was expected that this treatment would facilitate the healing of any portion of his lungs which might still be sore as a result of his attack of influenza. Mr. Koontze was required to purchase the calcium gluconate.

During the first week of our internment at the Ateneo Hospital Mr. Koontze sought to improve his standing with our chief doctor by lending a bicycle to the doctor and by loaning a small gas stove to the hospital kitchen.

One day early in February Mr. Koontze complained of a sore tooth. He was sent, with the doctor's clerk as an attendant, to the dentist in Red Cross Hospital No. 4. Mr. Koontze arranged with the dentist to have his tooth treated once each week. This arrangement permitted Mr. Koontze to leave the Ateneo premises and walk the mile to and from the dentist's office once each week. He was accompanied by a hospital attendant, who was usually the chief doctor's clerk. Each visit to the dentist required Mr. Koontze to be absent from the Ateneo Hospital for about two hours.

At about 6.30 a.m. on March 11 Mr. Koontze and his attendant left the Ateneo premises for the weekly visit to the dentist. When lunch-time came at 11.30 a.m. the chief doctor discovered that Mr. Koontze and his attendant had not yet returned. When Mr. Koontze and his attendant did return at about 12.15 p.m. the chief doctor informed Mr. Koontze that he would be sent back to Santo Tomas at 2 p.m. that same day.

Mr. Koontze did not offer any explanation for his long absence from the Ateneo Hospital. We surmised that he had paid a surreptitious visit to his wife, who lived not far from the dentist's office. He was a young man and had not bedded with his wife for more than two months.

On the morning of March 12 a notice was posted on our bulletin board stating that any internee who left the Ateneo Hospital premises without first securing permission from our chief doctor would be sent back to Santo Tomas. It appeared that on the preceding day Mr. Koontze and his attendant had left the premises without notifying the chief doctor.

The chief doctor, for the purpose of enforcing the new regulation, defined the Ateneo Hospital premises as the rooms actually occupied by the hospital, the veranda upon which these rooms opened, and the court upon which the hospital faced. We were prohibited from visiting any other portion of the Ateneo campus and building without first securing specific permission from the chief doctor. Prior to the promulgation of this regulation we had been free to move about within the Ateneo campus without keeping the chief doctor informed of our exact whereabouts. Thus we were all required to suffer a portion of the penalty which had been imposed because Mr. Koontze had trespassed too far upon the good nature of our chief doctor.

The day before Mr. Koontze was sent back to Santo Tomas he borrowed one peso from me, promising to repay it when his wife next called to visit him. Now that he had been sent back to Santo Tomas it seemed probable that the peso would not be repaid until the end of the war, if at all.

We heard nothing more of Mr. Koontze until early in May, when we learned that he was again out of Santo Tomas and interned in Red Cross Hospital No. 4. "How does he do it?" we asked each other. A few days later our chief doctor visited Red Cross Hospital No. 4. When he returned he told us that he had seen Mr. Koontze, who was thin as a rail but otherwise apparently in good health.

We had no further word of Mr. Koontze until the morning of June 6. The Ateneo Hospital was being closed and we of the men's ward were to be transferred to Red Cross Hospital No. 4 that morning. While we awaited transportation Mr. Koontze came to visit us. He said that he had been released to his home from Red Cross Hospital No. 4, but that when his pass expired he expected to return to Santo Tomas. He told us that after his return to Santo Tomas from the Ateneo he had contracted dysentery and had lost a lot of weight. That was the reason he had been sent to Red Cross Hospital No. 4. He did not have money enough to support himself for any great length of time. Hence he would return to Santo Tomas when his pass expired so that what money he had left could be turned over to his wife for her support. He then took one peso out of his wallet and repaid the one peso which he had borrowed from me.

Chapter 39.

Concerning the School Teacher

Mrs. McGuire, somewhat more than fifty years of age, was a widow and a school teacher. After many years of service in the Bureau of Education and in various private schools, she established her own private school in Manila. For this purpose she leased a large two-storey building. She finished equipping it for school purposes only a few months before the outbreak of war. In this enterprise she had invested not only all her savings but also several thousand pesos which she had borrowed. The outbreak of war forced her to close her school early in December.

Just before the Japanese entered Manila Mrs. McGuire delivered a metal box containing personal papers and most of her meager supply of currency to the secretary of a Manila bank for safe keeping. The banks were already closed at that time. Early in January, when she was about to be interned, she locked her school, leaving in the building most of her clothing and other personal effects. A Chinese caretaker, employed by the owner of the building, lived in a room on the lower floor. He was left in charge of the building.

During her internment at the Ateneo Hospital Mrs. McGuire several times, without success, sought permission to visit her school to obtain some of her personal effects and to learn whether or not the building had been looted. Early in July she was given a pass which permitted her to reside in the Convent of the Sisters of the Sacred Heart, where she paid 15 pesos per month for her board and room.

Mrs. McGuire had conducted a class for Japanese students in her school. One day late in July she met one of her former Japanese students on the street. When she told him of her desire to obtain some of her personal effects from her school building he gave her a note addressed to the head of the Japanese Military Police. She took this note to the Military Police Headquarters and obtained a pass to enter her school and remove her personal effects. A Japanese military guard accompanied her to the school.

She found her school building occupied by a group of Korean employees of the Japanese military administration. A Korean solider was guarding the building. Upon entering she found that her personal living quarters were being used as offices Practically all of her personal effects and at least three-quarters of the equipment of the school had been stolen. Not one of the articles which she had obtained permission to remove from the building could be found.

The Chinese caretaker who formerly resided in the building had fled. Another Chinese caretaker, employed by the owner of the building, had taken his place. This new caretaker said that some of the furniture had been sold by the former caretaker, who claimed that Mrs. McGuire had instructed him to sell it.

The Japanese guard who accompanied Mrs. McGuire to the building told her that her pass authorized her to enter the building whenever she wished and to remove any of her personal property which still remained in the building. He instructed the Korean guard of the building to that effect and then returned to his office, leaving Mrs. McGuire to inspect the building at her leisure.

Chapter 40.

I Quit Smoking and Do Some Profitable Reading

For many years prior to my internment I suffered from chronic bronchitis. I also smoked about 40 cigarettes per day. Doubtless the smoking aggravated my bronchitis.

The war cut off our income. As an economy measure, I began immediately after our arrival at Manila on December 22 to reduce the number of cigarettes which I smoked. During the first two weeks I limited myself to 10 cigarettes per day, although my constant craving for tobacco often tempted me to exceed this limit. During the second week I limited myself to 5 cigarettes per day. My craving for tobacco decreased and I found it easier to limit myself to 5 cigarettes than it had been to limit myself to 10 cigarettes per day.

I was still smoking 5 cigarettes per day when I entered the Ateneo Hospital. At that time I had 80 cigarettes in hand. Immediately after entering the hospital I reduced my smoking to 2 or 3 cigarettes per day and determined that when my supply was exhausted I would not purchase any more. Two weeks later I stopped smoking. The 40 cigarettes which I still had I gave to another internee. I informed my fellow internees that I had quit smoking because I could not afford to buy cigarettes. Several of them offered to give me cigarettes. After repeatedly declining these kindly offers, I finally agreed to accept one cigarette per week, which I smoked after breakfast on Sunday morning. This became a formal rite which was regarded with delight by my fellow internees.

The reduction in the amount of my smoking was accompanied by a remarkable diminution of my bronchial inflammation and my nasal catarrh ceased.

....

The enforced leisure of internment combined with access to the library of the Ateneo University provided an opportunity, which I did not neglect, to do some profitable reading. Among the many books which I read during the more than four months that I was interned at the Ateneo were the following:

History:—
A History of the Philippines by Rev. Jose Burniol, S.J. (1912)
Philippine Civilization before the Spanish Conquest by Eufronio M. Alip (1936)
The Pacific Ocean by Felix Riesenberg (1940)
Mexico, Central America & West Indies by Brantz Mayer (Vol. 22, History of Nations, 1913)
South America (Vol. 21, *History of Nations*, 1913)
The Franciscan Missions of California by John A. Berger (1940)
The Jesuits and the Great Mogul by Sir Edward MacLagan (1932) (A History of the Jesuit Missions in India)

History, Geography, Economics and Politics:—
Brazil By L.E Elliot (1917)
The Dutch East Indies by Amery Vandenbosch (1941)
Japan by Inazo Ota Nitose (1931)
The Honorable Enemy (Japan) by Ernest O. Hauser (1941)

Science:—
The Renaissance in Physics by Karl K. Darrow (1936)
Atoms in Action by George Russell Harrison (1939)
These Amazing Electrons by Raymond F. Yates (1937)
Atomic Artillery by J.K Robertson (1937)

War in China:—
Wheat and Men by Corporal Ashihei Hino (Katsunori Tamai), translated by Baroness Shizue Ishimoto (1939)

It will be noted that my historical reading was concentrated upon Spanish America and the peoples bordering the Pacific Ocean and that my scientific reading was devoted to a study of the atom and its component parts. The scope of my historical reading was determined by the fact that I was a resident of the Philippines, which was located in the Western Pacific and had been conquered by Spaniards sent from Spanish America. The fact that I was a chemist who, during the eight years which had elapsed since I retired from my profession, had not kept myself informed of the most recent development in atomic research, caused me to concentrate my scientific reading upon the atom.

Chapter 41.

Concerning Robert, the Movie Director

Robert came from Santo Tomas to the Ateneo Hospital late in February. He was 37 years of age and had been born and educated in the Philippines. For several years he was a vaudeville artist. During the years immediately preceding the war he directed the production of several movie films produced in Manila.

Robert's mother, who visited him frequently, appeared to be of Spanish and Filipino ancestry. I inferred that his father was an American. Presumably, also, his father was dead. Robert's wife was a comely Spanish-Filipino mestiza. She brought him food regularly each week and very evidently was much in love with her husband. Robert told me that she had been fortunate in securing employment by which she was able to support their family during his internment. There were two children, a girl of 12 and a boy of 10.

Robert was not a handsome man. His coarse, stiff black hair stood up in wild disarray which refused to be tamed. One leg was crippled by rheumatism. This caused him to walk with an odd sidewise shuffle which accentuated the ungainliness of his lean frame.

Yet there was about him some indefinable charm which attracted women. And he appeared to prefer the company of women to that of men. His most intimate friends among the internees were two of the young women.

He devoted several hours each day to the study of books on the science of physics and painstakingly recorded notes of what he had read. Among the titles which he read were: *The Renaissance in Physics, Atom in Action,* and *Atomic Artillery.* Learning that I was a chemist, he came to me with questions concerning the structure and properties of the atom, which he did not fully comprehend.

In order to answer some of his questions I was forced to read the books which he was studying. Thus did I inform myself of the amazing discoveries concerning the atom which had been made during the decade which had elapsed since I retired as a chemist. I have Robert to thank for renewing my interest in chemical and physical research. We were both fortunate in finding the Ateneo Library well supplied with books recording the results of the most recent research.

Robert went with us to Red Cross Hospital No. 4 when the Ateneo Hospital was closed early in June. About a month later he obtained a pass authorizing his internment at his home.

Chapter 42.

My Health Deteriorates and I Undergo an Operation

On December 1,1941 I weighed 196 pounds, which was not greatly in excess of the normal weight of a man of my height and age. I am almost six feet tall and at that time was 51 years of age. When I entered the Ateneo Hospital on January 24,1942 I weighed only 180 pounds. I continued to lose weight steadily. On April 24, three months after I entered the hospital, I weighed only 164 pounds. I had not weighed so little in more than thirty years.

About the middle of April the Commandant of the Santo Tomas Internment Camp ordered the passes of all internee hospital patients to be returned to the Commandant's office. We learned that a Japanese doctor would examine all patients to determine whether they should be permitted to remain in the hospital or should be sent back to the Santo Tomas Internment Camp. All passes which had been issued for an indefinite period were to be replaced with passes limiting hospital internment to a specified period. If a patient still required hospitalization when his pass expired it might be renewed for another definite period upon application to the Commandant of the Santo Tomas Internment Camp. This system of issuing passes for specified periods only had been in force since early February, but there were still outstanding a considerable number of passes which had been issued for unlimited periods. My own pass was one of them.

The Japanese doctor examined the patients at the Ateneo Hospital on April 22. He ordered that as soon as possible I be operated upon for the removal of the hemorrhoids and inquired how much longer I should be kept in the hospital. Our chief doctor replied, "At least two weeks." The Japanese doctor made a note of this.

I underwent the operation on April 24. During the six-day fast which followed the operation I lost a further eight pounds in weight. The wound was slow in healing and my doctor discovered that I was suffering from anaemia. For several weeks I was given daily injections of both liver extract and hematin. The hematin was then discontinued and the injections of liver extract were reduced to one per week. During this period I was given a small piece of liver daily in addition to the regular hospital food ration. My wife provided me with one egg per day. She also purchased the liver extract, which she found both costly and difficult to obtain. On June 3 a test of my blood showed that I was still anaemic, although the anaemia was less pronounced than it had been a month earlier, when my blood contained only about one-half of the normal number of red corpuscles. The wound from the operation had healed, but the healing had required a full month. I had not regained any of the weight I had lost.

During the month of May, when I was convalescing from the operation, my morale was at a very low ebb. My discomfort was aggravated by the intense heat. Day after day the temperature hovered around 100 degrees F. It reached a peak of 106, the highest temperature ever recorded for Manila. Because of the approach of the rainy season the humidity was close to saturation. This made the heat much more distressing than it would have been had the air been dryer. I moved about very little, yet I was constantly tired. My feet dragged when I walked. My craving for tobacco returned and I began to smoke again. But I smoked sparingly—not more than five cigarettes a day. A packet of 30 cigarettes, costing 20 centavos, lasted me a week.

My pass had been issued early in May with a note that it would expire on June 5. My doctor offered to recommend that I be interned in my mother-in-law's home. But he said that this recommendation if granted would be for a limited period, probably just one month, at the expiration of which I would probably be ordered back to Santo Tomas. On the other hand, if I remained in the hospital he might be able to secure extensions of my pass which would keep me in the hospital indefinitely. My wife wished to avoid my being returned to Santo Tomas because she could not visit me there. So I chose to remain in the hospital rather than risk being sent back to Santo Tomas after a brief period of internment at home.

On June 4 my pass was sent to the Commandant of the Santo Tomas Internment Camp with my doctor's recommendation that it be extended for another month. On June 6 it was returned with the date of expiration extended to June 30. In his recommendation my doctor stated that I was suffering from pernicious anaemia in addition to being not fully recovered from the operation which I had undergone.

Chapter 43.

The Red Cross Closes the Ateneo Hospital and We Are Transferred to Red Cross Hospital No. 4

On June 1, Dr. Gracia, the Portuguese lady physician in Red Cross service, informed us that the Red Cross would soon close its Ateneo Hospital. We were filled with consternation. We feared that the closing of the hospital would mean our return to the Santo Tomas Internment Camp. That evening when the Father Superior of the Jesuits visited us we told him of the rumored closure and requested him to use his influence to keep the hospital open. A day or two later the Father Superior told us that the head of the Red Cross had informed him that the Ateneo Hospital would not be closed. However, on June 5 we were informed by our chief doctor that the Ateneo Hospital would be closed on June 6. He had secured releases to their homes for several of the patients. The rest of us would be transferred to Red Cross Hospital No. 4. The men of my ward were transferred to Red Cross Hospital No. 4 on June 6. The transfer of the women interned at the Ateneo was effected on June 9 and 10.

The staff of the Ateneo Hospital was sent to establish a Red Cross Hospital at Hagonoy, Bulacan Province, about 40 miles north of Manila, where there were a large number of persons suffering from malaria and dysentery. About a month later one of the members of the hospital staff visited us. He said that most of the 200 patients in the Hagonoy Hospital were Filipino soldiers who had removed their uniforms and escaped from Bataan after the surrender of the USAFE forces in April. A large number of these refugees from Bataan had fled to Hagonoy. As a result the town's water supply was now insufficient. The hospital sometimes was without water for several hours at a time.

Chapter 44.

Concerning Frenchy, The Retired Sergeant, and Mr. Em

Frenchy was never interned at Santo Tomas. He had suffered a paralytic stroke and was bedridden in his home when the Japanese occupied Manila. He was a retired sergeant of the United States Army. His only income was his pension and that was cut off by the war. Early in February Frenchy was brought from his home to the Ateneo Hospital in a Red Cross ambulance. An American ex-serviceman, who had escaped internment because his wife was Japanese, had reported finding Frenchy bedridden, with no money and nothing to eat but a few bananas. This American and his Japanese wife visited Frenchy and brought him a carton of cigarettes soon after his arrival at the Ateneo Hospital. About ten days after his arrival a young woman, whom we inferred to be Frenchy's daughter, paid him a visit. Thereafter Frenchy had no visitors for several months.

He was a pathetic little man, not over five feet two or three inches tall and weighing not more than one hundred pounds. Paralysis had affected his speech. He spoke rarely and with difficulty and sometimes could not be understood. Both his arms and his legs were partially paralyzed. Although he was able to walk a little, he did so with a curious sidewise shuffle. For months he never left his bed except to go to the bathroom and he never spoke except when someone spoke to him.

When he arrived at the Ateneo Hospital he was suffering from a skin disease of some sort. But this gradually cleared up. Gradually also his speech became less slurred and he gained more control over his limbs, although he still walked with difficulty.

Eventually we learned that Frenchy had been born in New England, of French-Canadian parents. He had married a Filipino woman, by whom he had had a daughter. His wife was now dead and his daughter married. She too had a baby girl.

One Saturday afternoon in April, while I was on duty at the gate of the Ateneo Hospital, a young man appeared at my desk and requested permission to visit Frenchy. Upon inquiry, I learned that this young man was the son of a prominent Spanish-American war veteran of Manila and that he was Frenchy's son-in-law. He had a package of fruit and cigarettes for his father-in-law. I was unable to admit the young man that day because his visit had not been authorized by the Commandant, but I was able to deliver the package to Frenchy. Within two or three days passes were approved by the Commandant authorizing the young man and his wife and daughter to visit Frenchy once each week approved by the Commandant. Thereafter Frenchy's daughter, his granddaughter and his son-in-law visited him every Saturday afternoon.

When the men's ward was closed on June 6 Frenchy was released to the home of his daughter.

Mr. Em was a Spanish-American war veteran who, like Frenchy, was never interned at Santo Tomas. He was brought from his home directly to the Ateneo Hospital in February. He was small, emaciated and so bent with the weight of his years that he appeared to be hump backed. He suffered acutely from asthma and was placed in the isolation ward so that he would not disturb the other patients during his asthmatic attacks.

Mr. Em's only income had been his pension of sixty dollars per month which had been cut off by the war, leaving him destitute. He had a Filipino wife and five grown children. The children, Mr. Em informed us, were lazy and had never supported themselves. Apparently they were content with the meager living provided by their father's pension. They visited Mr. Em only once during his four months of internment, and they did not visit him after his transfer early in June to Red Cross Hospital No. 4.

Chapter 45.

Concerning Guy White, the Two Johns and the Scotsman

Guy White was a white-haired, blue-eyed Spanish-American war veteran who lived in Pasay. He was a neighbor of Hank, the chief engineer. Guy and Hank were both interned at Santo Tomas on January 22 and I believe that both arrived at the Ateneo Hospital on the same day in February. Because he suffered from asthma Guy was placed in the isolation ward, where he shared a cubicle with Ford, the editor. Guy spent most of his time either in his room or on a bench on the veranda just outside the door of the isolation ward. He did not mingle much with the other internees.

Guy owned his own home and was reputed to have been comfortably off when war broke out. His wife was a Spanish woman, considerably younger than he, by whom he had two daughters, both grown to young womanhood. The elder daughter had married an American, who was interned at Santo Tomas. The younger daughter, perhaps 20 years of age, was still single and lived with her parents. She visited her father regularly and brought him food once or twice a week. Guy remained with us at the Ateneo Hospital until it was closed in June. He was then released to his home.

John Tabor and John Wilson arrived at the Ateneo Hospital on the same day early in May. Both were Spanish-American war veterans over sixty years of age. Both of them had married Filipino women and resided with their families in Los Baños, at the foot of Mount Makiling, about forty miles south of Manila. John Tabor lived on a farm of about fifty acres, which he owned.

When the Japanese forces occupied Los Baños late in December the two Johns took refuge in the forest on Mount Makiling. There they remained in hiding, supplied with food by their families for nearly four months. Unable to endure the hardships of their mountain refuge, they returned to Los Baños and presented themselves to the Japanese Commandant about the middle of April. After being interned for a few days at their homes they were sent to the Santo Tomas Internment Camp, where they remained for about a week before being sent to the Ateneo Hospital.

John Tabor said that the Japanese had confiscated about sixty of his white leghorn pullets. He also owned about 20 head of cattle. Fearing that these might also be confiscated, he had instructed his wife to sell them for ten pesos ($5.00) per head. The price was low because people feared to invest in cattle, which were frequently confiscated by the Japanese.

John Wilson was quite deaf and his vocal chords had been removed. He spoke in a strange high pitch and his speech was very difficult to understand.

John Wilson's wife and a nephew of John Tabor came from Los Baños to the Ateneo Hospital about the middle of May. They brought bananas, fresh eggs and two pesos in cash for each of the two Johns. John Tabor was a thrifty soul and immediately sold three dozen of his eggs to fellow internees at 1.20 pesos ($0.60) per dozen.

The two Johns were transferred to Red Cross Hospital No. 4 when the Ateneo Hospital was closed early in June. Early in July they were sent back to the Santo Tomas Internment Camp. Late in July, however, they were again sent to Red Cross Hospital No. 4, which had become the Remedios Hospital, where they joined the eight old men already interned there.

About the end of March an aged Scotsman was brought from his home to the Ateneo Hospital. He was 79 years old, almost blind and bedridden when he arrived. A middle-aged Filipino woman, who was the old man's servant, requested the Red Cross to bring him to the hospital because he had no money with which to buy food.

For about two days after his arrival the old man was unable to hold his urine. Frequently he either wet his bed or urinated on the floor beside his bed. He was so weak that he was unable to feed himself. Apparently his weakness was due in part at least to starvation. By the end of April he was able to feed himself and, feeling his way with his cane, was able to walk to the bathroom and back to his bed. Occasionally he also sat for perhaps an hour at a time in a chair on the hospital veranda.

The Scotsman had no relatives in the Philippines and his British friends were themselves interned. His only visitor was his faithful Filipino servant. She continued to care for his house and occasionally brought him a bit of fruit.

The Scotsman seldom spoke. But his hearing was very acute. We often heard him chuckling to himself at the jokes which were told in our ward.

When the Ateneo was closed early in June he was transferred to Red Cross Hospital No. 4. There he spent the greater part of each day sitting in a chair upon the veranda. He was one of eight old men who were permitted to remain at Red Cross Hospital No. 4 when it was closed to internees and converted into a hospital for Filipino war prisoners early in July. When I visited the hospital on August 1 the Scotsman was in a coma and was not expected to live out the day. He died that night.

Chapter 46.

Concerning the Internee Nurses

Two of the women interned at the Ateneo Hospital served as hospital attendants. They were not trained nurses but they performed a nurse's duties. Both were volunteer Red Cross workers who served without pay. Both had passes which permitted them to leave the hospital premises when they were not on duty. One of them, whom we detested, we called "Snuffy." The other, whom we loved, we called "Mabel."

Snuffy was a small, slender, blue-eyed English woman. Her American husband was a mining engineer employed by one of the gold mines near Baguio. He had joined the United States Army as a lieutenant immediately after the outbreak of the war and had gone to Bataan with the USAFE forces.

Snuffy's graying hair indicated that she might be about 45 years of age, although her face appeared more youthful. Undoubtedly at one time she had been very pretty but time, and possibly poor health, had robbed her of much her beauty. She was very fastidious about her dress. Even her nurse's uniforms were well tailored. During the hours when she was off duty she appeared in a variety of stylish costumes which she wore with grace and distinction. She was, I believe, the only really well-dressed woman whom we saw during our internment at the Ateneo Hospital.

Most of the internees disliked Snuffy. She possessed an acid tongue and did not have the knack of making friends. The great-hearted Mabel, with whom she roomed, was the only person who spoke kindly of Snuffy.

Snuffy possessed a dog upon which she lavished her affection and which she fed, presumably at the hospital's expense, better food than the patients received. This dog was an evil- tempered bitch which was kept tied up most of the time. But Snuffy usually released her dog for an hour or two each day, At such times anyone who approached the dog was in danger of being bitten. Two persons, including Snuffy's maidservant, who cared for the dog, were bitten. Several other persons escaped being bitten only by the timely intervention of Snuffy. She was required by our chief doctor to pay for the anti-rabies injections which were given to the two persons who were bitten.

Snuffy was rather indifferent in her care of the patients in the men's ward and she was inclined to be spiteful in her attitude toward the male internees. About the middle of February our chief doctor issued an order requiring all patients to remain in their beds and to preserve absolute silence in the ward from 12.30 to 3 p.m. each afternoon. The male internees resented this restriction and suspected that Snuffy was the instigator of the new rule. A few days later, when we were eating our midday meal, she came to the door of the men's ward and sweetly informed us that thereafter we would be required to remain in our beds and preserve absolute silence only from 12.30 to 2.30 p.m. The shortening of the "siesta" period by one-half hour, she said, was to permit us to prepare to receive our visitors at 3 p.m.

The lights were turned out at 9 p.m. each evening and we were supposed to go to bed at that hour, though this rule was never rigidly enforced. Patients were permitted to remain on the veranda and in the courtyard until long after 9 p.m. provided they kept quiet so as not to disturb those who wished to sleep. One evening two of the male internees remained on the veranda until about ten minutes after nine talking to one of the nurses. Snuffy was not on duty at the time. But the next morning she came into the men's ward and demanded information as to which of the internees had been talking to one of the nurses after 9 p.m. the previous evening. We resented her inquisition. It chanced that the nurse with whom two of the men had chatted was Mabel, Snuffy's room mate.

It was after this incident that Snuffy received her nickname. One of the male internees expressed his resentment by calling her "Snuffy, the Cab Driver." This was immediately shortened to the single word, "Snuffy." Just why she should be called a "Cab Driver" I never learned. But the reason for calling her Snuffy was obvious. She spoke through her nose with a nasal twang. Several of the male internees eventually came to detest her so intensely that they mimicked her nasal speech even when she was present.

Snuffy was not always indifferent to the welfare of her patients. The hospital was short of mattresses when I arrived late in January. Fortunately I had brought my own mattress. A few days after my arrival Snuffy came to the men's ward and asked if one of us would loan his mattress to a lady in the women's ward who was very ill and did not have a mattress. I volunteered. When the hospital acquired additional mattresses Snuffy saw to it that I was the first to be provided with a mattress.

When the aged, almost blind, Scotsman arrived he was so feeble that he required a great deal of attention. Some of the nurses neglected him. But Snuffy gave him the same diligent care which she might have been expected to give her own father. She fed him and bathed him and rendered those sometimes unpleasant services which a feeble and bedridden old man requires.

Snuffy did not hear from her husband after he went to Bataan. When we heard on the radio General Wainright's announcement of the surrender of Bataan, Snuffy wept. She left the hospital about noon the following day.

When she returned to duty at 4 p.m. she was too intoxicated to do her work properly. Frequently she became despondent. On several occasions she was heard to remark that if she did not hear from her husband soon she would not be responsible for her conduct.

During the last month of our stay at the Ateneo Hospital Snuffy was ill and unable to report for duty most of the time. When the Ateneo Hospital was closed early in June she was transferred with us to Red Cross Hospital No. 4., but she was rarely well enough to go on duty as a nurse.

Early in July Snuffy and several other internees, who had been inmates of the Ateneo hospital, were sent back to the Ateneo where they were housed in the quarters formerly occupied by the hospital. Snuffy was detailed as a nurse to care for the ailing internees. About the middle of July, when I went to the Ateneo to visit several internee friends, I found Snuffy in her nurse's uniform sitting on the veranda. She answered my greeting listlessly. Although more than three months had elapsed since the surrender of Bataan, and although several women of her acquaintance had heard from their husbands after the surrender of Bataan, Snuffy had still not heard from her husband. She feared that he was dead.

Her automobile still stood beneath the acacia tree in the courtyard, where she had parked it more than six months before. The tires were now flat and the body was filthy with the droppings of the sparrows which roosted in the tree.

....

Mabel was a plump, robust and jolly little widow. She had two grandchildren even though she did not appear to be more than 40 years of age. Prior to the war she operated a beauty parlor in Manila's swankiest hotel. Her daughter, son-in-law and their two children were interned at Santo Tomas, where Mabel went to visit them once a month.

Mabel performed her duties as a nurse unobtrusively, efficiently and pleasantly. Her good sense and genuine kindliness enabled her to get along well with everyone. She never spoke an unkind word concerning anyone and no one ever spoke unkindly of her. She mothered us all. We loved her for it and called her Mabel.

When Mabel and Snuffy were transferred as nurses to Red Cross Hospital No. 4 early in June, Mabel's son-in-law secured a pass from Santo Tomas to assist them in moving their baggage. He was a tall, handsome young man, garbed in shorts and an enormously wide-brimmed straw hat, such as Filipino farm laborers often wore to protect themselves from the tropic sun. When he had finished unloading their baggage at Red Cross Hospital No. 4, Mabel put her arms around his neck and kissed him heartily.

Early in July, a bedridden old lady was released to her home Mabel and Snuffy were sent to care for her.

Chapter 47.

Concerning Red Cross Hospital No. 4

Red Cross Hospital No. 4 occupied a two-storey concrete building which prior to the war had been the parish school of the Malate Catholic Church. There were almost one hundred internee patients in this hospital. The internees transferred from the Ateneo Hospital to Red Cross Hospital No. 4 early in June were distributed to several different wards. Slim and I were quartered in a ward on the second floor.

The hospital operated a public dispensary which was visited daily a large number of non-resident patients. Most were Filipinos but among them were a few Spaniards and other neutral nationals. There were also a few Americans who had been released to their homes and who visited the dispensary for medical attention.

A few non-internee patients occupied beds in the hospital. One of these was an Italian whom the Japanese military police had imprisoned for a time at Fort Santiago. Soon after his release from Fort Santiago this Italian was struck and severely injured by a Japanese military truck. He was brought to Red Cross Hospital No. 4 for treatment. A few days later a major of the Japanese Army entered the hospital and was placed in a bed next to the Italian. It was rumored that the Italian had been imprisoned for making statements derogatory to the axis powers and that the Japanese major had been sent to the hospital to keep an eye on him. It was also rumored that both the Italian and the Japanese major were in the hospital to spy on the internees.

An atmosphere of nervousness and distrust pervaded the ranks of the internees in Red Cross Hospital No. 4. The Japanese military administration had issued a decree imposing severe penalties for disseminating anti-axis propaganda and rumors which might disturb the tranquility of the public mind. The Commandant of the Santo Tomas Internment Camp had forbidden internees from discussing the war. The Filipino chief doctor in charge of the hospital requested internees not to discuss the war with members of the hospital staff. Internees who discussed the war glanced nervously about to make sure that no member of the hospital staff and no person who might not be loyal to the Allied cause was within earshot.

The progress of the war was, of course, the chief topic of interest to the internees. Rumors were abundant but authentic news was scarce. There was no radio in Red Cross Hospital No. 4. Those of us who had come from the Ateneo Hospital no longer received the daily summary of the radio news which the Jesuit Fathers has furnished us at the Ateneo Hospital.

The parish priest of the Malate Catholic Church and his assistant were citizens of the Irish Free State and, therefore, were not interned. They visited the hospital each day. In response to the eager inquiries of internees these Irish priests imparted fragments of the radio news from San Francisco and London which they picked up with their short wave receiver. They were very nervous about imparting such news, however, and the news which they gave us was very brief and incomplete.

At my request my wife obtained from one of the Jesuit Fathers at the Ateneo a complete typewritten transcript of the news from San Francisco and London which the Jesuit Fathers had picked up with their short wave receiver during the preceding seven days. I permitted several of my fellow internees to read this transcript but the possession of it made me so nervous that I destroyed it a few hours after I received it. The Jesuit Fathers who gave the transcript to my wife warned her that it must be carefully guarded and must be destroyed as soon as we had read it. Because I felt that it was dangerous for my wife to have such a transcript in her possession I did not request her to obtain any subsequent transcripts.

The food provided by Red Cross Hospital No. 4 was even more scant than the meager ration at the Ateneo Hospital. We were informed that the hospital's budget provided only 14 centavos ($0.07) per patient per day for food. For breakfast we were given a cup of coffee, a teacupful of rice porridge and about a teaspoonful of scrambled duck's egg. Each duck's egg, after being scrambled, was divided into eight portions and one of these small portions was given to each internee. For lunch we were served with a teacupful of boiled rice and a teaspoonful of boiled fish. The ration for dinner was the same as that provided for lunch.

Many of the internees purchased additional food from Filipino food vendors who visited the hospital daily. Additional food was brought to other internees by friends or relatives. Twice a week a Spanish lady brought bread to the hospital. One slice was provided for each patient.

My wife brought food to me twice each week. The cooked meat which she brought I placed in the electric refrigerator located on the veranda of the women's ward. Occasionally a portion of the meat was stolen from the refrigerator. The thief was never caught, but we suspected a woman who was interned in the women's ward.

One of the internees, a man over 65 years of age, had dug up a narrow strip of lawn in front of the hospital and had planted vegetables in it. This garden was too much shaded by trees and did not grow plants as well as it would in a more sunny location. However, he watered it and cultivated it carefully. Soon after I arrived at the hospital he began to harvest small quantities of green vegetables. There were cucumbers, Chinese cabbage, sweet potato leaves and New Zealand spinach.

Interned in my ward was a Greek who spoke Spanish but did not understand English. Also interned in my ward was a young American who spoke Spanish fluently. Each evening for at least an hour this young American and the Greek sat on the veranda and conversed in Spanish. Their favorite topic was the delicious foods which they expected to eat when the war was over. They discussed this subject with enthusiasm and in minute detail, much to the annoyance of fellow internees who understood Spanish.

Another internee in my ward was an American business man who planned to start a poultry farm when the war was over. He had studied his subject and had drawn up the plans for a poultry plant in considerable detail. He never tired of discussing this subject with his fellow internees.

Occupying the bed next to mine was an American merchant marine seaman who said that he was a veteran of the First World War. He informed me that on December 31, when the warehouses of the U.S. Army in the port area were thrown open to the public, he and another American seaman acquired a truck load of foodstuffs, including several cases of beer, which they transported to the home a Filipino friend in Manila. They remained in hiding in the house of this friend for several days. Eventually, however, they got drunk on the beer, went out into the street and were picked up by the Japanese military police. During the night of the preceding the day he was to return to Santo Tomas, but he was absent from the ward. When he returned early the following morning, he informed us that he had spent the night with the Filipino friend with whom he had stored the truck load of food. He said that he had visited this friend in order to obtain some money from him. After his return to Santo Tomas he escaped from the internment camp, was picked up by the Japanese military police, and was interned for a time in a psychiatric hospital. He again escaped, was again picked up by the Japanese military police, and this time he was shot.

Also interned in my ward was Bill Reese. He was one of the Old Timers with whom I had played solo whist in the Shamrock Hotel at Baguio. Bill's daughter brought food to him each day. She and her three small children were living near the hospital. The husband of Bill's daughter was an American automotive mechanic who joined the USAFE force in Bataan. Some time after the surrender of Bataan, Bill's daughter received from her husband a message stating that he was a prisoner of war in Cabanatuan. About the middle of June Bill obtained a pass releasing him from the hospital and interning him for two months in the home of his daughter. He obtained this pass on the plea that he was over 60 years of age and was suffering from pernicious anemia, which required a diet not obtainable either in the hospital or in the Santo Tomas Internment Camp.

Late in June we were informed that on July 1 Red Cross Hospital No. 4 was to be closed to internees and was to be converted into a hospital for Filipino war prisoners. Some of us were sent back to Santo Tomas Internment Camp. But the majority of us, on one plea or another, obtained passes authorizing our internment for a limited period of time either in our homes or elsewhere outside of the Santo Tomas Internment Camp.

There were only two pleas on which a male internee might hope to obtain a pass interning him outside Santo Tomas. One plea was that he was over 60 years of age. The other plea was that he was suffering from some ailment which required medical attention or a diet, or both, not obtainable within the Santo Tomas Internment Camp. The regulations governing the release of women from the internment camp were slightly more liberal. Because of the overcrowded conditions of the sleeping quarters within the internment camp, it was the policy of the Japanese Commandant to release to quarters outside of the camp those internees who pleas conformed to his requirements for internment outside of the camp. It was also his policy to ease overcrowding by issuing releases for limited periods of time. After all other internees had been removed from Red Cross Hospital No. 4, there still remained in the hospital on July 1 eight old men who were deemed too feeble for internment at Santo Tomas and for whom no other quarters had been found. These eight old men were permitted to occupy one of the wards of the hospital after it was converted into a hospital for Filipino war prisoners.

Early in July the administration of Red Cross Hospital No. 4 was transferred from the Philippine Red Cross to a group of Catholic Sisters. Thereafter the hospital was known as the Remedios Hospital as it was located on Remedios Street. The Catholic Sisters provided the patients with sufficient food—something which the Red Cross administration never did. The Catholic Sisters also improved the administration of the hospital in other respects.

The organization in Manila of hospitals for the care of Filipino war prisoners was due to the release from Camp O'Donnell in Tarlac Province of all Filipino war prisoners who were suffering from malaria and dysentery. Prior to their release these war prisoners were required to sign a pledge that they would not oppose the Japanese military administration in any manner. At least one relative or friend was also required to sign a pledge guaranteeing the good conduct of the war prisoner after his release. After their release the war prisoners were brought to Manila for hospitalization.

Within a few months all of the Filipino war prisoners were discharged from the Remedios Hospital, which was then converted into a hospital for the internment of about 60 old men considered too feeble for internment at Santo Tomas.

Chapter 48

I Visit Santo Tomas and Secure a Pass Interning Me in My Home for Ten Days

Late in June, when we were informed that Red Cross Hospital No. 4 was to be closed to internees on July 1, I requested the chief doctor to give me a letter recommending my internment at my home. He acceded to my request rather reluctantly. The letter which he gave me recommended that I be interned in my home because I was suffering from chronic constipation and required a special diet which I could best obtain at home. He refused to mention that I was suffering from pernicious anemia. He said that, because I had been receiving injections of liver extract, an examination of my blood would probably show a nearly normal count of red corpuscles. It was better, he said, to say that I was suffering from chronic constipation because the Japanese could not check up on that!

On June 29, with the doctor's letter and my pass in my pocket, I set out for the Santo Tomas Internment Camp. Charlie, the policeman, whose pass expired that day, accompanied me. No guard accompanied us. We went first to Charlie's home, where he had a brief visit with his wife. He had not been home for almost six months. We arrived at Santo Tomas at about 8.30 a.m. Charlie reported almost immediately to the Commandant's office.

As no one apparently paid any attention to us, I decided, before reporting to the Commandant, to request a letter from Dr. Fletcher recommending my internment in my home. It was Dr. Fletcher who had sent me to the camp hospital in January. Although Dr. Fletcher was interned at Santo Tomas, he spent the greater part of each day attending internee patients in hospitals outside the internment camp. From his wife I learned that he left the camp at 8 o'clock each morning and usually returned at about 1 o'clock in the afternoon.

While waiting for Dr. Fletcher's return, I strolled about the camp, here and there meeting an acquaintance. The camp was still terribly over-crowded, of course, but was more comfortably arranged to promote good health. In one corner of the campus a village of shanties had been erected by internees at their own expense. There the owners and their friends spent a considerable portion of the daylight hours, although they were not permitted to sleep in their shanties. A long shed, which served as a dining room, had been erected at the rear of the main building. This shed was furnished with long tables and benches made of rough lumber. Nearby were several long troughs, provided at intervals with water taps, where each internee might wash his own dishes and clothing. The kitchen was located on the ground floor of the main building and opened on to the hallway leading to the rear entrance. In the hallway, opposite the entrance to the kitchen, was a long serving counter. At mealtimes the internees lined up, each with a plate and a cup, and filed past the serving counter, where food and drink were dispensed.

I found Mr. Stocking in charge of the lost-and-found department, where he was on duty from 8 to 11 each morning. He was a Spanish-American war veteran who must have been at least 60 years of age, although he did not appear to be more than fifty. For many years prior to the outbreak of the Japanese-American war he was a department head in one of Manila's largest mercantile establishments. He was a bachelor and for many years had resided at the American YMCA which had now been converted into a hospital for Japanese soldiers. Mr. Stocking was one of the leading stamp collectors of the Philippines. It was our mutual interest in stamps which brought about our acquaintance. The residents of the American YMCA were among the first to be picked up and interned by the Japanese. Mr. Stocking had been forced to leave his valuable stamp collection in his room at the YMCA.

It was rumored, Mr. Stocking told me, that the feeding of the internees would be taken away from the Red Cross and turned over to the Commandant of the Santo Tomas Internment Camp. The funds of the Red Cross were almost exhausted. According to rumor, the Japanese Army was willing to provide 70,000 pesos per month for the feeding and maintenance of the camp since there were about 3,000 persons in the camp. This allocation amounted to just 70 centavos ($0.35) per person per day. The allocation would be increased only if the population of the camp should be increased by re-interning some of those who had previously been released from the camp. Mr. Stocking was informed that many of those who had been released were being required to return to the camp at the expiration of their passes.

While I was chatting with Mr. Stocking, Fred Passemore came and greeted me. He was wearing shorts, was deeply tanned, and radiated good health and good cheer. At the outbreak of the war he was a civilian employee at the Nichol's Field Army Airport, but had been lucky enough to escape injury during the bombing of the airport. He pointed to a cot in the hallway nearby and said that was where he bunked. He chatted only a few moments and then resumed the building of a screen which would provide his sleeping quarters with a small measure of privacy.

I then saw Mr. Boerecki approaching. He was clad only in shorts and tennis shoes, the latter a bit soiled with mud. His lean face, prominent nose, black eyebrows and white hair enabled me to identify him. But I was amazed to find his face and body tanned to a deep golden brown. He was even leaner than when I had last seen him in January, but he looked very fit. He told me that he was in charge of the camp garden and that he was sending the camp hospital about 1,000 pounds of fresh vegetables each week. "I would like to have you join my gang of gardeners," he said. "I think you may find a pal among them. They include a mining engineer, a clergyman and a university professor." Mr. Boerecki himself was a mining engineer with an international reputation as an expert in the valuation of mining properties. Until the Japanese occupation of Manila he had been the valuation expert of the Bureau of Mines of the Philippine Government.

In the hallway on the ground floor of the main building I encountered Mr. Witteman. For several years prior to the war he was the assistant treasurer of the firm which was the Philippine distributor of Ford Automobiles. I found him busily engaged in making chocolate cream candy. He said that he used only the very finest of ingredients and that for twenty chocolate creams weighing about a pound his price was 2.50 pesos ($1.25). Although his fellow internees were his only customers, he was able to sell at that price all the chocolate creams which he could make. I watched him dip the cream centers in the melted chocolate and lay them out to cool. They certainly looked delicious.

It was the noon hour and while we chatted a 14-year-old girl came to show Mr. Witteman her midday meal. It consisted of fried beef steak, mashed sweet potatoes and a cup of cocoa. Mr. Witteman said that the children and the men who worked three hours or more a day received three meals a day. All other internees received only two meals a day. His own camp work of cleaning toilets on his floor each afternoon did not take three hours. Hence he received only two meals a day.

Our conversation was terminated by the appearance of Charlie, who had come with me to the camp that morning. A lady accompanied Charlie. "Come with us," she said, "and I think I can rustle some chow for you." She conducted us to the serving counter at the entrance to the kitchen. All those entitled to a midday meal had already been served and the supply of beef steak was exhausted. The lady provided Charlie and me each with a plate and cup. We were then served with sweet potatoes and cocoa. My cup contained nearly a pint of cocoa and on my plate was a huge helping of sweet potatoes. It was more than I could eat. So I hunted up Sam Deebel on the second floor and shared my meal with him. Sam contributed to our joint meal several slices of roast beef which one of the internees had given him.

Those internees who could afford it supplemented the camp ration with additional food which they purchased and cooked themselves. Some of them supplied all of their own food. Scattered about the camp I had noted many little earthen cooking stoves, each about ten inches in diameter and ten inches tall. Charcoal or wood was used for fuel. These earthen cooking stoves, which are quite economical in fuel consumption, had for generations been used by the poorer native inhabitants of the Philippines. Now the American and European internees, impoverished by the war, found in these primitive stoves an inexpensive means of cooking their food.

Sam, like nearly every other internee in the camp, was eager for news of the war. The internees within the camp were without a radio and most of them were cut off from any trustworthy source of news. Hence their craving for news of allied victories and particularly, their ardent desire for news indicating a probability of their own early release, caused many of them to give credence to the wild rumors, as amazing as they were false, which circulated throughout the camp. Most of this false news apparently originated outside the camp and was smuggled into camp by notes hidden in packages of food. Sam told me that, according to one report which reached the camp that morning, Guam had been recaptured and the Japanese had been driven out of Mindanao by the American forces and American submarines were blockading Manila Bay so that Japanese ships were unable to either enter or leave the harbor. When I told Sam that these reports were false he replied earnestly and rather pathetically, "Here in camp, when anyone tells you any news you do not tell him that you do not believe it because, if you do, he won't bring you any more news."

Near Sam's quarters I found a middle-aged internee making cigarettes. He had constructed a very simple device which he said rolled cigarettes in essentially the same manner as a cigarette machine. This device was operated by hand. With it he was able to roll about 100 cigarettes an hour. The cigarettes were neatly rolled and the paper was firmly glued. The surplus tobacco projecting from each end of the cigarette was trimmed off with a pair of scissors. He said that he was using a mixture of Philippine and Virginia tobaccos and that he sold his cigarettes for 35 centavos ($0.175) per packet of 20. Machine-made cigarettes of a similar mixture were then selling in the camp for 60 centavos ($0.30) per packet of 20. I inferred, however, that this internee did not pay any internal revenue tax on his handmade cigarettes, which may have been one reason why he was able to sell his product so much cheaper than the machine-made cigarettes.

As Dr. Fletcher was late in returning to the camp I was unable to consult him until after 4 p.m. Meanwhile the Commandant's office closed at 4 pm, so I was unable to report that day. Fortunately my pass did not expire until the next day. Dr. Fletcher said he would personally accompany me to the Commandant's office and recommend my release. He believed, however, that the letter which the chief doctor at the hospital had given was sufficient, provided I also mentioned that I was suffering from anemia. He told me to inform the guard at the gate, if I was questioned, that I had come to consult

Dr. Fletcher. When I showed my pass to the guard, however, I was permitted to depart without being questioned. I returned as I had come, unguarded, to Red Cross Hospital No. 4.

When I returned to Santo Tomas at about 1 o'clock the following afternoon, Dr. Fletcher's wife informed me that he had been called upon to perform an operation at Saint Luke's Hospital and probably would not return to Santo Tomas before 3 p.m.

I went to Sam's quarters and gave him a hard-boiled egg. From the eagerness with which he accepted it I surmised that he had not eaten an egg for a long time. There were more than twenty men quartered in the room which Sam occupied. He informed me that camp regulations prohibited talking in quarters between 1 and 2 p.m. He suggested that we play a game of pinochle at a table on the balcony of his room. I preferred to return to the lobby at the main entrance, where I could watch for the return of Dr. Fletcher. Sam did not accompany me. He preferred to take a *siesta* (afternoon nap).

In the lobby I encountered Earl Dayton. For more than twenty years he had been employed on the Calamba Sugar Estate, about 35 miles south of Manila. I had also been employed on the Calamba Sugar Estate when Earl began working there as a field overseer in 1920. He was then a young man in his early twenties and had recently graduated from an agricultural school in California. I left the Calamba Sugar Estate in 1921 and had not seen Earl for at least ten years. He was now a middle-aged man and very fat. He was dressed in beautifully tailored and freshly laundered clothing, in stark contrast to the careless clothes of many of the internees. Evidently someone outside the camp was taking care of his laundry as well as bringing him food.

The Calamba Sugar Estate was sold by its American owners to a Filipino-owned corporation about a year before the outbreak of the Japanese-American War. Earl was one of the five American employees retained by the new corporation. He said that the Calamba Sugar Estate was milling sugar cane when the war began and that it continued to operate until December 27, 1941. On that morning Earl and other members of the staff were ordered to evacuate to Manila by members of General MacArthur's staff, who informed them that the Japanese forces were approaching. As soon as Earl and other members of the Calamba staff departed the USAFE detachment dynamited the bridges on the road leading to the Calamba Sugar Estate. The detachment then came on into Manila, dynamiting each bridge en route as soon as they had passed over it. Earl told me that the Japanese forces had not damaged the Calamba Sugar Estate and that the harvesting of the crop had been resumed and completed after the occupation of Manila by the Japanese forces.

When Dr. Fletcher had not returned by 2.30 p.m. I decided to wait no longer. With considerable trepidation I reported to the Commandant's office, where I presented my pass and the letter which the chief doctor at the hospital had given me. I was told to wait outside the office until called.

There were about twenty other internees waiting for action on their applications for renewal of their passes. Jack Howard, who had been re-interned at Santo Tomas after having been released to his home from the Ateneo Hospital, informed me that five out of every six who applied for renewal of their passes were being ordered back to Santo Tomas. So I felt that my chance of being released to my home was rather slim.

I expected that I would have to wait until the applications of all those who had reported ahead of me were acted upon. But I was ushered into the Commandant's office after waiting only about five minutes. I was taken to the desk of the Japanese civilian who prepared the passes. There I was questioned by Mr. Stanley, an Englishman who spoke Japanese fluently and who had been brought from Japan to act as an interpreter.

Mr. Stanley asked me if Red Cross Hospital No. 4 was to be closed immediately. I replied that I was not certain, but that I understood that it was to be closed as soon as a place could be found for several old men who were interned there and that I understood the old men were to be sent to the San Juan de Dios Hospital. For some reason, not disclosed to me, this information seemed to displease him, but he made no comment. He then informed me that I would be temporarily released to my home but was required to return on July 10 for examination by a Japanese physician, whose report would determine whether or not I would be released to my home for a longer period.

The Japanese civilian then made a note on my pass extending it to July 10. After being instructed to return on July 10 at between 12.30 and 12.45 p.m., I was given a slip of paper on which was noted the time I was dismissed from the Commandant's office. I was instructed to present this slip to the guard at the gate. I was told that I must leave the camp within five minutes.

Jack Howard was waiting in the lobby to learn how I had fared. When I told him that I had been given ten days at home and must return for a medical examination by the Japanese doctor, Jack said, "You have only about one chance in six to get passed by the Japanese doctor, but you will have ten days at home anyway, and that is something." Jack told me that Charlie, who had accompanied me to Santo Tomas the preceding day, had also been given ten days at home and was required to report for medical examination on July 9. It appeared that since his return to Santo Tomas Jack spent most of his time waiting in the lobby outside the Commandant's office to learn the fate of each internee whose pass came up for renewal. There appeared to be about a dozen other internees who also loitered in the lobby for the same purpose. I broke away from them and hastened to the gate.

I returned to Red Cross Hospital No. 4, where Socorro, my wife, had promised to meet me and escort me home if I was released. Socorro, who was employed as a bookkeeper in the central office of the Red Cross, did not reach the hospital until about 5 p.m. She had walked the mile and a half from her office in order to save five centavos ($0.025) which she would otherwise have paid for transportation. We said goodbye to about a dozen internees who still remained in the hospital.

As we were about to leave the hospital Mabel, one of the two internee nurses, came to say goodbye. She pulled my head down and gave me a motherly kiss. Then she turned to my wife with a friendly laugh and said, "Now you can get a divorce."

We walked to Taft Avenue, renamed Daoitoa Avenue by the Japanese, where we secured a horse-drawn *tartanilla* to transport us to my mother-in-law's home.

Chapter 49.

Concerning the First Ten Days of My Internment at Home

"Daddy, daddy," shouted my son when we reached our home. My mother-in-law welcomed me with tears of joy streaming down her cheeks. Behind her, awaiting their turn to welcome me, stood our two young servant girls, smiling shyly and my mother-in-law's aged servant, Tia Onung (Aunt Onung), her wrinkled face beaming.

Only one who has himself been a prisoner can fully comprehend the delight of returning to one's home and family after having been in prison. Just to saunter through the rooms of the house and gaze upon each worn and familiar article of furniture filled me with a vast content. The shabby shelves loaded with my son's battered toys, the ancient rug with a hole carefully darned and concealed beneath a table, the *rataan* chairs which needed a fresh coat of paint, the lithographed landscapes upon the walls, the oddly assorted dishes within the china closet, the worn silverware within its drawer, the white tiled bathroom with its gas water heater, my son's bed and the chest of drawers where his clothes were kept, the radio, the gas stove in the kitchen—all these commonplace furnishings to which I had formerly given but scant attention—now were pleasing and somehow oddly precious.

I strolled out into the garden. The flowers in which my mother-in-law had delighted were there no longer. They had been displaced by vegetables. Green corn was ready to be harvested; peanuts were already in bloom, which a little later should yield a bushel or more. There was okra, eggplant, beans and several varieties of "greens". In a seed bed were a hundred or so young eggplants waiting to be transplanted. Three papaya trees were loaded with fruit and there were more than seventy young papaya trees grown from the seed of an Hawaiian papaya which had been the gift of a fellow internee at the hospital—in six or seven months these young papaya trees should be bearing fruit. The pomelo tree was covered with a multitude of tiny pomelos—in three months each tiny pomelo should become a huge orange five or six inches in diameter. There were several bunches of bananas in varying stages of development. The macopa tree and the balingbing tree were both loaded with fruit which was almost ripe. There were even two late melons ready to be harvested.

In his pen was the pig, which had only been a little fellow when I saw him last in January but which was now grown to several times his former size. We planned to butcher him for my son's birthday in November, still more than four months hence. In their coop were the white rooster and his seven white hens. As I approached, the rooster picked up and dropped a grain of corn, calling lustily to his hens.

Truly we were fortunate, I reflected, that in our straightened circumstances we had a house for which we did not have to pay rent and a garden, a few chickens and a pig which would provide us with part of our food.

For dinner that first evening after my return to our home we had green corn on the cob, fresh spinach and bananas from our garden. To these were added boiled rice and fried beef steak. It was a substantial meal and there was enough of it so that all of us—my wife, my son, my mother-in-law, our three servants and myself—could eat as much as we wished. How much better it was than the meager ration which the hospital had furnished during the five months of my internment there!

The next day, July 1, my first day at home after more than five months of internment, was my birthday. No one remembered this, however, and I did not mention it. My wife left the house for her office at 7.30 in the morning and did not return until 6.30 in the evening. I spent the day writing. In the hospital I had made only very brief notes in my diary. Now I was able to expand these notes and to record incidents which I had not dared to enter in my diary because of the possibility that it might fall into Japanese hands.

July second and third passed quietly. I did not leave the house and spent most of my time writing.

Then came July 4, the anniversary of the American Declaration of Independence. For forty years July Fourth had been celebrated as a holiday in the Philippines. But there was no public celebration this year. The Japanese military administration had decreed that July 4 was no longer a holiday.

In the morning I called on Dr. Fletcher at Saint Luke's Hospital. He gave me an injection of liver extract and had a blood test made. The test showed only 63% of the normal count of red corpuscles and indicated that I was still suffering from anemia. The hospital laboratory provided me with a certificate showing the result of the blood test and the fact that the test had been made at the request of Dr. Fletcher. I intended to present this certificate to the Japanese doctor when I went to him for medical examination on July 10.

July 5 was our twentieth wedding anniversary. As it was Sunday my wife was able to spend the day at home. I took the opportunity during the day to discuss with her our precarious financial situation.

Like many other people who, prior to the war, had been well off, we now found it difficult to obtain sufficient cash to meet our living expenses, even when these had been reduced to the minimum. Fortunately my mother-in-law owned her home, so there was no rent to pay. The garden, the chickens and the pig would provide us with a part of our food. Nevertheless, there were seven people to feed—my wife, my son, my wife's mother, the three maidservants and myself. We could, of course, discharge the three maidservants and thus avoid the expense of feeding them. But they had served us faithfully and we were determined to provide them with food and shelter for as long as it was possible to do so.

Immediately after the outbreak of war, in order to prevent a run on the banks, President Quezon by executive order limited to 400 pesos per month the amount which each person might withdraw from his bank account. We were living in Baguio at that time. Our only bank account was carried in a Manila bank. Mail, telephone and telegraph services between Baguio and Manila were suspended so that we were unable to communicate with our bank. Because of the limited amount of cash on hand in the two branch banks at Baguio we were able to obtain there, by means of a check drawn on our Manila bank, only 200 pesos. We had always paid our bills by check and never kept much cash on hand. Thus when we arrived in Manila on December 22 we had only a little more than 200 pesos ($100) in cash. We might have drawn another 200 pesos from our bank but because of our preoccupation in building an air raid shelter to protect ourselves from the constant bombings by Japanese planes we neglected to do this before the banks closed on December 27. So when the Japanese occupied Manila on January 2 we had only about 200 pesos in actual cash on hand.

The gold mines which were our only source of income had suspended operations and ceased to pay dividends. The Japanese military administration refused to permit the reopening of the bank in which our funds were deposited, so we could not obtain money from that source. My mother-in-law's small savings account was carried in the same bank, so we were also denied access to that. Her only income was the rent which she had received from a house which she owned in the town of Isabela on the island of Negros. Communication with that island had been cut off by the war. There were no means of forwarding money even if the tenant still had some with which to pay the rent. Thus, my mother-in-law was also without income. It was an unpleasant situation to say the least. Before the war we had spent at least 500 pesos per month. We now had no income and only 200 pesos in hand.

During the six months which had elapsed since the Japanese occupation of Manila my wife had done a wonderful job of husbanding our slender resources. She began the year with 200 pesos and six months later, on June 30, she still had 160 pesos—a shrinkage of only 40 pesos. Nevertheless, she had spent during the six months about 360 pesos—an average of 60 pesos per month. Including the three servants there were seven mouths to feed. Thus our living expenses had been down to less than nine pesos ($4.50) per person per month. Since our cash reserve had been reduced by only 40 pesos my wife had been able during the six months to secure 320 pesos in additional cash. One hundred pesos had been realized from the sale of fifteen pounds of Klim powdered milk, twenty pesos had been obtained from the sale of 20 kilograms of green coffee beans; the remaining 200 pesos had been obtained by inducing several Filipino friends to cash checks drawn on our impounded bank account.

These checks could not be paid by the bank until after the end of the war. Hence the only cash which she had obtained on these checks was really a loan secured by the checks. Several persons in Manila who had money to loan were cashing checks drawn on impounded bank accounts at 30 to 35 percent interest. My wife had been fortunate in finding friends who cashed her checks without interest. Nevertheless, money was very scarce in Manila. To obtain even so small a sum as 200 pesos my wife had been compelled to canvas a considerable number of friends. Most of them were in the same financial straits as ourselves.

On June 15, my wife secured a position as a bookkeeper at 40 pesos ($20.00) per month in the central office of the Philippine Red Cross. After paying her transportation she would have left a salary of about 33 pesos per month. Since our expenditures were about 60 pesos per month we must still obtain about 30 pesos per month from some other source.

My wife had always kept on hand in our home at Baguio a supply of imported canned goods and other non-perishable foodstuffs sufficient to last at least six months. And since we always spent three or four months of each year with my wife's mother in Manila we kept on hand in her home a similar, but smaller, supply. When we fled to Manila from Baguio in December 1941, we brought two sacks (242 pounds) of rice and all the canned goods which we could carry in our Lincoln Zephyr. Thus, when the Japanese occupied Manila we already had on hand in my mother-in-law's house a substantial supply of canned goods and other non-perishable foodstuffs.

My wife had carefully conserved our supply of imported canned goods and had limited our consumption of food almost entirely to those foodstuffs which were produced in the Philippines. Almost the only imported foodstuffs which we continued to consume after the Japanese occupation of Manila were wheat flour and baking powder. At the beginning of the year we had on hand a sack and a half of flour. Late in January, my wife purchased a 5-pound can of baking powder—which had probably been looted—for two and a-half pesos ($1.25).

During the first two months that I was interned at the Ateneo Hospital my wife each Sunday brought us two cakes, one for the internee patients and the other for the members of the hospital staff. At home she frequently made hot cakes for breakfast. But when our supply of flour had dwindled to about one-half sack she ceased to bring cakes to the hospital and she ceased to eat hot cakes at home. Flour was then selling at 30 pesos ($15.00) per 49-pound sack. On January 3 we had paid only four pesos for a sack. My wife and son both dearly loved hot cakes for breakfast, but she felt that she could not afford to eat them when flour was selling at 30 pesos per sack. So she ceased to consume flour.

After the Japanese occupation of Manila no foodstuffs, with the exception of rice from Indochina, were imported. As a result the price of the imported foodstuffs still on hand in Manila rose rapidly. Our own limited supply of imported foodstuffs constituted an asset which was very saleable at much higher prices than we paid for it. The money realized from the sale of imported foodstuffs could be used for the purchase of much less expensive foods which were produced in the Philippines.

On July 6, we took our half sack of flour to a grocery store and sold it for twenty pesos ($10.00). It had cost us two pesos in January.

With a part of the proceeds of the sale of our flour, Socorro purchased a pair of shoes for herself and another pair for our nine-year-old son, Leonard. Socorro's shoes, of white leather with rubber soles, cost 6.00 pesos, which we thought was quite cheap. The internal revenue law promulgated by the Japanese military government imposed a tax of 40 per cent upon the selling price of all shoes selling for 4 pesos or more per pair. This tax was included in the price of 6 pesos which we paid for Socorro's shoes. The pair of shoes purchased for Leonard cost 2.50 pesos. The uppers were of brown canvas and the soles were made from a worn-out automobile tire casing. Both rubber and leather were now very scarce in the Philippines.

On July 9, Silvestre … visited us. He had been one of the hospital attendants at the Ateneo Hospital. He was now in charge of foodstuffs at the Red Cross Hospital which had been established in June in the coastal town of Hagonoy in Bulacan Province about 40 miles north of Manila. This town was located on the marshy delta of the Rio Grande de Pampanga, which discharged into Manila Bay.

When the USAFE troops in Bataan surrendered to the Japanese in April a number of Filipino soldiers had escaped capture by making their way through the coastal swamps from Bataan to Hagonoy. Silvestre said that almost all 200 patients in the Hagonoy Hospital were Filipino soldiers who had escaped from Bataan. They had, of course, discarded their guns and uniforms. Most of them were suffering from malaria, dysentery, or both. The number of refugees in Hagonoy who needed hospitalization far exceeded the capacity of the hospital. Many of those who were ill were being cared for in the homes of the residents of the town.

Silvestre said that there was an abundance of both rice and fish in Hagonoy and that the prices were lower than in Manila. Rice was being retailed in Hagonoy at 33 centavos per ganta (a ganta of rice weighs about 5.3 pounds.)

In Manila both rice and fish were scarce. Rice was rationed—300 grams per person per day could be purchased and rice could be purchased lawfully only from the government-owned National Rice and Corn Corporation which retailed the rice at 34 centavos per ganta. An embargo had been placed on the transportation of rice into Manila by private persons. Nevertheless rice was being smuggled into Manila and could be purchased at prices higher than the government charged for the rationed rice.

Chapter 50.

I Am Granted a Pass Authorizing My Internment in My Home for One Month

On July 10, I went to the Santo Tomas Internment Camp for medical examination by the Japanese doctor. I reported at the gate at 12.30 p.m. in accordance with my instructions. I was admitted at once but had to wait in the lobby of the main building until the Japanese doctor arrived at 1 p.m. There were about twenty other internees awaiting their medical examination that day.

Before going to Santo Tomas I obtained from Dr. Orobia, who had been my doctor when I was interned at Red Cross Hospital No. 4, a letter stating that I was suffering from pernicious anaemia.

At 1 p.m. all the internees awaiting medical examination were ushered into the Japanese doctor's outer office by an American woman who was herself an internee. She had a typewritten list of our names and seated us around that room in the order in which we were to be examined. I was the first to be called into the doctor's inner office. Seated on the opposite side of a small table were the Japanese doctor and his assistant, the latter an American physician who was one of the internees.

I presented to the Japanese doctor the letter stating that I was suffering from pernicious anemia and the certificate stating that a blood test had shown only 63% of the normal count of red corpuscles. After reading these the Japanese doctor inspected the inner lining of my lower eyelid—a means of detecting pronounced anemia. I informed the doctor that since the removal of my gall bladder in 1929 it had been necessary for me to be very careful what I ate. The Japanese doctor then inspected the long scar which was evidence of the gall bladder operation. After this brief examination he returned without comment to his seat at the small table. The American assistant doctor instructed me to go to the Commandant's office and wait there until my name was called.

I found a seat in the lobby near the entrance to the Commandant's office. One by one, I was joined by the twenty other internees as rapidly as their medical examinations were completed. When all of the internees had been examined the two doctors entered the Commandant's office, presented their report, and then departed. They had accomplished the examination of more than twenty patients in less than an hour.

While I waited outside the Commandant's office Jack Howard came and greeted me. He was one of perhaps a dozen internees whose chief occupation was loitering near the entrance to the Commandant's office for several hours each day in order to learn whose passes were renewed and for how long they were renewed.

"Have you been examined by the Japanese doctor?" asked Jack.

"Yes," I replied.

"Your real examination," said Jack, "will take place in the Commandant's office. There the decision will be made as to whether or not your pass will be renewed. Recently the officials in the Commandant's office have been somewhat more liberal than they were in June, when only about one pass out of every seven was renewed. During the past few days about one pass out of every *four* has been renewed. It all depends on how they feel in the Commandant's office on the day that your pass happens to expire. If they are in a generous mood your pass may be renewed. If not, you will be thrown back into the internment camp."

As I glanced over the twenty internees whose passes were to be acted upon that day I noticed that most of them appeared to be older and less robust than myself and I thought that my chance of having my pass renewed was rather slim.

At about 2.30 p.m., a young English internee who acted as usher in the Commandant's office called my name and escorted me to the desk of the Japanese official who issued the passes. Seated at his desk were Mr. Stanley, the Englishman who acted as interpreter, and Mr. Grinnell, the American chairman of the internee governing committee of the camp.

When I had seated myself, Mr. Grinnell said, "You are number one on the list today."

I was facing the Japanese official who prepared the passes and I noted that he already had his pen poised over one of the printed forms which were being issued to those who were granted releases to their homes. In that instant I realized with an inward thrill that my pass was to be extended!

Mr. Grinnell followed his opening observation with questions as to my age, nature of my illness, place of residence and former occupation. The Japanese official busily entered my replies in Japanese on the pass. Mr. Stanley then made the corresponding entries in English. The pass recorded my name, age, gender, citizenship, the nature of the illness on account of which I was released to my home, and the date on which the pass expired. This pass would expire on August 10. I had been granted an extension of one month.

"Thank you, gentlemen," I said when my pass was handed to me and I was dismissed.

An American internee handed me a time slip on which was noted the exact time of my dismissal and instructed me to present this to the guard at the gate. "You must leave the camp within five minutes," he said.

As I emerged from the Commandant's office the other internees who were awaiting action on their passes regarded me curiously.

"Did you have any luck?" asked one.

"I did," I replied.

Jack was waiting near by. "How did you fare?" he asked.

"I was given one month's extension," I replied.

Several of the internees eyed me enviously.

When I reached the gate I took off my hat and bowed to the inner guard, as we were required to, and I presented my time slip. As I passed through the gate I observed a young Japanese soldier standing on guard just outside of the gate. I turned and bowed to him also. He bowed in return with a smile. For good measure I said "Goodbye" pleasantly in English. I was so happy because my pass had been extended that I was able at that moment to greet even a Japanese soldier with genuine goodwill.

Chapter 51.

I Visit Several of My Former Internee Companions

When I called on the morning of July 10 at the former Red Cross Hospital No. 4 to obtain a medical certificate form Dr. Orobia, I learned that several of those who had been interned with me at that hospital had been transferred back to the Ateneo University. Because I was not certain that my pass would be extended, I called at the Ateneo before reporting to Santo Tomas. I found Paul, Ford, Bo and Slim occupying one of the rooms which formerly had been occupied by the Ateneo Hospital. Their food was being provided by the Jesuit mess, but since there was a gas stove in the former hospital kitchen they could cook for themselves if they wished. Bo said that their passes permitted them to leave the premises for medical attention and to purchase food, clothing and medicines, exactly as in the case of those who were interned in their homes.

Ford and Bo sought and obtained permission to live at the Ateneo, not only because they had no homes to go to, but also because they could obtain at the Ateneo the war news which the Jesuit Fathers received daily by radio from San Francisco and London. Paul was interned at the Ateneo because he too had no home to which he could go. Slim secured internment at the Ateneo because his wife and two sons, although they were not interned, had been given a refuge there.

Bo told me that his pass was to expire on July 13 and that Dr. P—, former head of Red Cross Hospital No. 4, had written a letter stating that he believed Bo was well enough to be sent back to the Santo Tomas Internment Camp. As a result Bo applied for a transfer from Red Cross Hospital No. 4 to the Santo Tomas Internment Camp for a medical examination on July 5. Bo was a physical wreck and was barely able to hobble about. He informed the Japanese doctor that he had only one kidney, that his gall bladder had been removed and that his one remaining kidney had been operated upon for the removal of kidney stones. The Japanese doctor, having inspected the scars which were evidence of these major operations, said that Bo was in no condition to be returned to Santo Tomas. Bo's request for internment at the Ateneo was granted.

It was at Bo's suggestion that I informed the Japanese doctor that my gall bladder had been removed. Whether or not that fact was what decided the Japanese doctor to recommend an extension of my pass I do not know.

On Saturday, July 11, I went to Dr. Orobia at the Remedios Hospital—formerly Red Cross Hospital No. 4—for my regular weekly injection of liver extract. Most of the patients in the hospital were Filipino war prisoners who had been released from concentration camp because of illness. There were still eight or ten American and European internees in the hospital, however. All of them were old men who had no homes to which they might go and who were considered too feeble to be interned at Santo Tomas. I visited them in the ward to which they had been assigned. They informed me that, when the Red Cross Hospital No. 4 was being closed, the chief doctor transferred them to the San Juan de Dios Hospital without consulting the Commandant of the Santo Tomas Internment Camp. This action displeased the Commandant and he ordered their return to the Remedios Hospital.

The building occupied by Red Cross Hospital No. 4 was owned by the Malate Catholic Church and had formerly housed the parochial school. Father Kelley, the parish priest, when he learned that the Red Cross planned to close the hospital at the end of June, arranged for the Catholic Women's League to take over its administration and convert it into a hospital for Filipino war prisoners who, because of illness, had been released from Camp O'Donnell in Tarlac Province. The Catholic Women's League had also assumed responsibility for the care of the few American and European internees who still remained in the hospital. It was renamed the Remedios Hospital.

Chapter 52

My Wife Recovers My Valuable Collection of Philippine Stamps

In December Socorro had deposited in the safe-deposit vault of the Manila branch of the National City Bank cases containing the set of silverware which was a wedding present and my own valuable collection of Philippine stamps. This stamp collection was worth more than ten thousand pesos. Socorro had been unable to obtain a safe-deposit box in which to place these valuables. At the suggestion of the bank officials, she placed them in a suitcase which, after being sealed by the officials of the bank, was placed in the vault which housed the safe-deposit boxes. Socorro was given a receipt for the suitcase which she had placed in her safe-deposit box in the vault of the Manila Building and Loan Association.

The National City Bank was not permitted to reopen after the Japanese Occupation of Manila. The American officials of the bank were interned at Santo Tomas. In June the Japanese Bank of Taiwan moved into the quarters of the National City Bank.

Early in July the Bank of Taiwan announced that it would open the safe-deposit vault of the former National City Bank on July 14. All Filipino citizens and citizens of neutral countries who had valuables deposited in the safe-deposit vault of the National City Bank were requested to appear on that date and claim their property.

Socorro went to the headquarters of the Japanese Military Police at Fort Santiago, where she stated that she was a Filipino citizen and that she had deposited for safe keeping in the vault of the National City Bank a suitcase containing silverware and a stamp collection. She also stated that she was unable to present her receipt for the suitcase because the receipt had been deposited in her box in the safe-deposit vault of Manila Building and Loan Association which had not been permitted to reopen. Socorro was then informed that she would be able to recover her suitcase without the receipt, provided she identified the suitcase and its contents to the satisfaction of the officials of the Taiwan Bank. Fortunately her name was painted with India ink on the suitcase. At the suggestion of the military police, she wrote a letter describing the suitcase and its contents, which letter the military police promised to transmit to the Taiwan Bank.

Socorro then obtained from Mr. Jorge B. Vargas, Filipino head of the Executive Commission of the provincial Philippine Government, a letter identifying her as a Filipino citizen and a person of good repute and stating that she wished to recover her suitcase from the vault of the National City Bank.

Armed with this letter Socorro went to the Taiwan Bank on July 15. An official of the bank, after she had presented the letter from Mr. Vargas and had described the suitcase and its contents, inquired whether it contained any currency. Socorro replied that there was no currency in the suitcase. The official then asked whether she was indebted to the National City Bank. When Socorro replied that she was not indebted to the bank she was permitted to take possession of the suitcase without its seal being broken or its contents examined.

I was, of course, jubilant when Socorro brought the suitcase home that afternoon. I had feared that because I was an American citizen the suitcase and its contents would be confiscated as enemy property by the Japanese military authorities.

In my stamp collection we now had a valuable liquid asset which could be sold and converted into cash if we needed the money. I immediately placed about 100 pesos worth of stamps in a book to be turned over to a Filipino stamp dealer for sale on a commission basis. I took the book of stamps to the dealer's store on July 16, but found the store padlocked and its windows boarded up.

Chapter 53.

The Japanese Military Administration Seeks to Curb the Dissemination of Uncensored News

The Japanese military administration had imposed severe penalties for the dissemination of uncensored news. Such news continued to be circulated, however. News from Allied sources overseas was picked up by short-wave radio receivers. Typewritten and mimeographed sheets containing such news were extensively, although secretly, circulated throughout the city of Manila. In order to curb the use of mimeographs and other duplicating machines for this purpose the Japanese military administration issued a decree requiring the registration of all such machines and prohibiting their use if they did not have a permit from the Japanese military administration. This decree was followed by two other decrees aimed at curbing the reception and dissemination of uncensored news.

When Socorro returned from her office on July 20 she reported that an order has been issued requiring the registration of all typewriters at the headquarters of the Metropolitan Police. Each registrant was required either to present his typewriter or to furnish a sample sheet typed on his typewriter. We inferred that this order had been issued in an attempt to learn the source, and prevent the circulation, of clandestine typewritten news sheets which reported news received by radio from Allied sources.

Socorro wished to conceal our portable typewriter because she feared that it would be confiscated if she registered it. It was several days before I was able to persuade her to register it so as to avoid the severe penalty to which we would have been subject.

In the meantime, on July 24, the Japanese military administration issued a decree which prohibited listening to foreign radio stations after August 1, 1942, requiring all radio receivers to be registered and requiring, also, that all radio receivers be submitted to the Japanese military administration for alteration so that short-wave radio broadcasts from overseas could not be picked up. The only radio stations to which it was permitted to listen were the local Japanese-controlled radio KZRH and stations broadcasting from Japan. The Japanese military administration was determined to prevent the people of the Philippines from obtaining news from Allied sources overseas. And there was also the clandestine local *Juan de la Cruz* radio station which had been broadcasting bitter attacks upon the Japanese and which the Japanese military administration had so far been unable to suppress.

Socorro and I decided, in order to avoid any possible chance of listening to prohibited radio stations after August 1, to place our radio receiver in storage. We had not been using it because two tubes were burned out and we could not afford to buy new ones. Accordingly, my wife's mother, in whose name the radio had been registered prior to the outbreak of the war, made the necessary affidavit that the radio had been placed in storage and it was registered as such with the metropolitan police.

Chapter 54.

The Son of Our American Neighbor Dies and a Wake is Held Over His Body

On July 25, Arthur Fishback, 22 years old and the adopted Filipino son of an American neighbor, died of pulmonary tuberculosis. His adoptive Father was an American veteran of the Spanish-American War who had been interned in his home because he, too, was suffering from tuberculosis. The family was destitute. We, and other neighbors contributed the money to pay Arthur's funeral expenses. Our own contribution of five pesos we took from our slender store of cash rather reluctantly. It meant that I would have to go without the new shoes I needed for another month or two at least.

A wake was held over Arthur's body throughout the entire night of July 25. His male friends took turns singing lugubrious songs. Someone was singing almost constantly throughout the night. Food and drink were, of course, provided for those who participated in the wake. We did not attend the wake because Socorro had to work the next day but we got very little sleep. The Fishback home, where the wake was held, was next door to ours.

Arthur was buried on the afternoon of July 26. He was another victim of the war. If his adoptive parents had been able to provide him with proper food or had been able to send him to a sanitarium his life might have been saved. They had sought to have him admitted to a tuberculosis sanitarium as a charity patient in January, but the institution had been taken over by Japanese military authorities and admission was refused.

Arthur's father, until the Japanese occupied Manila, was a civilian employee of the Quartermaster Corps of the United States Army in Manila. He was the engineer in charge of the power plant at the quartermaster shops in the port area. The war deprived him of both his job and his pension as a Spanish-American war veteran and caught him with very little cash in hand. Because he was a skilled mechanic he managed to exist with a little help from the Red Cross and the small income which he derived from such repair jobs as were brought by Filipino friends to his home where he was interned. One day he earned 50 centavos ($0.25) for soldering up a hole in a small water tank. On another day he cleaned and repaired a clock. But there had not been sufficient money to provide Arthur with proper care.

Chapter 55

The Commandant of the Santo Tomas Internment Camp Assumes Control of the Public at the Remedios Hospital

On the morning of July 25 I went to the public dispensary at the Remedios Hospital for my weekly injection of liver extract. I furnished my own liver extract. Hitherto it had been administered without charge. Now I was required to pay a small fee of 20 centavos for the administration of each injection. When I inquired the reason for this fee, I learned that the administration of the dispensary had been transferred to the Commandant of the Santo Tomas Internment Camp, although the hospital itself had been turned over to the Catholic Women's League. Apparently this arrangement was an aftermath of the clash between the Red Cross and the Commandant over the closing of Red Cross Hospital No. 4. This dispensary provided medical service for a considerable number of internees who had been released to their homes.

I suspected that the control of the dispensary had been transferred to the Commandant in order to provide him with a check upon the health of internees who had been released to their homes for medical reasons. Furthermore, our income was so small that even a fee of only 20 centavos must be avoided if possible. So I determined to see another dispensary for the administration of my liver extract.

The Red Cross dispensary, I learned, had been transferred to a hospital for Filipino war prisoners which the Red Cross had established in a portion of the buildings formerly occupied by the Meisic Police Station in another part of the city. Dr. Orobia, who had given me a good letter recommending my internment in my own home, was the chief physician at this Red Cross dispensary. It was located about two and a half miles farther from my home than the Remedios dispensary, but by walking a mile after I got off the street car I could reach it at no greater expense for transportation than I now paid to reach the Remedios dispensary. The liver extract would be administered without charge and the route to the dispensary would take me past one of the largest public markets, where I might possibly purchase food a little more cheaply than elsewhere. So, beginning in August, I went to the Red Cross dispensary for the administration of my liver extract.

The walk to the Red Cross dispensary took me through what had formerly been the most prosperous wholesale and retail business section of the city. Almost all of the larger business establishments were padlocked. Their stocks of goods had been confiscated by the Japanese Army. From most of the buildings the Japanese Army had already removed the stocks of goods. But here and there I observed goods being loaded into a military truck drawn up before the entrance of what had once been a large and prosperous business establishment. I saw the Japanese Army removing goods from Heacock and Company, large wholesale and retail jewelers; from the Botica Boie, large wholesale and retail druggists; from the Philippine Education Company; wholesale and retail dealers in books and stationery and from the Heilbronn Paper Company, wholesale and retail dealers in paper and office equipment. The establishments of the large dealers in hardware and machinery had already been completely stripped. Peering through their dusty windows I saw only rubbish upon the floors.

Chapter 56.

Concerning Substitutes for Wheat Flour

During the prosperous years of American dominion the Philippines had become an important market for wheat flour, which was imported from the United States and from Australia. Rice continued to be the principal food consumed by the vast majority of Filipinos but many people, particularly of the more prosperous middle and upper classes, had become accustomed to eating wheat bread. A salt-raised bread, called *pan de sal* (salt bread), was extensively eaten for breakfast. A large quantity of wheat flour was also consumed in the manufacture of crackers, cookies, cakes, and a wide variety of sweetened pastries. Relatively few Filipino homes were equipped with facilities for baking. Hence most of the foods made from wheat flour were distributed by commercial bakeries which were established in all except the smallest towns.

Many of the poorer people, *and* some well-to-do people, continued to eat for breakfast a variety of steamed bread, called *puto*, which was made from rice flour and was leavened with yeast or with baking powder. A somewhat similar bread made of rice flour and baked in a pan over a charcoal fire was called *bibinka*. The latter was far less popular than *puto* because it had a tendency to be tough and did not rise as well as *puto*.

The making of both *puto* and *bibinka* was a household industry. Almost all of the rice flour used for this purpose was ground in small hand-operated stone mills imported from China. Vendors, each carrying a pair of baskets loaded with *puto*, appeared on the streets of the poorer sections of Manila just before dawn each morning. The vendor trotted along the street, shouting "*puto, puto*," at frequent intervals. Those who wished to purchase *puto* opened their doors and called to the vendor.

After the Japanese occupation of Manila, the growing scarcity, and rapid rise in price, of wheat flour and its products greatly increased the consumption of both *puto* and *bibinka*. Vendors of these foods therefore also started to appear in the well-to-do areas of the city. Vendors of *puto* and *bibinka* were on the streets, not only early in the morning, but throughout the entire day.

The increase in the output of *puto* and *bibinka* was accomplished principally by an increase in the number of homes engaged in the manufacture of these foods, rather than by an increase in the output of those homes where the manufacture of *bibinka* and *puto* had been established prior to the increase in the demand for them. Hundreds of people who had been thrown out of work by the war discovered that they could make a living for themselves and their families by the manufacture in their homes of foodstuffs which they and members of their families peddled upon the streets and in the office buildings. A middle-aged Filipino of my acquaintance was a well-paid government employee with a family of several children. When he lost his position, as a result of enforced head-count reduction in government at the start of the start of the Japanese occupation, he turned to the manufacture of *puto* as a means of supporting himself and his family. His wife and daughters made the *puto* in their home. He and his son sold it in the government offices to those government employees who had been retained in the service. His son informed me that they made on the average a profit of two pesos per day. This was much less than his father had formerly earned, but it was enough to provide the family with food and cover the unavoidable expenses of light, water and fuel. Many families in Manila were compelled to exist on much smaller incomes.

By May wheat flour had become so scarce that it was almost unobtainable. Many of the bakeries had been compelled by lack of flour to cease operating. Officials of the government then began to consider the possibility of finding substitutes for wheat flour. The Bureau of Plant Industry announced that it possessed experimental equipment for the manufacture of flour from the dried roots of the cassava plant. For a fee of 12 centavos per kilogram the Bureau of Plant Industry would grind into flour any dried cassava root which was brought to its experimental plant. There was not much cassava root available, however. This plant had not been extensively grown in the Philippines prior to the war and the crop required about 18 months to grow.

There was a limited quantity of cracked wheat on hand in Manila. Some of this was converted into whole wheat flour by re-grinding it in corn mills. By July, however, the supply of cracked wheat was exhausted.

People then began to experiment with the use of corn flour and rice flour ground in motor-driven corn mills. Several corn mills were set up in Manila for the custom grinding of corn, rice and cassava. The Bureau of Plant Industry also made its equipment available for the grinding of these crops.

The price of 12 centavos per kilogram which was charged for grinding alone made the resulting flour rather costly. Furthermore, the fact that most of the rice brought into Manila was that sold on a ration basis by the Japanese military administration limited the quantity of rice which could be converted into flour. Most of the rice which was converted was smuggled into Manila and sold at 50 centavos, or more, per ganta (5.3 pounds). This was nearly twice the 34 centavos per ganta at which the government sold the rationed rice. Even corn was not available in any considerable quantity. During July and August corn meal sold in the public markets at 50 to 60 centavos per kilogram ($0.116 to $0.136 per pound). Corn flour, which was ground finer than corn meal, sold at 70 centavos to one peso per kilogram ($0.16 to $0.228 per pound). This was four to five and a half times the price at which wheat flour had been sold immediately before the war. Thus even the substitutes for wheat flour were costly. Wheat flour was selling at 2 pesos per kilogram ($0.44 per pound), so the price of the substitutes was less than half the current price of wheat flour.

When I was released to my home at the end of June I found that my mother-in-law had purchased a small hand-operated stone mill to grind rice into flour for making *puto*. For this purpose the rice was soaked in water to soften it prior to grinding and some water was added during the process. The resulting product was a paste rather than a flour. As this paste would sour quickly it had to be converted into *puto* on the day that it was ground.

Since I had little else to do, I determined to experiment with the dry grinding and use of both corn flour and rice flour. Grinding the flour in the small stone mill was slow and tedious work. About two hours was required to grind a kilogram (2.2 pounds) of rice flour. To produce a kilogram of corn flour required about four hours of patient grinding. Nevertheless, I kept at it day after day, using the flour which I ground for experiments in the making of bread and cakes.

Our only oven was a gas oven. The Japanese who took over the operation of the Manila Gas Company had cut off the gas because we could not afford to pay the balance prior to the outbreak of the war. But we had a small earthen charcoal stove about 10 inches in diameter by 7 inches in height. Such charcoal stoves were extensively used by Filipino families for cooking purposes. Each stove heated only one pan or kettle. Hence a family usually had a battery of two or three charcoal stoves in its kitchen. Considerable smoke is generated when the charcoal is lighted but once the charcoal is burning freely there is practically no smoke. It occurred to me that if I allowed the charcoal to burn until the smoke ceased to form I could then place the charcoal stove in the gas oven and do my baking on a grate placed above the charcoal. I tried it and it worked.

The oven had a tendency to burn the bread on the bottom. This was remedied by placing a sheet iron baffle between the charcoal stove and the grate to distribute the heat more uniformly throughout the oven. The baffle prevented the bread from burning on the bottom but necessitated the addition of a second charcoal stove to provide sufficient heat. With two charcoal stoves, however, it was possible to bake two pans of bread at the same time.

I experimented first in the making of muffins, for which I used equal parts of corn flour and rice flour. The result was satisfactory, but I found that the muffins were improved by using a mixture of 60 percent rice flour and 40 percent corn flour. I also discovered that in order to rise properly the dough must be quite soft, about the consistency of waffle batter. Both corn flour and rice flour offer greater resistance to the leavening agent than wheat flour. The recipe which I eventually worked out was as follows: 1 ½ cups of rice flour, 1 cup corn flour, 5 level teaspoons baking powder, 1 egg, 1 heaped tablespoon shortening, 2 heaped tablespoons sugar, ½ teaspoon salt, 1 ½ cups water. The baking powder which I used was a local product diluted with corn starch. A larger quantity was required than would have been the case had a more potent baking powder been available.

I next experimented with cake, using the same mixture of rice flour and corn flour which I had used for muffins. Further experiment demonstrated, however, that better cakes resulted from the use of rice flour alone, without any corn flour. The following two recipes produced very delicious cakes:

Plain rice cake:—
2 ½ cups rice flour, 1 duck egg (or two small hen's eggs), ½ cup shortening, 1 cup sugar, 5 level teaspoons baking powder, ½ teaspoon salt, 1 ½ cups water.

Chocolate rice cake:—
2 ½ cups rice flour, 1 duck egg (or two small hen's eggs), ½ cup shortening, 1 cup sugar, 5 level teaspoons baking powder, ½ teaspoon salt, 1½ cups water, 2 heaped tablespoons cocoa.

I used duck eggs, rather than hen eggs, because duck eggs were cheaper. One duck egg was about equal to two native Philippine hen eggs. Both duck eggs and hen eggs at that time were selling for 8 centavos ($0.04) each. The "white" of a duck egg cannot be used successfully for making the frosting of a cake, however, as it is not possible to beat the white of a duck egg into a sufficiently light froth.

A peculiarity of cakes made from rice flour is that they dry out with extreme rapidity. They must be eaten on the day that they are baked.

We had a small quantity of cassava root growing in our garden. I sliced and sun dried some of it and ground it into flour in the stone mill. I found that a mixture of equal parts of rice flour and cassava flour produced a cake which did not dry out as rapidly as cakes made from rice flour alone.

Further experiment demonstrated that rice flour was a satisfactory thickening for gravies and that both rice flour alone and a mixture of rice flour and corn flour could be used to produce satisfactory hot cakes.

Eventually I found the grinding of corn into flour in the stone mill to be too tedious and we started to take our corn to the Bureau of Plant Industry to be ground. I continued, however, to grind rice flour in the stone mill, partly to save the cost of milling and partly because of the muscular exercise which it gave me.

When I had learned how to make satisfactory cakes from rice flour I began to bake them for sale. Cupcakes, for which the materials and fuel cost 35 centavos per dozen, I sold for 70 centavos per dozen. Since I was not permitted to go in search of customers, my wife undertook to sell the cakes which I baked. She was busy all day in the office of the Red Cross, however, and so did not have much time to look for customers. People were also so poor that customers were not easy to find. Furthermore, the quantity of rice cakes which I could bake was limited by the quantity of rice which we were able to obtain at reasonable prices. Rice was rationed and the rice which I used for making cakes we had to obtain on the black market. Often the price of such rice was prohibitive. Nevertheless, I baked and sold several dozen cupcakes each week.

Chapter 57.

My Pass Is Renewed for Two Months

My pass, granting temporary release to my home, expired on August 10. I was required to report to the Commandant of the Santo Tomas Internment Camp on that day. It was the typhoon season. Heavy rains had been falling for several days when the morning of August 10 dawned cloudy and threatening more rain.

I dressed in shorts and donned my raincoat for the trip to Santo Tomas. In order to save 5 centavos in transportation, I walked the two kilometers from my home to the street car line. When I got off the street car I had to walk another kilometer before reaching the camp. I walked though water which in some places was knee deep. The water was ankle-deep over the sidewalk in front of the camp, although most of the camp itself was above the water level.

It was raining heavily when I reached the gate. Water which leaked through my old broad-brimmed western hat was running down my neck and dripping from my chin. Situated at the gate was a small concrete building which was used as sleeping quarters by the Japanese guards and they had now taken shelter from the rain in this building. I was met at the gate by a young American internee also dressed in shorts and a raincoat. He conducted me to a guard who, after inspecting my pass, gave me a slip of paper on which was noted the exact time of my arrival at the gate. I was instructed to present this slip of paper at the Commandant's office within five minutes.

Beside the door of the Commandant's office was posted a notice which stated that internee residents of the camp were prohibited from conversing with non-resident internees who had come to register at the Commandant's office.

It was about 9.30 am when I arrived. Already waiting at the entrance to the Commandant's office were about a dozen non-resident internees whose passes, like my own, expired on August 10. Others continued to arrive until the total number awaiting action on their passes was about twenty. An internee attendant took possession of our passes as soon as we arrived. Seated at a small table in the hallway outside the Commandant's office was another internee, who registered each arrival. I was required to give my name, age, citizenship, former occupation and home address; the name, age and citizenship of my wife; and the name, age, citizenship of my son. All of this information I had furnished on at least two other occasions when I had reported to the camp. Just why this information was again required I did not learn.

The regulation prohibiting resident internees from conversing with non-resident internees was not being enforced very rigidly. Resident internees were constantly greeting their friends among the non-resident internees waiting in front of the Commandant's office.

Johnny O'Toole, who, prior to the war, was employed as a salesman at a Manila machinery firm, came to greet me.

"Have you been interned in Baguio?" asked Johnny, who had formerly been the Baguio representative of his firm.

"No," I replied "We came from Baguio to Manila on December 22, before the Japanese occupied Baguio. I was interned at a hospital here in Manila for more than five months. On June 30, I was released to my home in Pasay but my pass expires today and I do not know whether or not it will be renewed."

"Recently," said Johnny, "the Commandant's office has been quite liberal in renewing passes. I understand that some passes have been renewed for periods as long as six months."

"How are you making out?" I asked. "Not so bad, now," replied Johnny. "We are better fed since the Commandant took away the running of the mess from the Red Cross. Eddie Tait, one of our internees, is in charge of the mess now. The Japanese Army has appropriated from its funds seventy centavos ($0.35) per internee per day for the operation of the camp. That amounts to about 70,000 pesos per month. We now have some fat in our diet and we have beefsteak, hamburger steak and beef stew twice a week."

"What discount," continued Johnny, "is now being charged for cashing checks drawn on the National City Bank and the other banks which have not been permitted to reopen by the Japanese military authorities?"

"I have never tried to cash a check," I replied. "So I cannot speak from personal experience. I have been informed, however, that there are several persons in Manila who will cash checks drawn on the National City Bank at a discount of 35 percent."

"I anticipated in December," said Johnny, "that it was going to be hard to get money out of the bank after the Japanese entered Manila. I had on hand in my room at the hotel 500 pesos in Philippine currency and 250 dollars in United States currency. Like a fool, however, instead of staying in my room, I went out on the street, where I was picked up by the Japanese. I have never been permitted to return to my room to get my money. And now it probably isn't there anymore."

I had baked and brought to camp a loaf of muffin bread made of a mixture of corn flour and rice flour. I sent Johnny in search of my old friend,

Sam Deebel, to whom I intended to give the bread.

"Do you have any news?" asked Sam, when he arrived.

"I haven't any news," I replied. "For some time I have not been getting any news. Since August 1 we have been prohibited from listening to foreign radio stations. We put our radio in storage and we don't even take the Japanese-controlled *Daily Tribune*."

"According to the reports we get here," said Sam, "all of us will be out of the internment camp by the end of September."

"I don't believe it," I replied.

As usual, the camp was full of wild rumors of the impending arrival of American aid for the Philippines.

Professor Clark came and greeted me. He had been interned with us for two weeks at the Ateneo Hospital while he was having a set of false teeth made by the dentist. Prior to the war he was professor of mining engineering at the University of the Philippines. Although seventy years of age he was still a very active man. He told me that he had delivered a number of lectures before groups of internees at the camp. His last lecture had been delivered before a study group on July 29. The general subject being studied was *The Shape of Things to Come*. Professor Clark's lecture was entitled *World Trade with Latin America and the Reconstructed Monroe Doctrine*. He gave me a set of mimeographed sheets containing extracts from his lecture. On these sheets was a map of North and South America and statistics concerning the nature and volume of the foreign trade of each South American country.

When I had waited for an hour or more, an attendant came out of the Commandant's office and conducted me and half a dozen other internees to a room adjoining the Commandant's office. At the head of a long table sat an elderly Japanese in the uniform of an officer of the Japanese Army. I had been informed that he was the Assistant Commandant of the internment camp. He very pleasantly requested us to be seated at the table.

The attendant who had conducted us to the room then explained that before our passes were renewed each of us would be required to sign a pledge, which he requested me to read to the assembled internees. This pledge was as follows:

I, undersigned, solemnly swear not to violate the following rules:

1. I will not commit any hostile act against the Imperial Japanese Army and will not say or do anything anti-Japanese.
2. I will not do anything that will benefit Japan's enemies.
3. I will not do anything which tends to disturb public sentiment, normal economic conditions or public order.

4. I will not employ or persuade others to do any acts stated in the preceding paragraphs.
5. I will not leave the area designed by the Commandant of the internment camp, unless in case of absolute necessity.

Signature   _____
Name in block letters _____
Address   _____
Date   _____

To the Commander in Chief,
Imperial Japanese Army,
Manila, Philippines.

The attendant, who was himself an internee, explained that the fifth paragraph of the pledge meant that we would not change our places of residence without first notifying the Office of the Commandant of the Santo Tomas Internment Camp. We were permitted, however, to leave our homes to obtain medical attention, to purchase food and clothing, to go to church, and to take exercise in the vicinity of our house.

After each of us had signed this pledge we were told to wait outside of the Commandant's office until our name was called.

About ten minutes later another attendant, a young British internee, came out of the Commandant's office and returned my pass to me, saying as he did so that it had been extended until October 10, that is, for two months. He then gave me a time slip and instructed me to leave the camp within five minutes, presenting my time slip to the guard at the gate as I left.

As usual, Jack Howard was among a group of resident internees loitering near the entrance of the Commandant's office to learn how the internees whose passes were up for renewal had fared.

"Did you get fixed up?" he inquired.

"My pass extended for two months," I replied.

It was raining slightly when I reached the entrance to the building. I stopped to put on my raincoat. The entrance was crowded with internees. At my elbow were two men who, to my surprise, were conversing in Spanish and who appeared to be Spaniards. I wondered if they, too, were interned. Nearby was a very tall young American girl. She was smiling shyly when I glanced at her, but her smile faded when she saw that I did not recognize her. I wondered who she was. Her face was vaguely familiar but I could not identify her. By that time I had struggled into my raincoat. Mindful of my time limit, I hurried toward the gate, which was perhaps 150 yards from the entrance to the building.

At the gate I took off my hat and bowed to the Japanese guard. He inspected my time slip and waved me out of the gate. Apparently he did not speak English. I did not understand Japanese.

When I reached the end of the street car line on my way home I stopped at a drugstore and tried to telephone my wife at the office of the Philippine Red Cross. When no one answered my call I discovered by glancing at a clock on the wall nearby that it was the noon hour. The rain had ceased. I walked the remaining mile and a half to my home.

"Daddy, daddy," cried my son when I reached home, "was your pass renewed?"

"Yes," I replied, "I have come home to stay for two more months."

Chapter 58.

I Sell Some Postage Stamps

As I plodded through the water of the flooded street after leaving the Santo Tomas Internment Camp on the morning of August 10, I decided to visit again the store of my friend, Rogelio de Jesus, the stamp dealer. Several months earlier his store had been included in a list published in the *Daily Tribune* of bookstores which had obtained permits from the Japanese military administration to reopen and resume business. Prior to the issue of its permit to reopen, the stock of each bookstore was censored and only books approved by the Japanese military censors could be offered for sale. It now occurred to me that Rogelio's bookstore might have been closed when I visited it at about 8 am on July 19 simply because Rogelio had not yet arrived to open it. I reached Rogelio's store a few minutes before noon and found it open for business, although, Rogelio, himself, had gone out for lunch.

On the following Saturday, August 15, I called again at the store and was fortunate enough to find Rogelio at his desk. I had brought a stock book containing some of my Philippine stamps, most of them duplicates of stamps in my collection. These postage stamps I proposed to leave with Rogelio on consignment, he to fix the selling price and retain 25 percent of the proceeds as his commission on any stamps sold. Rogelio accepted my proposal.

I pointed out one rare stamp, a 10-pesos stamp bearing the circular "O. B" (official business) overprint of the Philippine National Bank.

"This stamp," I said, "cost me twenty pesos. I probably paid too much for it. You may sell it for less if you wish."

"The price is O.K." replied Rogelio. "I can sell that stamp to J---. I have his collection in my safe and he has commissioned me to assemble a fine collection of Philippine stamps."

"Who is J—?" I asked.

"He is a German," replied Rogelio, but did not give any further information concerning him.

Rogelio then gave me a packet of twenty cigarettes. They were bootleg cigarettes made from Virginia tobacco which had been imported prior to the war and had been looted from the warehouse of the importer during the disorder immediately preceding the Japanese occupation. The Japanese-controlled Philippine government had increased the tax on cigarettes and tax-paid cigarettes made by Manila factories from a mixture of Virginia and native Philippine tobaccos were now selling at one peso per packet of 20. Cigarettes imported from the United States prior to the war were selling at 1.50 pesos per packet of twenty and the hand-rolled bootleg cigarettes which Rogelio gave me were being sold at 80 centavos per packet. Presumably the internal revenue tax on them had not been paid. They found a ready market among people who could afford them and who preferred cigarettes made of Virginia to the cheaper cigarettes made of native Philippine tobacco. Rogelio said that he did not smoke many of these bootleg cigarettes because they were too expensive. Cigarettes made of Philippine tobacco could be obtained for a quarter of the price of the bootleg Virginia cigarettes. Even the price of cigarettes made of Philippine tobacco had increased greatly since the occupation. Cigarettes, which prior to the Japanese invasion sold at 10 centavos per packet, were selling in August at 30 centavos per packet.

The Japanese military administration made an indifferent attempt to control the price of cigarettes. In April or May an order was issued fixing the retail prices of cigarettes manufactured by the licensed cigarette manufacturers of Manila. The manufacturer was required to print or stamp the lawful retail price on each packet of cigarettes. These prices were ignored, however, almost from the date that the price-fixing order was issued and no real attempt to enforce the order was made by the government. Early in July cigarettes whose lawful price was 16 centavos per packet of 20 actually retailed at 18 centavos. By the middle of August the actual retail price was 24 centavos.

Retail dealers complained that they were unable to obtain sufficient quantities of the established brands of cigarettes. This was one reason for the flourishing trade in bootleg cigarettes.

When I had thanked him for the cigarettes, Rogelio said, "If you need money at any time I can always advance you five or ten pesos. We have been helping out several of the National City Bank people in that way."

"I could use five pesos today," I replied.

Rogelio took five pesos from his pocket book and gave it to me.

"How have you been making out in your business since the occupation?" I asked.

"Business had been poor," replied Rogelio, "But, so far, I have been able to make enough money so that there is a little left after I have paid my living expenses. My wife and I are living more economically now than we did before the war. You may, perhaps, remember that I bought a lot in Santa Mesa Heights and we are now living in a very small house which I built there. We are rather crowded, but we don't pay rent anymore. Our second baby was born in January. Nevertheless my wife has discharged her cook and is doing the cooking herself. We have a vegetable garden where we raise most of the vegetables which we eat. I have a bicycle on which I ride to and from the store in order to save the money I formerly spent on bus fare."

While I chatted with Rogelio my nine-year old son had been examining the toys in the showcase. He now implored me to buy him a Chinese checker board with its accompanying marbles. I refused because I felt that I should not buy toys for my son when we had barely enough money for our food. Rogelio then insisted on presenting the Chinese checker board to my son as a gift.

Thereafter I visited Rogelio's store each Saturday when I came downtown to purchase food in the nearby Quiapo market.

On August 22 I found Rogelio occupied with a customer who was buying stamps. Rogelio left his customer long enough to give me another packet of bootleg Virginia cigarettes and to tell me that he would have some money for me the following Saturday.

On August 29 I brought Rogelio a cake which I had made of rice flour. Rogelio gave me two pesos on account and a list of Philippine stamps which he did not have in stock and which he wished to purchase for Mr. J—, his German client.

"I can supply some, but not all, of these stamps," I said, after I had examined the list.

"Can you bring the stamps on Monday?" asked Rogelio.

"I am still an internee," I replied. "Selling stamps is not one of the purposes for which I am permitted to leave my home. I come down town once a week, on Saturday, to obtain an injection of liver extract at the Red Cross Hospital and to purchase food at the Quiapo public market near your store. I stop at your store en route. So far I have never been asked when on the street to show my pass but I wish always to have a legitimate reason for being on the street. I have been informed that several internees were sent back to Santo Tomas because they were seen too frequently in the downtown section of the city. But if you will come to my home and take *merienda* (afternoon tea) with us tomorrow, Sunday, I will have the stamps ready for you. Bring your wife with you. We will probably have several other guests. I am going to bake a chocolate rice cake for the occasion."

"My wife will not be able to come, but I would like to bring my cousin with me if I may," said Rogelio.

"Your cousin will be welcome," I replied.

"If the weather is good we will probably ride to your house on our bicycles," said Rogelio.

As I arose to depart, Rogelio gave me another packet of Virginia cigarettes.

My son, who again accompanied me, had selected a toy which I now agreed to buy for him. But Rogelio insisted on presenting it to him as a gift. I decided that, thereafter, I would leave my son at home when I went to visit Rogelio.

I had just placed the chocolate rice cake in the oven to bake when Rogelio and his cousin arrived at our home on that Sunday afternoon, August 30. I immediately got out my stamps. We became so occupied with them that I forgot about the cake. It was scorched slightly on the bottom when I took it out of the oven.

Rogelio selected fourteen stamps for which the net price to be paid to me was 73.70 pesos. Rogelio was to fix his own selling price and was to pay me when he had collected the money from his German customer.

Having disposed of our business, I took Rogelio and his cousin out to see our garden. Rogelio had brought us some ripe corn from his garden. My wife reciprocated by giving Rogelio some eggplant and the first fruit from a young papaya tree.

Rogelio's cousin, I learned, was a student in the University of the Philippines until the Japanese invasion forced the University to close. His father, a well-paid government employee, had lost his position when the personnel of the government was drastically reduced after the invasion. He and his cousin now supported the family by selling *puto,* thereby earning about two pesos a day.

Our only other guest that Sunday afternoon was Mrs. Josephine Hemmingway. She was a Filipino woman whose American husband had been the principal of the Leyte High School when I taught there in 1915. He was made a superintendent of schools the following year. In 1919 he died of smallpox, leaving to his wife and three children life insurance policies which yielded about 40,000 pesos. With this money in hand Mrs. Hemmingway moved to Manila, purchased a home and invested the balance of her funds in bonds. She never remarried.

Each of her three children, two girls and a boy, had married an American. The eldest, Josephine, was now interned with her husband and their young daughter at the Santo Tomas Internment Camp. Henry, the son, had graduated with honors from the United States Naval Academy at Annapolis. He remained in the United States, where he married an American girl and where he was now employed as a design engineer by a ship-building firm. Ester, the youngest, following her graduation from high school, had gone to Washington, D.C. as the social secretary of the Philippine Resident Commissioner. When the Commissioner returned to the Philippines, Ester remained in Washington where she obtained a position as a stenographer in the United States Federal Service. She had also married an American and she and her husband were now both employed by the Federal Government in Washington.

Mrs. Hemmingway's income had been cut off by the war but she had rented her home for 40 pesos a month and managed to live on the rent.

I had not seen Mrs. Hemmingway for five years prior to her visit that Sunday afternoon and I welcomed the opportunity to renew an old acquaintance. I recalled that it was 27 years since I was a teacher in the Leyte High School where Mr. Hemmingway was my principal. I and another young American teacher often played auction bridge with Mr. and Mrs. Hemmingway. Josephine, their eldest child was then only four years old. Henry was a baby and Ester had not yet been born. Now Josephine was 31 years old and had a daughter of her own.

Mrs. Hemmingway informed me that Henry was a reserve officer in the United States Navy. However, he had not been called to active duty when she last heard from him just before the outbreak of the war. It was possible, because he was employed by a ship-building firm, that he would not be called up.

For our *merienda* we had coffee made from imported pre-war coffee, *puto*, coconut fritters made with eggs and rice flour, chocolate rice cake and ice-cream flavored with *duhat* juice. The *duhat* is a small, purple fruit which has a stone like a plum. For the coffee we opened a can of evaporated milk. We still had on hand a few cans which we had purchased before the war. Evaporated milk was now so costly, however, that we used it only when we had guests, and not always even then.

Rogelio and his cousin started home at about five o'clock. Their homes were on the opposite side of the city and they wished to get home before dark. Mrs. Hemmingway remained to talk over old times. At about 8 pm my wife, my son and myself walked with her to the bus station about a kilometer from our home. The bus would take her to within three blocks of her home.

Before he left Rogelio requested me to bake three rice cakes for him. He said that he wished to give the cakes to three American stamp collectors who were interned in Santo Tomas. I delivered the cakes to him on the following Saturday, September 5. He sought to pay me for the cakes but I refused to accept any payment because of the many favors he had extended to me.

Rogelio's German client proved to be a little slow in taking delivery and in making payment for the stamps which he purchased, but Rogelio paid me on account, 5 pesos on September 5, 10 pesos on September 12, and 20 pesos on September 19.

In the meantime, I delivered to Rogelio on consignment twelve additional Philippine stamps for which the net price to be paid me was 272.55 pesos. And, on September 14, I delivered to him nine more for which the net price to be paid me was 21.35 pesos. These last stamps were delivered at Rogelio's request, subject to the approval of his German client.

I now had a steady, if small, weekly income from the sale of my stamps. This, added to my wife's small salary as a bookkeeper for the Red Cross, gave us just about enough money to meet our living expenses if we continued to live very economically.

Rogelio continued, after I was re-interned at Santo Tomas, to make regular weekly payments to my wife until not only had he paid to her all that he owed me but he had also loaned her money as well. Altogether, he paid us about 600 pesos for stamps which I delivered to him.

Chapter 59.

Concerning Various Occurrences During August and September

On August 12 Socorro took 48 small tins (½ case) of Carnation Evaporated Milk from our storeroom and sold them to a Chinese-owned grocery store at 43 centavos per tin—21.04 pesos for the half case. Prior to the Japanese invasion these small tins of evaporated milk had retailed at 10 centavos each tin. The retail price was now 50 centavos per tin.

About the middle of August Socorro, when she returned from her office, reported that she had witnessed the brutal beating of a Filipino. She had gone for lunch, as she often did, to a restaurant near the Paco public market. There was a police outpost near the market. On the street in front of the outpost she saw four Japanese soldiers beating and kicking a Filipino into a state of unconsciousness before leaving him lying in the street. The Filipino policeman at the police outpost witnessed the beating but did not intervene.

On Sunday afternoon, August 16, Guy White and his daughter took *merienda* with us. Guy was an American Old Timer who lived near us and who had been interned at the Ateneo Hospital until it closed. He was then released to his home. He told us that when his pass expired on August 5 it was renewed for a period of six months.

On August 13 Mr. Fishbach, our neighbor, called to exchange magazines. He said that when his pass expired on August 13 it was renewed for four months.

On August 27 we had fried chicken for dinner. It was the first time my family had eaten chicken since late in December. I, however, had on two or three occasions received a small piece of chicken during my internment at the hospital.

On September 1 a young Filipino came to our house to sell firewood. He asked if we had heard about the guerrilla attacks upon Calumpit in Bulacan Province and upon Antipolo in Rizal Province. We replied that we had not heard about these attacks. He then said that he, himself, had joined the guerrillas and had participated in both the attacks. In Antipolo, he said, two of the Filipino municipal officials were killed by the guerrillas. He said that he had two pistols and offered to give me one of them. I declined the offer. I warned him that he should be very careful to whom he spoke of his guerrilla activities. He departed rather hastily. On the following day he delivered the firewood which we had agreed to purchase from him. When the wood arrived we discovered that the sticks were very small and that the price which we had agreed to pay was very high. We accepted the wood, however, and paid him the agreed price for it.

Chapter 60

Concerning the Neighborhood Associations and the Distribution of Rice

On August 17 a census enumerator called to make a count of the persons living in our house. He said the census was being taken for the purpose of controlling the rationing of rice in the city. A similar census had been taken at the end of June and a new system of rationing rice had been put into effect on July 5.

The people of Manila were required to form neighborhood associations of 23 families each. Each neighborhood association was required to choose a leader. This leader purchased from the Japanese military administration the rationed rice for his entire group. He then distributed it to the members of his association. Each leader was permitted to purchase one sack of rice containing 23 gantas every second day, the ration being half a ganta (2.6 pounds) per family per day. The ration was now fixed at 1/5 ganta (300 grams) per person per day. It was assumed that the average family consisted of four persons and the rice was distributed on that basis. This system did not allow sufficient rice to those families which consisted of more than four persons. The method of distribution was subsequently modified to permit families of more than four to purchase 1/5 ganta (300 grams) of rice per person per day. Each neighborhood association leader had been required to submit to the Japanese military administration a list of the members of each family in his association.

In some cases the head of the family had reported non-existent persons as members of his family in order to obtain a larger allocation of rice. The rationed rice was sold by the Japanese military administration at 34 centavos per ganta, but the current black market price was 50 centavos per ganta. Hence any person who obtained more rice than he needed could sell his surplus at a substantial profit.

There were always in Manila a considerable number of transients and other persons who, for one reason or another, were not members of any neighborhood association and hence were not able to purchase rationed rice at the government price. Furthermore if a family had chickens, cats and dogs to feed the ration of 300 grams per person per day was not sufficient.

The Japanese military administration sought to prevent the entry into Manila of any rice except that sold by the government on a ration basis. Nevertheless rice was constantly being smuggled into the city and the ration restrictions were constantly being evaded by families padding out the lists with fictitious names.

It was for this reason that a new census of the residents of Manila was being taken. I was required to sign the census sheet on which were listed the members of my family. On this sheet was printed a warning that any person making a false declaration was subject to a penalty of six months imprisonment, or a fine of 200 pesos, or both, at the discretion of the court.

We were not members of any neighborhood association because my wife, as an employee of the Red Cross, was permitted to purchase the rice ration for her family each week at the office of the Red Cross. She was allotted 6 gantas per week at 33 centavos per ganta. This was slightly lower than the 34 centavos per ganta which the members of the neighborhood associations paid. The difference of one centavo per ganta represented the cost of transporting the rice from the place of purchase to the home of the leader of the neighborhood association where it would be distributed to the members of the neighborhood association.

The rice ration which Socorro purchased each week at the office of the Red Cross was not sufficient for our family, so each week we purchased each an additional 6 gantas elsewhere. The 12 gantas were more than sufficient to feed the seven members of our family and to provide food for our chickens, pig, cats and dog. The surplus we stored away against the time when rice would be much more costly and more difficult to obtain. We already had on hand a reserve supply of 100 gantas of rice and each week our reserve increased.

On August 20 Socorro, returning from her office reported that an executive order had been issued which required the people to organize themselves into neighborhood groups of ten families and to choose a leader for each group. Several days later the *Daily Tribune* announced that officials of the government would soon issue instructions concerning this. This executive order was not welcomed by the Filipino people as these leaders would be required to become spies on the members of their neighborhood groups and would be obliged to report their conduct to the Japanese military authorities.

In order to effect the organization of the people into these neighborhood groups, the *Kalisapi* was created. At the head of the organization was placed Benigno Aquino, one of the foremost Japanese collaborators in the Philippines. One of the chief purposes of this organization was to inculcate Japanese ideology. Each municipality was divided into districts and each district was organized as a district chapter of the *Kalisapi,* at the head of which was a district leader. Considerable pressure was brought to bear on all adult males in each district to induce them to join the *Kalisapi.*

Chapter 61.

*I Visit the Internees at the Ateneo University
and Obtain Authentic News of the War*

On August 29 I went to the Ateneo University to weigh myself on the scales in the Observatory where I had periodically weighed myself during my internment. On June 29 I had weighed, dressed in shorts, 158 pounds. On August 29, dressed in the same manner, I weighed 166 pounds, in two months of internment at my home I had gained 8 pounds. When I entered the Santo Tomas Internment Camp on January 21, I weighed 180 pounds. During the succeeding five months of my internment at the hospital I had lost 22 pounds.

While at the Ateneo I visited Bo, Paul, Ford and Slim, who had been interned there since the closing of Red Cross Hospital No. 4 in July. From Bo I obtained news of the progress of the war, the first reliable news I had received in more than a month. In spite of the decree of the Japanese military administration which, since August 1, had prohibited listening to foreign radio stations, the Jesuit Fathers at the Ateneo were still using their concealed short-wave radio receiver to pick up the news from San Francisco and London. This news they passed on to Bo and his roommates.

On August 10 the Japanese-controlled *Daily Tribune* reported that the American fleet had been destroyed in a naval engagement with the Japanese among the Solomon Islands. On August 15 the *Tribune* reported that a total of 35 American ships had been sunk in the Solomon's engagement. Bo now informed me that this engagement had resulted in a victory for the Allies, that landings had been effected and Allied bases had been established in three of the Solomon Islands. He said that another engagement had been going on for four days in the Solomon Islands and that to date the Allies had sunk or damaged 16 Japanese ships. On August 29 the *Tribune* reported this second Solomon Seas Battle as follows:

> "*Tokyo, August 27 (Domei)*—further details of the naval engagement off Solomons in which three American vessels were heavily damaged were given by informed sources who disclosed that Japanese reconnoitering planes patrolling the southern waters first caught sight of a large enemy fleet in battle formation streaming northward last Monday afternoon ... the Japanese fleet then encountered the enemy east of the Solomons. It was revealed that the battle planes

of both sides took off from aircraft carriers to stage terrific air battles. Heavy damage was inflicted on one battleship, one large-size new-type aircraft carrier and one medium size aircraft carrier of uncertain type, it was disclosed. Japanese losses consisted of one destroyer sunk and one medium size carrier damaged, it was said."

This was the most conservative Japanese report which I read concerning any of their naval engagements. But it certainly differed materially from the Allied claim that 16 Japanese ships had been sunk or damaged in that engagement.

Chapter 62.

Concerning Mrs. Bowers and Her Daughter, Bessie

On Sunday, September 6, Mrs. Bowers came and spent the afternoon with us. She was a Filipino woman whose husband, General Clarence Bowers, was at one time the chief of the Philippine Constabulary. When the war broke out General Bowers was in Washington, D.C., in the service of the United States Federal Government. His pension as a retired officer of the Philippine constabulary was being paid to his wife. Immediately after the Japanese occupied Manila the pension ceased. Mrs. Bower's bank account was frozen in a bank which had been closed and not permitted to reopen. Thus Mrs. Bowers found herself without income and with very little cash in hand. During the early months of 1942 she resorted to selling her furniture, piece by piece, in order to obtain money with which to buy food. But furniture was difficult to sell at that time. Money was scarce. Furniture looted from homes of persons interned at Santo Tomas was also being offered for sale. Some of the internees whose homes had not been looted had commissioned Filipino friends to sell their furniture. In order to help Mrs. Bowers my wife had purchased from her a dresser and a desk for thirty pesos. When I objected that we could not afford to buy furniture my wife replied, "Never mind. We will get more money somehow. Mrs. Bowers needs the money very badly."

On that Sunday afternoon Mrs. Bowers told us that her daughter, Bessie, had just arrived with her two children and two servants from the island of Romblon. Bessie was living on her small farm near the town of Romblon when a ship loaded with Japanese soldiers anchored in the harbor of Romblon about the end of May. Bessie said that all the people of the town, except the policemen, fled to the hills behind the town. The Japanese remained in Romblon for about one month. Then all of them departed. Bessie said that when the people returned to their homes they found that everything of value had been looted. The Japanese had loaded their plunder aboard a ship and had taken it away. Bessie was more fortunate than the rest. Soon after the Japanese occupied the town she returned to her farm and it had not been molested.

Mrs. Bowers wrote to Bessie of her desperate need for money. As there was no safe way to send money from Romblon to Manila, Bessie decided to come to Manila and live with her mother. She sold her farm, but had difficulty in securing the agreed amount in currency which would be valid in Manila. In December, when communication between Manila and the Southern Islands was cut off by the war, President Quezon authorized the printing and issue of emergency paper currency in the Southern Islands, including Romblon. Most of the currency in circulation at Romblon when Bessie sold her farm was this emergency paper currency, which had already been outlawed by the Japanese and was not valid in Manila. Bessie refused to accept this emergency currency in payment for her farm. After some delay, during which the buyer combed the town of Romblon for pre-war Philippine currency, Bessie at last secured payment in that currency.

Bessie had some emergency currency on hand. Since this would not be valid in Manila she purchased tobacco with it. The tobacco could be taken to Manila and sold at a profit. Most of her pigs and chickens she sold for emergency currency which she also invested in tobaccos to be sold in Manila. Her household goods, two pigs and forty white leghorn chickens she decided to take to Manila.

Bessie chartered a *battelle* (small schooner) to transport herself, her two children, two servants, and her goods from Romblon to the town of Lucena on the island of Luzon about 100 miles south of Manila. Because the normal means of transportation had been destroyed by the war, the owners of such transportation as was available were charging exorbitant prices from Romblon to Lucena. There was barely enough room aboard the small *battelle* for her household goods, two pigs, 40 chickens, tobacco, and the five members of her family!

The *battelle* encountered stormy weather and adverse winds. It took three days to make the trip, from. One night a Japanese coastguard cutter fired six shells at the *battelle*. Two of these shells nicked the masts of the *battelle* but did not seriously damage the masts. The *battelle* hove to, expecting to be boarded, but the Japanese warship went on without stopping. The *battelle* was flying the Japanese flag at the time it was shelled by the Japanese warship. The next day the *battelle* scraped her bottom on a sunken reef, but fortunately passed over the reef without damage. A larger *battelle* which followed was wrecked on the same reef. It broke in two and sank. All hands were believed to have been lost.

When they arrived at Lucena Bessie hired a truck, paying 150 pesos for transportation from Lucena to Manila. At Lucena she was informed that her pigs and chickens would probably be confiscated by Japanese sentries stationed along the road if she attempted to transport the pigs and chickens to Manila. So she sold the pigs and chickens in Lucena.

At Manila Bessie found her mother living in a room above a stable. The stable bred a host of flies and the rank odor of rotting manure tainted the air. Garbage collection in Manila and its suburbs had ceased when the Japanese arrived and had not been resumed. The disposal of garbage and manure was left to private initiative, with often very unfortunate results.

Bessie went house-hunting. She leased for one year, for the small rental of 20 pesos per month, the home of an Englishman who was interned in Santo Tomas. The home had been well cared for since the Englishman's internment by his gardener. The house was large, well furnished and was located on a lot of almost one acre. There were a number of fruit-bearing trees and ample space for a garden. The gardener had planted a crop of sweet potatoes which would mature in about two months. Bessie, her family and her mother had moved into this house on the day before Mrs. Bowers visited us.

Bessie had already sold part of her tobacco at a good price. Mrs. Bowers was very happy. Now she would no longer have to worry about how to obtain money for next week's food and to pay next month's rent.

Mrs. Bowers said that Bessie had not come to visit us that day because she was very busy putting her house in order. Perhaps she would visit us the following Sunday.

"I heard yesterday," said Mrs. Bowers, "that President Roosevelt in a radio address stated that if he did not clear the Pacific of Japanese within 100 days he would resign the presidency."

The following evening, Socorro, when she returned from her work, said she had heard the same rumor. I doubted, however, that President Roosevelt had made any such statement.

Chapter 63.

Concerning the Smuggling of Rice into Manila

On Thursday, September 10, William Summerville, a young American-Filipino *mestizo* boy about 16 years old, called at our house. I had not seen him since he was about eight years old. His father, who died about a year before the outbreak of the war, was a Spanish-American War veteran. William was the oldest of three children. With their mother they lived in a house, which they owned, near the Nichols Field Airport.

William told me that during the bombing of Nichols Field by the Japanese in December they left their home and took refuge in Marikina, about ten miles away. When they returned early in January they found that their home was untouched, although bombs had fallen all around it. Their home was the only one in that vicinity which was not damaged by the bombs.

William said that his mother's pension had been cut off by the war and that their only income was what he made by smuggling rice into Manila. There was a steady demand for rice in addition to that which could be purchased from the Japanese military administration by means of ration cards. But the Japanese military authorities sought to prevent any rice, other than that which they themselves distributed, from entering the Manila market. Sentries stationed on all roads leading into Manila inspected the baggage of all persons entering the city and confiscated any rice which they found. Nevertheless, rice was constantly being smuggled into Manila

William had a bicycle. Every morning he went to Bulacan Province, about 15 miles north of Manila. There he purchased a sack of rice (121 pounds) which he tied onto his bicycle and brought to Manila. There was only one sentry to be passed. About half a mile before he reached this sentry he removed the rice from his bicycle and gave it to two men, each of whom carried one-half sack. Two sacks were used for this purpose. The two men carried the rice through the fields to a point on the road about a half mile beyond the sentry post. William, having passed the sentry with no cargo on his bicycle, then met the men who had smuggled his rice past the sentry, loaded the rice on his bicycle again and brought it into Manila.

Rice was sold by the Japanese military administration to ration card holders at 34 centavos per ganta. This was equivalent to only 7.82 pesos per sack of 23 gantas. But because the demand exceeded the quantity distributed by the Japanese military administration, William was able to sell the rice which he smuggled into Manila at 13 pesos per sack. The two men who smuggled his rice past the sentry were well-paid for their work and he paid in Bulacan a little more than the Manila ration price for the rice. Thus he made a profit of about 3 pesos on each sack of rice which he smuggled into Manila. He admitted that his business was "a little dangerous", but said that it was his only means of supporting his mother, sister and brother.

William travelled on his bicycle a total distance of more than 40 miles each day. His largest expenditure was for bicycle tires. Tires, which before the war cost only 2.50 pesos each, now cost 24 pesos each and were difficult to obtain even at that price. The pair of tires which he was using had cost him 12 pesos each.

Chapter 64.

Concerning Wartime Transportation in Manila

One of the last acts of the United States Army of the Far East (USAFE) before evacuating Manila was to set fire to the stocks of gasoline, kerosene and crude petroleum stored in the vicinity of the city. In a similar manner USAFE destroyed the stocks of gasoline, kerosene and crude petroleum in other parts of the islands. As a result, when the Japanese occupied Manila early in January only a very limited supply of these motor fuels was available.

The USAFE had requisitioned a large number of buses, trucks and taxis for the movement of troops and supplies during their rapid retreat to the Bataan Peninsula. The Japanese during their advance through Luzon and after their occupation of Manila had confiscated a large number of motor vehicles.

Partly because of the shortage of motor vehicles and fuels, and partly because of the unsettled conditions attending the Japanese occupation of Manila, there was, during the first week of January, an almost complete cessation of civilian motor transportation but during the second week of January a few privately owned trucks and automobiles reappeared on the streets.

On January 14, the commander-in-chief of the Japanese Army issued a proclamation forbidding the operation after January 17 of all motor vehicles using gasoline, except those whose use was licensed by the Japanese Army. The same proclamation prohibited "buying, selling, giving, receiving, or transporting, gasoline and lubricating oil" on and after January 15, and provided that "those who possess or have in custody on behalf of the possessor, gasoline and lubricating oil must report by January 20 the quantity of stock thereof as on January 15, 1942, at the municipal office of Manila." Another provision of this proclamation required the registration on or before January 31, 1942, at the municipal office of Manila all automobiles, automobile tires and spare parts, repair shops and tools. It was stated in the *Daily Tribune* of January 15 that this proclamation was issued "owing to the present shortage of gasoline and materials and to avoid inconvenience to the operation of Japanese forces."

Permits to operate motor vehicles were issued by the Japanese military authorities for "use by the government, consular representatives, news agencies, physicians and hospitals, for public transportation and for transportation of necessary articles of price necessity," and for such other purposes as were considered "necessary" by the Japanese military authorities.

The Japanese military administration also assumed control of the sale of motor fuel and lubricating oil for the use of such motor vehicles as were permitted to operate.

The shortage of gasoline soon necessitated the substitution of alcohol as a motor fuel. For this purpose the Japanese military administration organized the Manila Liquid Fuel Distribution Union, which began the sale of alcohol motor fuel through ten distributing stations in Manila on February 20. The supply of motor alcohol proved to be inadequate, however, and by August charcoal gas producers had been installed on many trucks and even on a few automobiles. Charcoal gas was not a very satisfactory motor fuel. Engines operated on charcoal gas developed so little power that the speed of motor vehicles was greatly diminished and heavily loaded buses and trucks had great difficulty in ascending the approaches to bridges.

The shortage of motor vehicles resulted in the substitution of other means of transportation. The demand for bicycles became so great that before the end of June even second hand bicycles were selling at 150 pesos each. New bicycles were practically unobtainable. The price of bicycle tires, which normally sold for 1.50 to 2.50 pesos each, rose to 24 pesos in August. Bicycles came into rather extensive use for public transportation. Three types of conveyance were developed for this purpose The side-car; the pusher; and the trailer. A side-car carrying one passenger was attached to a bicycle in the same manner as a side car was attached to a motorcycle. A pusher replaced the front wheel of the bicycles with a two-wheeled conveyance for two passengers. This conveyance was riveted to the bicycle frame in such a manner that the vehicle was steered by means of a bar attached to the back of the passenger seat. The trailer was a two-wheeled conveyance for one or two passengers towed by the bicycle. These bicycle-propelled conveyances were operated chiefly on certain streets in the residential districts occupied by the well-do-to residents of the city.

Horse-drawn vehicles of various types became the principal means of public transportation. The most generally used form was the *tartanilla*, a two-wheeled cart drawn by a single horse. It consisted of a rectangular, box-like body provided with a top and curtains which were rolled up in good weather. The seats, three in number, consisted simply of boards about ten inches wide laid across the frame of the box-like body. Two of these seats were removable so that the vehicle could be used for transporting goods as well as passengers. Three passengers could just about be accommodated on each of the two removable seats. Two additional passengers could sit beside the driver on the fixed front seat. Thus the *tartanilla* could, and often did, transport nine persons, including the driver. It was pulled by a native Philippine pony, usually weighing not more than 500 pounds. The wheels of the *tartanilla* were equipped with solid rubber tires, but the springs were stiff and the seats were without either backs or cushions. Hence the *tartanilla* is by no means a comfortable vehicle in which to ride, but It was an inexpensive means of transportation. One might ride a mile for five centavos ($0.025).

The increased demand for horse-drawn vehicles created a flourishing business for carriage-makers, harness-makers and blacksmiths. Many persons whose income from other sources had been cut off by the paralyzation of business resulting from the war turned to the operation of public horse-drawn vehicles as a means of earning a living. A Spaniard, who himself acted as the driver of his *tartanilla*, told a friend of mine that his gross receipts from fares averaged about five pesos per day. A Filipino retired major of the Philippine constabulary, whose pension had been cut off by the war, operated three *tartanillas*. The horses were stabled on the lower floor of his house and the *tartanillas*, when not in use, were parked in his small back yard.

Rubber for the solid tires used on the *tartanillas* soon became exceedingly scarce. The tire consisted of a strip of solid rubber which was forced into a slot in the steel tire of the wheel. Even before the war it was not an uncommon practice to make solid rubber tires for *tartanilla* wheels by cutting strips of the required width (about 1¼ inches) from discarded automobile and truck tires. Several such strips were used to make one tire for a *tartanilla* wheel, which was about five feet in diameter. In July rubber *tartanilla* tires made in this manner from discarded motor vehicle tires sold for as much as 25 pesos each – 50 pesos for the pair of tires required by each *tartanilla*.

Due to the scarcity of facilities for transportation during January 1942, very high fares were collected by the operators of horse-drawn vehicles. A trip across the city, of perhaps five miles by horse-drawn vehicle, cost as much as two pesos. By normal means of transportation, that is to say, by bus or streetcar the same trip had formerly cost only eight centavos. A trip of perhaps two miles from the residential suburbs to the business center of the city cost as much as 80 centavos in January. In normal times this trip by bus or street car cost only eight centavos.

Before the end of February licenses had been issued for the operation of a limited number of small motor-driven *auto-calesas* and the number of horse-drawn vehicles on the streets had greatly increased. As a result the cost of transportation within the city of Manila dropped to about double its pre-war cost. As additional facilities for transportation became available there was a further reduction of fares. Before the end of June the trip from the residential suburbs to the business center of the city could be made for ten centavos. The pre-war cost of this trip was eight centavos. Trips of one mile or less by *tartanilla* could be made for five centavos, provided the trip was along an established route where there was a considerable volume of traffic.

The scarcity of materials for the construction of horse-drawn vehicles, combined with the large number of automobiles meant that many were equipped with wheels removed from other automobiles. It is probable that in many cases the wheels used were stolen. After I was released to my home at the end of June, I noted a considerable number of automobiles in various parts of the city which apparently had been parked at street curbs by owners who, for one reason or another, perhaps because of being interned, had abandoned them. These cars had been stripped of wheels, engines, and all other salvageable parts until little but the body and chassis remained. Although this automobile wreckage scattered about the streets of the city was unsightly and constituted an obstruction to traffic, it still remained on the streets as late as December 1942.

Manila's two race tracks were prohibited from operating during the first nine months after the Japanese occupation. This fact coupled with the increased demand for horse-drawn vehicles for public transportation resulted in the use of a number of native Philippine race horses in this service. Many owners of such horses could not afford to feed them unless they were put to some work which would pay for the cost of feed. Here and there imported American horses might also be seen pulling various types of public conveyance. Prior to the war imported American horses were seldom used except as riding horses and most of those so used were the property of the United States Amy and its officers. Most of the Army horses were now in the hands of the Japanese Army. It was not an uncommon sight to see Japanese Army officers riding imported American horses on the streets of Manila.

Japanese officers, soldiers and sailors when in uniform were, by order of the Japanese military administration, accorded free transportation on the electric street cars and motor buses. Whether or not this privilege of free transportation extended to horse-drawn vehicles I did not learn. One afternoon in June, during our internment in Red Cross Hospital No. 4, several of my fellow internees seated on the veranda of the hospital observed a Japanese soldier hail an empty *tartanilla*. The driver of the *tartanilla* apparently refused to accede to the soldier's demand for transportation. The soldier pulled the driver from his seat and slapped him. Then the soldier climbed into the *tartanilla* and compelled the driver at the point of a bayonet to proceed. The soldier seated behind the driver had the point of his bayonet pressed against the back of the driver. Japanese soldiers not on duty, when moving about Manila, seldom carried rifles, but they usually carried a bayonet in a scabbard attached to the belt of their uniforms. A Filipino policeman witnessed this incident but did not intervene.

One of the results of the increased cost, as well as the scarcity of transportation facilities for freight, was the appearance upon the streets of a large number of carts of many different sizes and types either pulled or pushed by manpower. These vehicles were used for transporting firewood, rice, vegetables and other merchandise, household goods and baggage; and for vending foodstuffs on the streets. Some of these carts were crude, home-made contrivances. They were used extensively for transporting rice from the government-operated distribution centers to the homes of the leaders of the neighborhood groups, where each sack of rice was opened and distributed to the members of that group. The leader of one of these neighborhood groups was a woman who lived across the street from our house. Her son made a four-wheeled cart in which to transport the rice from the distribution center about a mile from their home. We purchased firewood which was delivered to our home in such a cart. Most of these carts were pulled or pushed by just one man but a few were so large that two, or even more men were required to move them when loaded.

While the cost of transportation along the principal streets of the city was by July very little higher than it was before the war, it was necessary to pay considerably more for transportation to many parts of the city. The electric street cars operated only on a few streets. The limited number of buses and *auto-calesas* in operation, and the horse drawn vehicles providing cheap transportation, operated only along fixed routes where there was a large volume of traffic.

For those who could afford to pay more than the minimum price for transportation the time-honored, two-wheeled, horse-drawn *calesas* were available and would take the passenger directly to his destination. However, because of the greatly reduced incomes of the people these vehicles were far less frequently patronized than they had been prior to the occupation.

Because of their reduced incomes people did much more walking than they had done in pre-war days. In order to reach the Red Cross Hospital form my home I would walk about half a mile to a *tartanilla* route. There I would pay five centavos for a *tartanilla* which would take me about a mile to the end of the street-car line. For another five centavos the street-car would take me to the Plaza Santa Cruz in the business center of the city and from there I would walk the last mile to the hospital. Frequently I walked the entire mile and a half from my home to the end of the street-car line in order to save the five centavo *tartanilla* fare. In such cases, including the walk from the Plaza Santa Cruz to the hospital, I walked more than half of the five miles from my home to the hospital and occasionally I would walk the entire five miles.

The very limited number of private automobiles which were permitted to operate resulted in a large increase in the number of private horse-drawn vehicles. These were of several types, the most common of which was called a *dokar*. The *dokar* was either a two-wheeled or a four-wheeled vehicle drawn by a single horse. It was provided with a top and curtains to protect the occupants from sun and rain. There was a driver's seat in front and a long-cushioned seat running length-wise along each side of the box-like body. The occupants sat facing each other with their knees interlocking. Access to the cushioned seats was to be had by means of a step through a door at the rear of the vehicle. The more luxurious of these vehicles were equipped with pneumatic tires salvaged from automobiles.

Chapter 65.

I Make Cup Cakes of Rice Flour, Cornstarch and Coconut Milk for my Friends Interned at the Ateneo

Because of the scarcity and high cost of cow's milk, both fresh and canned, a milk substitute made from fresh coconut was extensively used in Manila during the Japanese occupation of the city. Early in 1942 the Bureau of Science began manufacturing a coconut milk which was fortified by the addition of vitamins and was sold at 40 centavos ($0.20) per quart. This coconut milk was also distributed gratis by the Philippine Red Cross to destitute mothers for the feeding of infants. Coconut milk looks and tastes much like cow's milk. The fat and sugar content is about equal to that of cow's milk but the protein content is lower and vitamins are lacking. For making cornbread, hotcakes and cakes coconut milk is a satisfactory substitute for cow's milk.

Most of the coconut milk consumed in Manila was produced by the users in their homes. Our own procedure was typical of that followed by other families. The flesh of a fresh coconut was grated and minced with about a pint of hot water, or with the slightly sweet water drained from the coconut. The fluid was then pressed out of the mixture. Each coconut yielded about a pint of milk.

Early in 1942 my wife purchased 500 coconuts, which she stored on the lower floor of her mother's home. Stored in a dry place coconuts will remain in good condition for more than six months. We used two or three coconuts each day. The cost delivered to our home was about two centavos ($0.01) each. Before the end of 1942, however, the price rose to ten centavos each. And during the latter part of 1944 the price reached ten pesos each!

On Saturday morning, October 3, I went to the Red Cross Hospital for my weekly injection of liver extract. En route, I stopped at Rogelio's bookstore. Rogelio had stepped out of the store on some errand, but he had very thoughtfully instructed his clerk to pay me ten pesos on account for stamps which I had delivered to Rogelio to be sold. After visiting the hospital I went to the Azcarraga public market, where I purchased a half-dozen duck eggs at the rate of 1.30 pesos per dozen. A week earlier the price had been only 1.05 pesos per dozen, but a typhoon during the week ad temporarily halted the transportation of foodstuffs to Manila. The quick rise in price occurred as the stocks in the markets decreased.

The storm, although not a really severe typhoon, brought heavy rainfall and the highest winds of the season. The wind blew down one of our banana plants on which there was an almost mature bunch of bananas. Several of our young papaya trees would also have blown down if I had not tied them to the fence with ropes. One of our *patola* vines was so whipped by the wind that it had died. We regretted losing it because it had just begun to bear fruit. The *patola* was a large cucumber, 15 to 16 inches long. The vine, grown on a trellis often reaches a length of 75 feet.

During the afternoon of October 3, I experimented with a new recipe for chocolate cup cakes, using rice flour, cornstarch and coconut milk, as follows: 1 cup rice flour; 2 heaped tablespoons cornstarch; ¼ teaspoon salt; 2 teaspoon baking powder; ¾ cup brown sugar; ¼ cup shortening; 1 duck egg; 2 tablespoons orange syrup; 1 cup coconut milk; 2 heaped tablespoons cocoa. This recipe makes twelve cup cakes.

The resulting cup cakes were so delicious that on Sunday morning, October 4, I took a dozen of them to my friends at the Ateneo University, among whom were Bo, Ford, Paul and Slim. I found that since my previous visit to the Ateneo Professor Clark had been transferred form Santo Tomas to the Ateneo. He had been interned with us at the Ateneo Hospital for two weeks during April.

One of the American Jesuit Fathers interned at the Ateneo was visiting my friends when I arrived. He gave us the first authentic news from overseas sources which I had heard in more than a month. Allied planes in the Solomon Islands and in New Guinea were shooting down nine Japanese planes for every Allied plane lost. One Japanese formation consisting of 25 bombers accompanied by 25 fighter planes was hugely depleted when the Allied fighters shot down 23 of the 25 bombers. In Egypt the fighting had reached a stalemate. The Chinese were doing well. In Russia the situation was critical at Stalingrad, with heavy fighting going on in the outskirts of the city.

It was rumored that a Japanese transport carrying a large corps of engineers had been sunk by a submarine off the coast of Japan and that practically the entire corps of engineers had been lost. This information was said to have come from a Japanese recently arrived from Japan. The Jesuit Father did not vouch for its truth.

Bo informed me that on or about October 1 the sending of food and packages to the internees at Santo Tomas had been suspended for ten days. This order was issued by the Commandant when he discovered that messages concealed in packages of food and laundry were being sent to the internees by their friends outside the camp. An examination of the packages of food and laundry sent to Santo Tomas during a single day had disclosed more than one hundred messages. Among them were reports of news broadcast by foreign radio stations, listening to which had been prohibited on August 1. The sending and receipt of uncensored messages by internees had been prohibited very soon after the camp was organized in January. However, the internees and their friends outside the camp immediately began to evade this regulation by concealing messages in packages sent into the camp and in bundles of laundry and empty containers sent out of the camp. It had taken the Japanese more than eight months to discover this evasion of their regulations.

The principal reason for the sending of bootleg messages into the camp was the intense craving of a large majority of the internees for authentic news of the war. Unfortunately most of the alleged news which reached the camp by means of these bootleg messages consisted of false rumors of the arrival, or impending arrival, of American aid for the Philippines. The credibility with which these rumors were received, both outside and inside the internment camp, was pathetic. The people so desperately desired help to come to the Philippines that they were ready to believe almost any rumor that help had arrived or was soon to arrive.

Chapter 66.

Concerning Chaotic Conditions on the Island of Negros

On Sunday afternoon, October 4, my wife's cousin, Mr. Custodio, and his family took a late *merieda* with us. We had *puto*, chocolate rice cake, and sherbet flavored with *duhat* juice. The color and flavor of *duhat* juice is quite similar to that of grape-juice.

Mr. Custodio was the son of a planter whose plantation and home were located on the island of Negros. At the outbreak of the war Mr. Custodio and his family were residing in Manila, where he was a law student at one of Manila's universities. They purchased tickets to return to their home in Negros but the steamer failed to sail and they were stranded in Manila when the Japanese occupied the city.

Mr. Custodio sought unsuccessfully to obtain a refund of the money he had paid for his tickets. The manager of the shipping concern informed him that the ship had been lost and that his firm had no money with which to refund the price of unused tickets.

Since the Japanese occupation of Manila Mr. Custodio had earned a meager living for his family by acting as a commission agent. He brought together buyers and sellers of all sorts of merchandise. On some days he earned a commission of two or three pesos, on other days nothing at all. He had been able to earn an average of about sixty pesos per month.

He had been planning to return to his home in Negros but was dissuaded by friends from that island who had recently arrived in Manila. They informed him that conditions were so chaotic on the island that it was unsafe for him to return. They themselves had fled from Negros. Guerrillas were active throughout the island and were little better than bandits. They pillaged the haciendas of the landowners to obtain food. If the landowners offered any resistance they were killed. Sometimes they were killed even when they did not resist. A Spanish planter had been killed for refusing to give the guerrillas a contribution of 25 pesos. A Filipino landowner had been killed because he was appointed municipal president of the town of La Castillana by the Japanese-controlled government. Persons known to be, or merely suspected of being, in sympathy with the Japanese were being killed.

The guerrillas were unwilling to permit anyone to remain neutral. If anyone refused to actively support the guerrillas he was subject to attack by them. If one actively supported the guerrillas and this became known to the Japanese he was liable to be shot by the Japanese.

There were several bitterly antagonistic political parties in the province. Members of these parties took advantage of the chaotic conditions to attack, rob, and sometimes kill their political enemies.

Automobile and bus traffic had been suspended between Bacolod, the provincial capital, and the southern towns of Negros because bandits lay in wait along the roads and robbed travellers.

Many farm laborers and tenant farmers who had joined the guerrillas pillaged and burned the homes of the landowners. Mr. Custodio was informed that his own family home had been burned.

Many of the landowners had fled from the province and had come to Manila. Several Spanish planters who expressed sympathy for the Axis cause prior to the outbreak of the Japanese-American war had been compelled to flee for their lives.

It was reported that in one town the guerrillas had ambushed and killed several Japanese soldiers and that the Japanese in reprisal had shot down, with machine guns, about 150 citizens in the market place.

Because of these alarming reports Mr. Custodio had decided not to return to his home in Negros until conditions on that island became more settled.

On the following afternoon, October 5, Mrs. Bowers again called on us. She also informed us that conditions on the island of Negros were very chaotic. The Japanese, she was informed, occupied only two towns—Bacolod (the provincial capital) and one other town. Elsewhere in the province the Japanese made no attempt to maintain order. The local law-enforcement agencies were unable to cope with the situation. Guerrillas, most of whom were bandits, were rampant throughout the province. It was unsafe for the landowners to live on their haciendas. For this reason, she was informed, the wealthy and politically prominent Montilla family had fled to Manila.

Chapter 67.

Concerning a Superstitious Belief

A large majority of the people of the Philippines are very superstitious. Superstitions persist even among the well-educated people of the islands. As might be expected, however, superstitious beliefs are more general among educated women than among educated men.

My wife, although educated in the public schools under American teachers, still retains the superstitions which were transmitted to her by her mother. She visits fortune tellers. She systematically picks up and preserves every horseshoe which she spies on the street. I have often been required to stop our car for my wife to get out and pick up a horseshoe. She believes that bad luck will attend the occupants of a house whose principal entrance does not "face the morning sun."

The number of steps leading to the entrance of a house, my wife believes, has a vital bearing upon the degree of prosperity and good luck which its occupants may expect to enjoy. The steps are counted by beginning at the bottom and saying: "*Mata* (kill, vex or molest)" for the first step; "*plata* (silver)" for the second step; and "*oro* (gold)" for the third step. The formula is then repeated: "*mata*" for the fourth step, "*plata*" for the fifth step, "*oro*" for the sixth step, "*mata*" for the seventh step, and so on, until the top is reached. The word applicable in this manner to the top step determines the degree of good fortune to be enjoyed by the occupants of the house. Where the number of steps is one, four, seven, ten or thirteen the top step is "*mata*", signifying that bad luck will attend the occupants of the house. But if the number of steps is two, five, eight, eleven or fourteen the top step is "*plata*", indicating that the occupants of the house will enjoy a moderate degree of prosperity. While if the number of steps is three, six, nine, twelve or fifteen the top step is "*oro*", indicating that the occupants of the house will enjoy great good fortune and will become wealthy.

Mrs. Bowers and her daughter, Bessie, had leased a house into which they moved about the middle of September. When Mrs. Bowers called on us on October 5 we went with her to see her new home. After greetings had been exchanged with Bessie, her two children, and a young woman named Olga, we seated ourselves on the veranda. My wife then broached the subject of the number of steps leading to the front entrance of the house.

"How many steps are there?" asked my wife.

"There are four," replied Bessie, doubtfully.

"Four is '*mata*' and that is bad luck," said my wife. "You better add another step. You can lay a board on the ground in front of the bottom step. The board will be another step, making five in all. Then the top step will be '*plata*', which means good luck."

"Does your house face the morning sun?" continued my wife.

"The front entrance does not, but the side entrance does," replied Mrs. Bowers. "And there are five steps leading to the side entrance. Do you think it would be better for us to use the side entrance instead of the front entrance?"

"Let's go and see," said my wife.

"What do you think, Mr. Warren?" inquired Olga, as the women arose to go and inspect the steps. I grinned, but made no reply.

"Do you believe there is anything in it?" inquired Mrs. Bowers, when she returned to the veranda where I had continued to sit while the women inspected the stairways. But before I could reply she said defiantly, "There *is* something in it!"

"Wars are not won in that way," I replied.

The rest of the women returned and the conversation turned to other subjects. I did not learn what the women had decided to do, if anything, about the steps.

Chapter 68.

I Do Some Errands and Hear Some News

I was to report to the Commandant of the Santo Tomas Internment Camp again on October 10. I was not certain that my pass would be renewed. So on the morning of October 8 I went down town to attend to several errands. My wife had locked my hat in the closet and had taken the key when she went to the Red Cross office that morning. As a result I was compelled to go without a hat. As usual, I was clad in shorts and the shirt from a suit of slacks. I walked most of the way and, as it was a bright sunny morning, I got sunburned a little.

Since I placed about 600 pesos worth of stamps with Rogelio to be sold on consignment and had so far received only 60 pesos on account I called at his store to check up on the sales which he had made and to request him to return the more costly stamps he had been unable to sell. I found several customers in Rogelio's store and told him that I would return after I had visited the hospital for my weekly injection of liver extract.

In front of the hospital I was greeted by a middle-aged Filipino who called me by name. I did not remember his name but he told me that he was still employed on the Calamba Sugar Estate. Hence I inferred that he must have been working there when I was employed there from 1918 to 1921. He had doubtless aged a lot in the more than twenty years which had elapsed since then. And so it was perhaps not surprising that I did not recognize him. But I was ashamed to ask his name and thus acknowledge that I did not remember him. He informed me that the Japanese had purchased the Calamba Sugar Estate for twenty percent of its value from Mr. Madrigal, President of the Filipino-owned corporation which owned it. He said that he owned a small store in front of the Pasay public market, not far from where I lived.

"But," he continued, "there is very little business because, as you know, the Japanese control everything now. When do you think the Americans will come back?"

"I don't know." I replied.

"Some say they will be here in December and others say April," he continued. "The Allies have control of the air and are mopping up in New Guinea now. Where do you think they will go next? To Java?"

"I don't know," I replied. "but I believe that the war will last at least a year longer. There are many Japanese-occupied islands between the Philippines and New Guinea."

"If the Japanese remain in control of the Philippines for two years more they will suck all our blood," he replied gloomily.

After visiting the hospital, I returned to Rogelio's store, but found him still engaged with several customers. I told him that I would call again on Saturday on my way to the internment camp. He gave me two-and-a-half pounds of butter and twenty small cottage cheeses. He said that his wife had removed the butter from her icebox because it had become rancid. They had not purchased any ice for their icebox for several months because ice was too expensive. He believed that I might be able to use the butter for making cakes. The butter was wrapped up in one-half pound packages. I found all except one-half pound to be still good enough for table use. The cottage cheeses, made from carabao's milk, had been molded into little cakes about 1½ inches in diameter by ½ inch thick. The cheese was very salty but otherwise delicious. I was glad to get it, because the lime it contained would be good for my small son, whose diet had been deficient in lime for some time. Rogelio also gave me some seed from the American eggplant he had raised in his garden.

After leaving Rogelio, I went to the Ateneo to return a book which Professor Clark had loaned me. It was the autobiography of a Texas boy, a Mr. Taylor who had become a mining engineer and was still one of America's leading manufacturers of mining machinery. He had made several million dollars during the First World War by the manufacture of artillery shells for the government. I found the story of his rise from poverty to wealth very inspiring.

At the Ateneo I chatted for a few minutes with Ford and Bo. As usual, Bo wanted to know if I had any news. I said I had been informed that conditions were very bad on the island of Negros, where guerrilla bandits were said to be rampant. I had been told that it was unsafe for the landowners to remain on their haciendas and that many of them had fled to Manila.

"And that is not all," replied Bo. "All of the Spaniards have been run out of the province of Negros by the guerrillas. I have talked with several of them who are now in Manila. Prior to the occupation of the island by the Japanese, the provincial government of Negros issued paper currency for use during the emergency, in accordance with authority granted by President Quezon. The Japanese, after occupying Bacolod, the provincial capital, prohibited the circulation of the provincial currency and introduced paper currency issued by the Japanese military administration of Manila. The Spaniards with whom I talked said that if they were caught by the guerrillas with any Japanese currency in their possession it was confiscated by the guerrillas. And if they were caught by the Japanese with any provincial currency in their possession it was confiscated by the Japanese. The Spaniards said they were caught between the devil and the deep sea. If they gave aid to the guerrillas they got into trouble with the Japanese. If they refused to help the guerrillas the latter pillaged their haciendas."

I walked all the way home from the Ateneo, a distance of two and a half miles. Altogether, I walked that day about seven miles.

Late that afternoon my young son and I planted corn and squash seeds in a plot which I had prepared in our front yard. While we were planting Hank called to me from the street. Although he lived on our street only about a half mile from our house, I had not seen him for two months. He stopped to chat for a few minutes.

"When does your pass expire?" I asked.

"About ten days ago it was renewed for another two months," Hank replied.

"My pass expires the day after tomorrow. I hope I may be lucky enough to get a renewal," I replied.

"The news during the past few days has been good," said Hank. "The Japanese at Buin in northern New Guinea tried to cross the Stanley Mountains to attack the Australians at Port Moressy, but the Allied forces attacked the Japanese in the mountains and drove them back. The Japanese fled in disorder, leaving their guns and equipment behind. Two Japanese cruisers were sunk during the past week in the vicinity of New Guinea and the Solomon Islands. In the Aleutians the United States Forces have occupied an island only one thousand miles from Tokyo and only 125 miles from Kiska, which is still occupied by the Japanese. A number of Japanese naval units, including a cruiser, have been sunk in the vicinity of Kiska. The Japanese barracks at Kiska have twice been machine-gunned and bombed by U.S. planes, with very heavy loss of life to the Japanese. In Egypt the Allied forces on one front drove the Germans and Italians back about four miles. In Russia the Russians have strengthened around Stalingrad and are now driving the Germans back."

"Winter must be almost upon them," I said.

"Yes," Hank replied. "Over France a few days ago the R.A.F lost eleven planes because their wings became so heavily coated with ice that they were forced down. In China the Chinese have retaken one of the important airports from the Japanese. In India an army is being equipped and trained to attack the Japanese in Burma as soon as the rainy season is over. A New York newspaper states that an Allied offensive on all fronts is expected in the very near future."

We had been chatting across the front gate while Hank stood in the street.

"Lower your voice," I warned Hank. "Two Filipinos are approaching. Most of them are loyal to America, but some of them are not."

"I must be getting on home," said Hank, after glancing at the approaching Filipinos. "I hope you are lucky and get your pass renewed."

Chapter 69.

My Pass is Renewed for Another Two Months

On the morning of October 10, I went to the Santo Tomas Internment Camp to request a renewal of my pass, which expired that day. As I approached the gate I observed a sign which read "Bow to the sentry before you enter". I removed my hat and bowed humbly to a wooden-faced sentry who did not acknowledge my salutation.

On Daitoa Avenue (formerly Taft Avenue) there was stationed, for several months, at the boundary between Manila and the suburban town of Pasay a Japanese sentry who punctiliously bowed in return to every salutation he received. Every day thousands of people bowed to him as they passed his sentry post. As a result, he was bowing almost constantly. He never smiled, but he bowed with exceptional grace and dignity.

It is seldom that an ordinary citizen is permitted to meet and deal directly with a Japanese official of high rank. There is always a subordinate official who meets the petitioner and transmits his petition to the higher official. I now discovered that at the gate of the Santo Tomas Internment Camp this practice had been extended to a Japanese official of very subordinate rank. This official was stationed just inside the gate. It was his function to inspect the passes and determine whether or not any person should enter or leave the camp. Formerly, when I entered the gate I presented my pass to this official he, with a wave of his hand, instructed me to proceed. I now found three American internees acting as intermediaries between this official and all persons who entered or left the camp.

One of these internees met me just inside the gate and asked for my pass. When I presented my pass he asked if I had come to seek a renewal. When I replied in the affirmative he pointed to a sign attached to the table of the Japanese inspector of passes, which read "Renewals and changes of address 2.30 to 3.30 p.m."

"I am sorry, I did not know." Said I.

"That regulation has only recently been put into effect. Come back this afternoon at about 2.30," the internee replied. He was Danny Adamson, who, prior to his internment, had been president in Manila of the Fraternal Order of Eagles, of which I was a member.

After leaving the internment camp, I went to Rogelio's bookstore. I found that the total amount due to me for the stamps which Rogelio had sold was slightly less than the 80 pesos which he had already paid me. He returned stamps valued at about 61 pesos and advanced me ten pesos on account of the stamps he still held on consignment.

When I returned to the internment camp at 2.25 that afternoon Danny was still on duty at the gate. He took my pass to the Japanese inspector and brought back a slip of paper on which was noted the time, 2.25 p.m.

"The Commandant's office," said Danny, "has been moved to the small concrete building at the right of the main building. You are to proceed directly to the Commandant's office and are not to talk to internees en route. Present your time slip and your pass at the entrance to the Commandant's office."

An internee sentry passed me through an inner gate in a high wood and *sawali* fence which enclosed an area about 100 feet square just inside the outer gate. This *sawali* fence had only recently been constructed. Internee carpenters were still working on it. The purpose of this fence was to prevent direct communication between the internees and those who brought food and laundry to the gate each morning. The packages were opened and inspected in the enclosed square before being passed through the inner gate for delivery to the waiting internees. This arrangement was the result of the discovery by the Japanese about two weeks earlier that numerous messages concealed in packages of food and laundry were being sent and received by internees without being passed through the office of the Japanese censor. As punishment for this infringement of the rules by a small group of internees, all internees were for ten days prohibited from receiving packages from outside the camp. During this period the *sawali* fence inside the outer gate was constructed. The prohibition against receiving packages had been lifted a few days prior to October 10. *Sawali*, of which the fence was constructed is a coarse mat woven from strips of bamboo. It is frequently used in the Philippines for the walls of inexpensive houses.

At the Commandant's office I found that the renewal of passes had become a routine procedure. At the "general office" I was received by an internee, who took my pass and time slip and instructed me to be seated. Half a dozen other internees who had preceded me were awaiting action on their passes. The internee who received us attached to each pass the corresponding internee's record card and deposited it upon the desk of a Japanese clerk. This clerk was assisted by a young Dutch internee, Mr. Ten-Grotenhuis, who had formerly been the assistant manager of the Manila branch of a Dutch bank. The waiting internees were called to the desk in the order of their arrival and at the rate of about one every two minutes. After the old date of expiration had been cancelled and a new date of expiration had been entered, a *chop* (handstamp) in red Japanese characters was affixed to authenticate the alterations to each pass. The pass was then handed to the waiting internee, who was instructed to obtain a time slip from the receiving clerk and proceed immediately to the gate without stopping to converse with internees en route.

My pass was extended for two months—to December 10. I left the general office at 2.40 p.m., just 15 minutes after I had entered the outer gate.

At the outer gate my time slip and pass were taken to the Japanese inspector by an internee, who returned my pass after it had been inspected and instructed me to pass through the gate.

I said, "Good luck, boys" to the three internees on duty at the gate and then bowed to the Japanese sentry.

As I passed through the gate Danny shouted, "Save some beer for us!" I was unable to repress a snort of laughter. Even the wooden-faced Japanese sentry grinned. The internees of the camp were forbidden to receive or drink alcoholic beverages of any sort. I was informed that a note discovered in an out-going package of laundry about two weeks earlier had instructed the Filipino servant of one of the internees to purchase a bottle of whiskey and secret it in the laundry when it was returned to the camp. The Commandant was particularly incensed at this note because there had been a number of cases of drunkenness in the camp.

After leaving the camp I purchased a half pound package of native Philippine smoking tobacco. I had begun smoking again during my convalescence from the operation which I underwent in May at the Ateneo Hospital. For my son I purchased two bars of peanut candy.

At the bus station I met Tommy, who had been interned with us at the Ateneo Hospital. He was released from the Ateneo to his home in April, was ordered back to the internment camp in June and was again released to his home in August. His pass, which had expired that day, had been renewed for one month.

"I am given a pass for only one month at a time," said Tommy. Then, seeing my package of smoking tobacco, he inquired, "Are you smoking a pipe?"

"No," I replied. "I am rolling my own cigarettes."

"I can't afford to roll my own, with genuine cigarette papers selling at 2.50 pesos ($1.25) per packet," said Tommy.

"I do not use genuine cigarette paper," I replied. "I buy cigarette papers made of onion skin at 45 centavos per package of 400 papers. Onion skin does not make a very satisfactory cigarette paper, but it serves the purpose when one cannot afford a better cigarette paper. One-half pound of smoking tobacco makes about 250 cigarettes. Including the paper, 30 cigarettes cost me about 10 centavos, which is much less than the 25 to 60 centavos which a packet of 30 Philippine cigarettes now costs."

Chapter 70.

Concerning Japanese Attempts to Suppress the Guerrillas by the Use of Filipino Constabulary Soldiers

When I reached home I found that two of my wife's cousins had come to call on us. One of them was Mr. Custodio, who had visited us on several previous occasions. The other cousin was a young man who had been a first lieutenant in the Philippine army at Bataan. After the surrender of Bataan in April the lieutenant became a war prisoner in Camp O'Donnell. In July he was released from Camp O'Donnell and was placed in a hospital in Manila because he was suffering from both malaria and dysentery. He had now recovered sufficiently to be discharged from the hospital, although he was still being treated for malaria.

The conditional pass on which the lieutenant had been released required him to report once each week to the Japanese military police. He feared that as soon as his health was fully restored he might be ordered to join the re-organized Philippine Constabulary and be required to fight against some of his former comrades-in-arms who were still carrying on guerrilla warfare. The re-organized constabulary consisted of Filipino officers and soldiers under Japanese commanders.

The Japanese-controlled *Daily Tribune* of October 8 reported:

> Isabela being rid of guerrilla band. — guerrilla forces operating in the province of Isabela have been dealt a severe blow by Constabulary soldiers cooperating with the Japanese forces engaged in mopping up operations in that province. ... the operations are continuing to rid Isabela of remaining guerrilla units. ... the operations began on September 22 with the aid of about 200 civilians from the municipality of Santiago and others. ... It was reported that Major Quisling of the USAFE had been shot by local forces, which are now chasing the band of another guerrilla commander, Colonel T. Manar, east of the town of Munuri. The Constabulary forces are led by officers recently trained in Manila. They are cooperating with the Japanese forces in that area.

At that time the Japanese Army was conducting, in Manila, a school for training both commissioned and non-commissioned Filipino officers for the Constabulary. The course of training, which extended over a period of about six weeks, was devoted chiefly to inculcating Japanese military ideology. The Japanese military authorities stated that the purpose of the course was to achieve the "spiritual rehabilitation of the trainees." The Japanese controlled press created the impression that enrolment for the course was voluntary.

The lieutenant informed us, however, that Filipino war prisoners who had been released on conditional passes were being forced to join the Constabulary. If they refused to join their passes were revoked and they were also subjected to other punishments.

Chapter 71.

Concerning the Danger of Being Overheard When Discussing the War

In its issue on the morning of October 10, the *Daily Tribune* reported that of 34 persons recently tried in the Japanese military courts for violations of Japanese military law, 14 had been sentenced to be shot and the remaining 20 had been sentenced to long prison terms. Among the violations of Japanese military law for which heavy punishment had been meted out were listening to and disseminating "false propaganda broadcast from the United States" and "spreading anti-Japanese propaganda among the people." The same issue carried a *Notice to the People,* issued by Mr. Jorge Vargas, chairman of the executive commission of the puppet government, in which he urged the people of the Philippines as follows: "Avoid speaking or talking about the war, and do not be led into spreading any rumor or news which has anything to do with the war efforts of the combatants in the war."

Late in July, the Japanese military administration had prohibited listening to foreign radio stations after August 1, and had ordered all radio receivers to be delivered to the Japanese military administration for alteration so that short-wave radio broadcasts from overseas could not be received.

One result of this restriction was an enormous increase in the dissemination of rumors of Allied successes and of Allied aid reaching the Philippines. Many of these rumors were, to well-informed and thoughtful people, obviously false. But they were received with credulity by a large majority of the people.

As the Japanese tightened their hold upon the Philippines the number of Filipinos who became secret agents of the Japanese increased. It was not safe to discuss the war in places where one could be overheard by persons who might not be loyal to the Allied cause.

We were not certain of the loyalty of some of our neighbors. Across the street from our house lived the family of a Filipino physician who had accepted a position as a health officer with the Japanese-sponsored government.

Our house was located very near the street and on one side the adjoining house was separated from ours by a distance of less than ten feet. Because of the hot climate, our windows were always open and we frequently entertained our visitors on the veranda facing the street. If we were not careful to speak in a low tone of voice our conversation might be overheard by our neighbors and by persons passing in the street. This danger was never absent from our minds when we had visitors, particularly since our visitors almost invariably chose to discuss prohibited war news. On more than one occasion we warned our visitors to lower their voices.

Because of the announcement which had appeared in the *Tribune* that morning, I was particularly nervous when my wife's cousins, Mr. Custodio and the lieutenant, called at our house on the afternoon of October 10. Mr. Custodio invariably raised his voice in vehemence when he discussed the war. And the war was always his chief topic of conversation.

That afternoon, when Mr. Custodio began to discuss the war in a tone which could be heard by our neighbors, I showed him my copy of the pledge which I had signed on August 1 and in which I promised to refrain from anti-Japanese acts.

After he had read the pledge I said, "We will not discuss the war. Your cousin, the lieutenant, signed a similar pledge when he was released and we are liable to be overheard by persons of whose loyalty we are not certain." The lieutenant concurred in my suggestion.

But it was difficult to repress Mr. Custodio. In spite of my effort to direct the conversation into other channels he insisted upon telling me that it was rumored a man in Manila had a copy of *Life* magazine of August 2, 1942, which he had obtained by sending a messenger for that special purpose to Aparri in Northern Luzon.

"And Sunkist oranges, recently received from the United States, have been eaten in Manila," continued Mr. Custodio.

"I give up," said I. "If you want to talk about the war, go ahead. The Japanese probably won't do anything worse than shoot us if they find out about our conversation!"

Chapter 72.

I Meet Captain Winship

On the morning of October 14, Captain Winship hailed me as he came by our house. I was in the garden pruning my papaya trees. The captain said he was on his way to Santo Tomas to request a renewal of his pass, which expired that day.

"Wait until this afternoon," said I. "The new regulations require applicants for renewal of their passes to report between 2.30 and 3.30 p.m. If you go this morning you will be told to return this afternoon."

"I am glad you told me," said the Captain.

"Come in and visit a while," said I.

"Let me first return some magazines to your neighbor, Mr. Fishback," said the Captain. "I will be right back."

When the Captain returned I said, "I understand that you are living on this street."

"Yes," said the Captain. "We moved out here in May. After the surrender of Bataan in April the Japanese began to move into the San Miguel district, where we were living at that time. Soon there were Japanese occupying all the houses around us. Frequently drunken Japanese soldiers would pound on our doors and demand admission. One night some things were stolen from a house across the street, which was occupied by Japanese. The next day Japanese military police searched our house for the stolen goods, but, of course, did not find them. For several days thereafter pedestrians who passed the house where the robbery had occurred were beaten up by the Japanese. I wanted to move to some part of the city where we would not be constantly annoyed by the Japanese, but we could not afford to pay rent."

"One morning Gloria (his wife) went to market. While she was gone her brothers came with bull carts and began to load our household goods into the carts. They said Gloria had told them to come. When Gloria got back from the market she told me that we were moving out to a little house, which Gloria owned, in Pasay. Gloria built the house several years ago for her mother, so that she would not have to live with us. But since the war began Gloria's mother has been living with one of her sons because she was afraid to live alone in the little house at Pasay. The house is small, but it does not leak, and no one disturbs us."

"How are you feeling?" I asked.

"I am much better than I was a few months ago," the Captain replied.

"I am still fighting the Sprue. A few months ago my weight got down to 125 pounds. Now I weigh about 145 pounds. I am still weak, however. My normal weight is about 175 pounds."

"I had some difficulty in convincing the Japanese doctor at Santo Tomas that I was really ill. During June and July I had to report at Santo Tomas for medical examination about every two weeks and once I was ordered back to Santo Tomas for internment. But when I arrived with my baggage a friend in the camp told me to hide my baggage and request a reconsideration of my case. I did so and was given a ten day extension of my pass. Finally the Japanese doctor decided that I was really suffering from sprue so on August 14 I was given a two-month extension of my pass."

"I think you will be given another extension of your pass this afternoon," I said. "For those whose internment in their homes was recommended by the Japanese doctor the renewal of passes has become a routine matter. I secured a two-month extension of my pass last Saturday. There were six or seven others awaiting renewal of their passes when I arrived at the Commandant's office. No questions were asked of the applicants and the renewals were issued at the rate of about one every two minutes. I received the renewal of my pass just 15 minutes after I entered the gate of the camp."

"I am going home to tell Gloria," said the Captain happily.

Chapter 73.

Several Red Cross Hospitals are Closed

On the morning of October 17 Silvestre called while I was working in my garden. He brought us some *lanzones* and requested my wife, Socorro, to recommend him for a position in the secret service of the puppet government of Manila. Socorro advised him to seek some other employment. He had been employed as a property clerk in the Red Cross Hospital at Hagonoy in Bulacan Province. The hospital was closed on October 15 because the Red Cross did not have sufficient funds to keep it open. Silvestre said there were about 200 patients in the hospital when it was closed. Because of the lack of funds the diet of both the patients and staff had been insufficient for several weeks beforehand.

"For some meals," said Silvestre, "only one kind of food, rice, was served. I have heard that the Red Cross Hospital in Bataan is also to be closed."

"Yes, it is," agreed my wife, who was a bookkeeper in the central office of the Red Cross.

My wife had already informed me that the funds of the Red Cross were running low. The daily income from donations was not sufficient to maintain all the work which the Red Cross was doing. In June the Red Cross had about 130,000 pesos in the bank. By the October 1 its bank balance had shrunk to 17,000 pesos.

Before he left, Silvestre told us that recently he heard over the radio that President Roosevelt had announced that the United States now had 4,000,000 fully equipped soldiers under arms and that he warned the people of France to get away from the vicinity of military objectives.

"I guess the big offensive is coming soon," said Silvestre.

Chapter 74.

Concerning the Manner in Which the Japanese permeated the City of Manila

I soon discovered, after my release from the hospital at the end of June, how completely the Japanese had permeated the city. There were, of course, certain areas in which the Japanese were much more numerous than elsewhere and it seemed that at least one house on almost every street was occupied by Japanese. Also Japanese military couriers, with their dispatch bags, could be seen either boarding or disembarking from street cars and buses in all parts of the city.

On my weekly trips from home to hospital I sought, in so far as possible, to avoid contact with the Japanese. I detested the sight of them. They only served to remind me of the disaster which had overtaken us. It seemed to me that the sun shone more brightly, that the breeze blew more freshly, that the grass was greener, that the flowers were more attractive, when there were no Japanese in sight. And so on my journeys across the city I sought the streets where I would be least likely to encounter Japanese.

There were three parallel routes leading from my home in Pasay to the point where I boarded the street car about a mile and a half from my home. These were Taft Avenue (renamed Daitoa Avenue by the Japanese), Calle Dominga (Dominga Street), and an unnamed footpath which traversed an abandoned railroad. I avoided Taft Avenue because on that street it was necessary to pass and bow to a Japanese sentry and because a constant stream of Japanese military traffic traversed the street. Because there was no Japanese sentry and practically no military traffic at Calle Dominga most of the *tartanillas* which transported passengers from the southern outskirts of Pasay to the end of the street- car line used that street. However, at the end of July I discovered that a Japanese family occupied one house and the German consul and his staff occupied three additional houses on Calle Dominga.

Therefore I then took the footpath along the abandoned railroad. This footpath was located at the extreme eastern edge of Pasay. For a distance of two or three miles only a single row of houses separated the eastern side of the footpath from the adjacent rice fields. Each Saturday for about two months I followed this footpath without once meeting a Japanese. Baguio sunflowers growing wild on the crown of the railroad bordered each side of the path. The ditches on each side of the railroad had been converted into vegetable and flower gardens. Through these gardens footpaths led to the houses beyond. Butterflies darted here and there and the air was filled with the pleasant hum of bees. The occasional Filipino wayfarers whom I passed greeted me with friendly smiles. Sometimes I heard one of them remark "Americano" (American) to his companion after they had passed me. On this street, I reflected with satisfaction, that there were no Japanese.

But one Saturday morning I discovered the name, S. Nakashima, painted on a board fastened to the gate of a house on the eastern side of the path. My dream was shattered. It wasn't possible to go from my home to the end of the street-car line, even by that obscure footpath, without passing a house which was occupied by Japanese.

That the Japanese had taken over the cream of such business as could still be carried on in Manila was only too evident. A Japanese-controlled organization had the exclusive privilege of selling rice to the people of Manila. Rice not distributed by that organization was considered contraband and both sellers and buyers were liable to punishment for dealing in it. The operation of the Manila Electric Railroad and Light Company was in the hands of a Japanese corporation. A Japanese manager took control of the Philippine Manufacturing Company, which produced vegetable lard and soap from coconut oil. Japanese managers took control of the Philippine Match Factory, the Manila Gas Company, a sugar factory near Manila, the Philippine Long Distance Telephone Company which operated the telephone service of Manila. They also took over a ship yard and the principal machine shops. These were only a few of the many business enterprises which were now controlled by the Japanese.

If a large and profitable business was owned by Americans, British, Dutch or Chinese it was confiscated. If it was owned by Filipinos the Filipino owners were forced to sell their property at a small fraction of its worth. When the Filipino owner of three daily newspapers published in Manila refused to sell his business to a Japanese organization he was arrested by the Japanese military police and imprisoned in the notorious Fort Santiago. In two weeks the Japanese military police persuaded him to sell his business to the Japanese. He was paid, of course, in Japanese war notes.

A horde of Japanese soldiers, returned to civilian status after the surrender of Bataan, ranged over the city seeking small business enterprises which they might acquire from the Filipino and Chinese owners, by force if necessary. About twenty prominent and wealthy Chinese had to disgorge hidden wealth. Not infrequently the same Japanese ex-soldiers resorted to looting. The Japanese devoured the wealth of the city like a swarm of hungry locusts.

Japanese soldiers, most of them off duty, crowded the streets of the down-town section of the city. They were particularly numerous in the Quiapo District, where there were many Japanese-operated hotels, barrooms and brothels. Even before the war a considerable number of Japanese resided and had their places of business in that district.

The large garrison of Japanese soldiers was systematically dispersed throughout the city. On almost every street were buildings occupied by Japanese troops or by units of the Japanese military administration. Before every such building stood a Japanese sentry.

There was an enormous increase in the number of night clubs, barrooms and brothels. Many of these facilities were located, for the greater convenience of their Japanese patrons, in what had formerly been two of the best residential districts of the city. In these two districts, Ermita and Malate, which fronted on Manila Bay, many fine homes and several large hotels and apartment houses were occupied by the Japanese Army and Navy.

The numerous night clubs, restaurants and barrooms patronized by the Japanese found it difficult to obtain sufficient waitresses and hostesses. The following random selections of the many similar advertisements which appeared in the *Daily Tribune* tell a part of the story:

Jan. 23, 1942— "Wanted to buy, table and chairs suitable for restaurant. Also bar and counter."

Jan. 23— "Wanted beautiful waitresses. Apply Rainbow Hotel."

Jan. 27— "Wanted beautiful hostesses. Apply to Mr. Yamasaki, Kenwood Hotel."

Jan. 28— "Wanted attractive, nice ladies. Good income assured. Apply at Alcazar Club."

Feb. 20— "Wanted immediately beautiful hostesses. Apply personally at Rainbow Hotel."

Mar. 5— "Wanted waitresses, hostesses and dancers. Good looking and up-to-date girls preferred. Apply personally at Quiapo Bar."

Mar. 21— "Wanted waitresses. Apply at Tokyo Saloon (Alcazar Club). Good income assured."

Apr. 1— "Wanted beautiful hostesses. Apply personally at 1136 Apt. D, Dakota, Malate."

Apr. 14— "Wanted nice girls. Apply personally Japanese Navy Club, 223 Porvenir, Pasay."

May 7—"Wanted 50 beautiful waitresses. Good income guaranteed. Apply Mr. Yamamoto, 319 Ronquillo."

May 8— "Wanted immediately 10 beautiful hostesses. Apply personally at 442 P. Gomez."

May 8 – "Wanted hostesses and waitresses immediately. See Miss. Sarmiento, 535 P. Paterno."

(Note: A large influx of Japanese soldiers into Manila was expected following the fall of Corregidor, which was announced on May 8)

May 26— "Wanted 20 beautiful waitresses. Tokyo Saloon (Alcazar Club)."

June 24— "Wanted beautiful *mestizas* as hostesses. Peacock Garden, Escolta."

(Mestizas were girls of mixed white and Filipino parentage. The Japanese considered them more beautiful than girls of pure Filipino parentage.)

July 4— "Wanted attractive *mestiza* waitress for night club, 223 Porvenir, Pasay."

Aug. 15— "Wanted hostesses. Apply Congress Hotel. 551 M.H. del Pilar."

Sept. 12— "Wanted immediately waitresses. Good Salary and conditions. 336 Carriedo, Quiapo."

Oct. 3— "Wanted: Andalusia needs girls who can dance Spanish dances or any good floor show. Also girls who can sing and some hostesses. 44 A. Mabini."

Oct. 3— "Wanted hostesses and waitresses, night club, 328-330 Carriedo,"

Oct. 24— "Wanted at once hostesses & waitresses. Apply 543 Rizal Avenue, Santa Cruz."

Chapter 75.

Concerning Hard Times for Many People in Manila

By the middle of 1942 a good many people who before the war had been in comfortable circumstances began to feel the pinch of poverty. We, ourselves, were in as dire straits as they were but they did not know it and frequently sought to borrow money from my wife. She of necessity refused most of these requests. But now and then she relented and loaned small sums varying from 20 centavos to, in one case, as much as five pesos.

There was one type of petition, however, which my wife found it difficult to refuse and that was the appeal of people who, in order to obtain money for food, besought her to purchase various articles of household furniture, at bargain prices. My wife bought some, nevertheless. In June she bought a lady's dresser for 15 pesos from a widow whose pension had been cut off by the war. In July the widow again appealed for assistance and my wife bought from her an office desk for five pesos. In August a man came to our house and sold my wife a new electric fan for five pesos. He said he needed the money to buy food for his wife and family. My wife planned to sell the fan, but she was unable to find a buyer.

In April a young woman who lived across the street from us had given my wife a half sack (11 kilograms) of wheat flour in exchange for 6 gantas (about 14 kilograms) of rice. In September this young woman came to our house and sold my wife a plain iron bed (¾ size) for 14 pesos. Our reserve of cash at that time was only 150 pesos. When I protested that we did not need the bed and could not afford to purchase it, my wife said, with tears in her eyes, "but our neighbor needs the money. She has no money with which to buy rice."

There was practically no chance of reselling second-hand furniture. The warehouses of second-hand dealers were glutted with furniture looted from the homes of well-to-do Americans and Europeans who had been interned.

Early in October a young man came to our house one Sunday and requested my wife to recommend him for a position in the service of the Japanese-controlled municipal government of Manila. He said that prior to the war he had been a market inspector in the employ of the city government of Manila. In December he evacuated his wife and children to the home of his parents in one of the southern islands. When he returned to Manila in February he found that his position had been abolished. He had applied without success for another position in the government service. In the meantime he had earned a little money by acting as a commission agent in bringing together buyers and sellers of various miscellaneous items of merchandise. Now, he said, nearly everyone on the street was an agent. His earnings had dwindled to almost nothing. Some friends had desired to return to their home in the town where his family was living. He had provided these friends with the money for their transportation and they had promised to give an equivalent sum to his wife upon their arrival at their destination. He took this means of sending money to his wife because there was no other means of sending it. Later he learned that his wife had not received the money. The friends to whom he entrusted the money returned to Manila. But they avoided him and refused to return the money he had loaned.

Mr. Custodio, one of my wife's cousins, had been a law student in Manila when the war broke out. He was married and had four small children. His father was a well-to-do planter on the island of Negros. The war not only closed the law school which he was attending but also prevented him from obtaining financial assistance from his father, or even returning to his home in Negros. He earned a precarious living as a commission agent. For several months his earnings from this source averaged about 60 pesos per month. Among his principal customers were Americans who had been released to their homes and who wished to sell some of their possessions in order to obtain money for their living expenses. However, as time went on it became more and more difficult for him to find buyers for such goods as he could offer for sale. In the meantime his wife had become pregnant and was expecting her fifth child in November.

Mr. Custodio visited our house several times and each time expressed his desire to find a job but jobs were scarce, and he was unable to find one. "About the only jobs open," he said, "are those offered by the Japanese, and I do not care to work for them."

He had considered returning to his home in Negros, but had been advised that guerrillas and bandits were so active in that province that it was not safe to return. A considerable number of landowners had already fled from Negros to Manila. His own home was reported to have been burned by bandits or guerrillas.

On October 18 Mr. Custodio's wife came to our house, bringing her youngest child, a boy of two years. She said that their money was running low and her husband had decided to apply for a position in a new branch of the government service which was about to be organized to regulate gambling and night clubs. Her husband was attempting to obtain a position as an inspector of gambling clubs, night clubs and bar-rooms. She requested my wife to recommend him to the proper authorities.

"It is a good job," she said. "He would go around and visit the gambling clubs, night clubs and bars and probably receive not only his salary but also tips!"

Mrs. Custodio stayed for lunch and for *merienda* and ate so heartily that I suspected that she might not be having enough to eat. Fortunately we had a very tasty beef stew with plenty of vegetables in it for lunch that Sunday.

My wife gave her some vegetables from our garden, rice, sugar, cornbread and rice cake to take home.

As Mrs. Custodio was about to leave she said, "I expect to deliver my child in November and that will take about all the money we have left. If my husband is unable to obtain a position I don't know what we will do. All of my children have been artificially fed and if we do not have money we cannot buy milk for the new baby."

That same afternoon Miss White called. Her father was an elderly American interned in his home on our street. She came to get her weekly Red Cross ration, which my wife brought home each week in order to save Miss White the cost of transportation to the Red Cross office. Each week the Red Cross office, where my wife worked, issued free rations to a large number of destitute persons in Manila. This week Miss White's ration consisted only of ½ kilogram of sugar. My wife informed her that because the funds of the Red Cross were almost exhausted no more free rations would be issued.

Miss White said that she was offered a position as a waitress in a downtown bar-room at 15 pesos per month plus tips. Her father, however, refused to permit her to accept it. He said it would not hurt them to go hungry for one day each week. Miss White was a beautiful blue-eyed blonde girl of 20.

Chapter 76.

Financial Assistance is Given to Some of Those Interned in Their Homes

Early in January, the Red Cross established a kitchen at the Santo Tomas Internment Camp for the feeding of all internees who were unable, or unwilling, to provide their own food. The Red Cross continued to provide the funds for food and to administer this kitchen until sometime in July. The Japanese military administration then appropriated funds for feeding the internees and the administration of the kitchen was placed in the hands of the Commandant of the internment camp. Seventy centavos ($0.35) per internee per day was allocated for the purchase of food and all other expenses of the camp. This allocation applied not only to those interned at Santo Tomas but also to a group of children who were interned at the Holy Ghost Convent. It was also rumored that a similar allocation had been granted to a few needy persons who, because of ill health, had been authorized to reside outside of the internment camp.

Early in September, my wife, who was employed at the Central Office of the Red Cross, informed me that, at the request of the Japanese military administration, the Red Cross was preparing a list of civilian enemy nationals residing outside the camp who were in need of financial assistance. It was rumored that either money or foodstuffs, or both, had been sent by ship from the United States via Lorenzo Marquez (in Africa) which was intended to secure exchange of diplomatic representatives. My wife placed my name on the list of those desiring financial assistance.

Late in September, a Mr. Nuger, one of the internees at the Santo Tomas camp, was given a week's pass to visit his wife, who operated a small *tienda* (store) near our home. One morning, while his wife was busy at her store, he called at our home. He informed me that those internees who had been released to their homes would be given financial assistance if they needed it. I was left with the impression, although I am not certain that he stated the source of such assistance, that it would be granted by the Commandant of the Santo Tomas Internment Camp. He did say, however, that a man and wife with three children could obtain 27. 50 pesos ($13.75) per month. The exact amount of the assistance to be granted would depend on the number of persons dependent upon the internee.

During the first six months of 1942, when the Red Cross was operating several hospitals for internees, a Mrs. MacDonald, herself one of the internees at the Santo Tomas Internment Camp, acted as a liaison officer who visited the various hospitals where internees were confined and transmitted to the Commandant the requests of internees for renewal of their hospital passes or for release to their homes. Mrs. MacDonald disappeared from my horizon when I was released to my home on June 30. On October 31 she reappeared on the scene. That day was Saturday. As usual, I went to the Red Cross Hospital for my weekly injection of liver extract. During my absence Mrs. MacDonald called at our home and left the following note for me:

"Please see Mr. Hawkins and he will explain why I was here. —Mrs. MacDonald, Sto. Tomas."

Mr. Tom Hawkins, a fellow internee at the Ateneo Hospital, had been released to his home in March. He lived on the same street as we did about a half mile from our house.

When I returned to my home at about 2.30 that Saturday afternoon my mother-in-law gave me Mrs. MacDonald's note. I immediately went to see Mr. Hawkins. He said that Mrs. MacDonald had informed him that it had been reported at Santo Tomas that some of the Old Timers who had been released to their homes were in need of financial assistance. A committee of internees had been appointed to investigate and recommend such assistance where it was needed. Mrs. MacDonald had been instructed to call on the internees and inform them of this arrangement. Those who desired assistance were requested to call at the Santo Tomas Interment Camp and see Mrs. MacDonald. She had not mentioned the amount of financial assistance to be granted. But she had asked to be directed to the homes of other internees living nearby. Mr. Hawkins had sent his servant to show her the way.

Several other internees, like myself, were absent when Mrs. MacDonald called. Thus it came about that, while I was chatting with Tom and his wife, Mr. White, Mr. Chambers and Mr. Fishback also called to inquire about the purpose of Mrs. MacDonald's visit. Mr. Chambers was an American Negro. Tom Hankins, Chambers and Fishback were Spanish-American War veterans who had arrived in the Philippines in 1899 and had been residents of the Philippines for more than 43 years. They began to recall their experiences as soldiers in 1899 and 1900. Mr. White, although he also was an old soldier, had not reached the Philippines until 1907. Hence he had resided in the Philippines for only 35 years. He remarked that he had been told that an Old Timer was a person who had resided in the Philippines for 40 years or more. Hence he could not qualify as an Old Timer.

"Mr. Warren, how long have you lived in the Philippines?" Asked Tom's wife.

"Not so very long," I replied with some diffidence in the presence of the veterans of 1899. "I have been here only 28 years."

Mrs. Hawkins giggled. She then turned to Mr. Fishback and asked, "Are you going to apply for aid?"

"I don't want to ask the Japanese for help," replied Mr. Fishback. "I would rather get the money somewhere else. I have managed to get along so far. I am a mechanic and people bring to my house a little repair work for me to do. Some days I make 25 centavos; on other days 50 centavos; and occasionally a peso. Some days I don't make anything. But the wife and I manage to eat."

"Don't you think that you are entitled to receive aid from the Japanese?" asked Mrs. Hawkins. "They interned you and deprived you of the means to earn your living."

Fishback had been getting aid from Tom and Mrs. Hawkins probably hoped that Fishback would accept aid from the Japanese so that Tom would not have to lend him any more money.

"Whether I am entitled to it or not, I would accept aid only as a last resort," replied Fishback.

"And what are you going to do about it?" Mrs. Hawkins inquired of Mr. White.

"I think I will wait awhile and see how those make out who do apply for help," said Mr. White. "I would rather not ask for help from the Japanese."

"And how about you?" Mrs. Hawkins asked of me.

"We have managed to get along so far. If nothing happens to cut off our present meager sources of income, or increase our monthly expenditures. I believe we can continue to get along without aid for some time. There are seven persons to feed at our house, but we manage to get along on about 60 pesos a month for food, light, water and fuel," I replied.

"It cost us 58 pesos last month," said Tom. "But we used to spend 200 pesos."

"When the Japanese entered Manila in January," I continued, "we were caught with only 200 pesos in cash in and we have not been able to draw any money from our bank account since then. By the end of June, in spite of borrowing a little money from our friends and selling some of our imported foodstuffs, our cash reserve shrunk to 150 pesos. There has been no further shrinkage in our cash reserve during the past four months, and we still have about 150 pesos in cash on hand. In June my wife obtained a position as a bookkeeper in the Central Office of the Red Cross. Her monthly salary, after deducting the cost of her transportation, is about 33 pesos per month. I have a stamp collection. I have placed some of my stamps for sale on consignment with a Filipino merchant who operates a small bookstore in Manila. Since August 15, he has paid me regularly about 10 pesos per week—a total of 125 pesos. He still owes me about 500 pesos. What I get from him, added to my wife's salary, just about covers our monthly living expenses. I also make a little money now and then selling cakes and muffins which I make from rice flour. I sell cupcakes at 70 centavos per dozen. They cost me about 35 centavos a dozen for ingredients and fuel so I make a profit of about 35 centavos on every dozen that I sell. The price of ingredients is increasing, however. Eggs, which cost 8 centavos each in August, now cost 11 centavos each. Baking powder and shortening are higher too. And cakes are harder to sell than they were a few months ago. People can't afford them now."

When my wife came home that evening she announced that she had resigned her position with the Red Cross, effective on November 15.

"Why did you do that?" I gasped, thinking that now we too would have to ask aid from the Japanese.

"The Red Cross has no more money," she replied. "There was a balance of about 17,000 pesos in the bank a month ago. Now the Red Cross is overdrawn about 10,000 pesos. But do not worry. You will be given a pension by the Japanese. I heard about it at the office this morning. As long as I was working you could not get a pension. But now that I have resigned you will be given a pension. I am going to the Santo Tomas Internment Camp tomorrow morning to register for the pension."

"Who is providing the money for these pensions?" I asked.

"The money, 1,000,000 pesos, was sent by Henry Ford from the United States through the International Red Cross," replied my wife.

"Are you sure of that?" I asked.

"That's what I heard at the office," replied my wife.

The next day, when my wife went to Santo Tomas, she learned that Mr. Duggleby was the chairman of the internee committee which was conducting the investigation to determine which of those who were interned in their homes should be given pensions. My name was not on the list of those already recommended, but Mr. Duggleby said that the committee had not yet completed its investigation. In answer to my wife's inquiry as to the source of the money for the pensions, Mr. Duggleby said that it was to be provided by the Japanese military administration.

Prior to the Japanese occupation of Manila Mr. Duggleby had been the vice-president of the Benguet Consolidated Mining Company, which operated two of the world's largest and most profitable gold mines, as well as several other mining properties. Now in the internment camp, Mr. Duggleby said, he received only two meals a day and, as chairman of the investigating committee, a salary of 10 pesos per month.

Chapter 77.

My Wife Seeks Another Source of Income to Replace the Salary Which She Would No Longer Receive from the Red Cross

When she found it was doubtful that I would be granted a pension from the Santo Tomas Internment Camp my wife lost no time in seeking another source of income to replace the salary which she would no longer receive from the Red Cross.

On the day that she visited Santo Tomas she also visited the home of her sister, Natividad, whose husband, Emelio Javier, was a practicing attorney in Manila. My wife had not visited them and they had not called on us, since the Japanese occupation of Manila. She found them, like ourselves, in straitened circumstances. Prior to the war Emelio in addition to the income from his law practice, had enjoyed a salary as the dean of a law school and his wife had been earning a salary as a teacher in the law school. The law school closed immediately after the outbreak of the war. Emelio and Natividad had received no salary since the school had closed. Emelio still maintained his law office, however. There was very little for a lawyer to do, but he earned a small income as a notary. His wife was earning 20 pesos a month teaching English to a Chinese student who came to her home for his instruction. They had dispensed with their maidservant, but still retained their chauffeur, although they were not permitted by the Japanese authorities to use their car.

Emelio still owed me about one-half of the price of an automobile which I sold him ten years earlier. Furthermore, during the past five years my wife had been the principal support of her mother, to whom she had given the money to buy a lot and to build the house in which we were now living. As she ate lunch with Emelio and Nating (Natividad) that day, my wife told them that now we were hard up and it was their turn to do something to help us and their mother.

Three or four days later Emelio and Nating called on us. My wife had told them that her mother, who was more than 75 years old, was ill. She had recently complained of a fever and one of her legs was swollen. Emelio and Nating had come to take her to a hospital for medical examination. Emelio feared that her kidneys were beginning to fail. He said that he and Natividad would pay for our mother's hospital expenses.

Although still swollen, our mother's leg had improved sufficiently for her to walk with Emelio and Natividad to the bus station, a distance of about half a mile.

We gave Emelio and Nating some vegetables from our garden—okra, eggplant, *patola* (a large cucumber) and a *pomelo* (a large citrus fruit about twice the size of a grapefruit).

A few days later, on Saturday, November 7, my wife visited her mother at the hospital. She found the old lady cheerful and asking to be permitted to go home. The doctor said, however, that she should remain in the hospital under observation for a few days longer.

On her way to the hospital my wife had called on Emelio and had obtained from him ten pesos, the first installment of twenty pesos which he had promised to give us for the purchase of liver extract for me. The money was to be credited to Emelio's debt to me.

This payment was almost a forced levy on Emelio, who was himself very hard pressed financially. My wife told him that if he would not help us she would go to Mr. Jose Yulo and borrow the money from him. At that point Emelio said, "Oh, don't do that. I will let you have the money."

Emelio was a prominent member of the principal minority political party in the Philippines. In 1941 he had been its candidate for vice-president of the Philippines. When Judge Sumulong died Emelio succeeded him as head of the party. Early in 1942 Emelio had been offered, and had refused, a position as a member of the Japanese-sponsored Philippine Executive Commission. Mr. Yulo was a prominent member of the majority party. Under the Japanese-sponsored government he had become the Chief Justice of the Philippine Supreme Court.

During the next six weeks Emelio made several small payments to my wife on the debt which he owed me. Sometime after when I was re-interned at Santo Tomas he paid to my wife the balance of more than 500 pesos which he still owed me. How he managed to raise the money I do not know.

Because he had refused to "cooperate" by accepting membership of the Japanese-sponsored Philippine Executive Commission, Emelio was constantly under surveillance by the Japanese military police. In 1944 Emelio cashed a check for an American internee on a frozen bank account. This was in violation of a decree issued by the Japanese military administration. The Japanese military police learned of it and imprisoned Emelio for more than five months in the notorious Japanese military prison at Fort Santiago.

Chapter 78.

We Have Visitors from Baguio

Late on the afternoon of Friday, November 6, Mrs. A—, a Filipino woman whose American husband had been employed by me as a mining foreman in 1933, called at our house. She was accompanied by a young Filipino, whom she introduced as a former lieutenant in the USAFE forces who had escaped when Bataan surrendered to the Japanese. I did not learn the young man's name. My wife entertained them while I finished watering the garden. When I rejoined the party Mrs. A— was telling my wife about conditions in Baguio, where Mrs. A— had been living since the Japanese occupation of that city gate in December, 1941.

Mrs. A— said that she had tried to support herself by operating a stall in the public market at Baguio but lost money on that venture. There were, she said, very few civilians living in Baguio. The Japanese Army took most of the foodstuffs offered for sale in the public market. The army compelled the vendors to accept whatever price it chose to offer for the foodstuffs which it requisitioned. Mrs. A— bought *camotes* (sweet potatoes) for five centavos per kilogram and was compelled to sell them to the Japanese Army for three centavos per kilogram. The regular retail price of *camotes* in the public market of Baguio at that time was 12 centavos per kilogram. When Mrs. A— sought to ship fresh vegetables to Manila, where they would fetch a higher price, she found that the Japanese military administration prohibited the shipment of foodstuffs from Baguio to Manila.

My wife inquired concerning our house in Baguio.

Mrs. A— replied, "I opened the back door and I think your piano and radio were missing." She proposed that if my wife would permit it she would enter the house when she returned to Baguio to see whether or not it had been looted. My wife replied that she expected to go to Baguio soon and would see for herself.

The lieutenant advised my wife not to go to Baguio. "Here in Manila," he said, "it is very quiet, but in the provinces it is different. There are three contending parties. To travel in the provinces now you need three flags— USAFE, Tulisafe, and Japanese."

The USAFE were the remnant of the United States Army of the Far East conducting guerrilla warfare in various parts of the islands. The Tulisafe were bandits operating under the guise of guerrillas. Similar bandits during the early years of American occupation of the Philippines had been called *tulisans*, a Filipino word meaning bandits. This word was combined with USAFE to produce the name *Tulisafe*, meaning Tulisan (bandit) Army of the Far East.

"What are you?" my wife asked the lieutenant.

"I am of the USAFE," replied the lieutenant. "We had a meeting last night."

"Don't talk about that," said Mrs. A—.

"Did the Japanese take your car?" inquired the lieutenant.

"Yes," I replied.

"Were you caught driving it?" asked the lieutenant.

"No," I replied. "We did not use it after the Japanese occupied Manila. I registered at the Santo Tomas Internment Camp on January 21. I was required to fill in a form describing my car, stating where it was located and giving the name and address of the person who held the key. At some time late in February, or early in March, the Japanese took all of the internees' cars. I was interned and so was not present when they took our car, but Socorro told me about it."

"Did they take it from your garage?" asked the lieutenant.

"No," I replied. "We had it in a garage across the street from our house."

"Did they give you a receipt for it?" asked the lieutenant.

"No," I replied.

"That is what we came to see you about," said the lieutenant. "We can give you a receipt showing that your car was requisitioned by the USAFE. When the war is over the United States government will pay you for it. And if you need money now we can make you an advance on your car."

"We can go somewhere and I can pay her," said Mrs. A—, referring to my wife. There had been some conversation concerning the car while I was watering the garden.

My wife then said that she would visit her mother at the Emanuel Hospital on the following day. Mrs. A--- took note of the name and location of the hospital and the name of my wife's mother. It was arranged that Mrs. A--- and the lieutenant would meet my wife at the hospital.

It rained during the morning of the next day and my wife did not go to the hospital until the afternoon. Mrs. A--- and the lieutenant had visited my wife's mother during the morning and had left a note for my wife saying that they could not wait for her.

I advised my wife not to accept the money if she was required to sign a receipt for it. "That receipt," said I, "could get you into trouble with the Japanese. We have no assurance that these people really represent the USAFE."

"Are they Japanese spies?" asked my wife.

"I don't know," I replied. "but we only have their statement as to whom they represent.

Mrs. A— and the lieutenant called again at our home on the afternoon of November 10 and asked to see Mrs. Warren. I was busy in the garden and did not go in to talk with them. They stayed for about an hour. When they left my wife gave them some vegetables from our garden.

My wife told me that they had called again concerning our car. They wanted to obtain its license number and description and said that it would be paid for when the war was over. They told my wife that they would call again. The lieutenant said that their present work was to go around and obtain a list of the cars which the Japanese had taken.

Chapter 79.

Concerning the High Prices Which Collectors Paid for Stamps

When I called at Rogelio's book store on Saturday, October 31, I found Ramon Catala waiting for Rogelio, who had not yet arrived. Mr. Catala was a prominent member of the Asociacion Filatelica de Filipinas (Philatelic Association of the Philippines). For several years prior to the war he was the business manager of the magazine, *A.F.F.*, published by the Asociación Fliatélica de Filipinas. Prior to the war members of the Philatelic Association met once each month for a luncheon, followed by a stamp auction. The publication of the association's magazine ceased with the Japanese occupation of Manila and for nine months thereafter the association held no meetings.

On a Sunday early in October, however, members of the association met at the Turin Restaurant for a luncheon and stamp auction. This was the first meeting to be held in ten months. Thereafter the Philatelic Association held an auction each Sunday. The demand for stamps was brisk and much better prices were obtained than during the year immediately preceding the war. Mr. Catala said that the most active buyers were a group of German Jews who were in business in Manila and who were investing the profits of their business in stamps, apparently because they did not wish to hold the paper currency (war notes) of the Japanese military administration. The people were compelled by military edict to accept this currency. But if they deposited it in banks the amount which could be withdrawn each month was limited by other military edicts.

"I wish I might attend the auctions," said I. "I have some stamps which I would like to sell. But my pass prohibits me from attending gatherings of that sort."

"It would not be wise for you to come," said Ramon. "The Turin Restaurant is frequented by Japanese and there are several Japanese stamp collectors who attend the auctions. But I will be glad to take your stamps and sell them for you."

"I would be delighted if you could sell some of my stamps," I replied. "Come out to my house and visit me. While you are there we will select some stamps which you believe can be sold."

"I will pay you a visit next Friday, if that is a convenient day," said Ramon.

"That will be fine," I replied. "Any day except Saturday is convenient for me. On that day I make my weekly trip to the hospital and do my marketing."

When Ramon came to see me on the following Friday he brought me as a gift several envelopes bearing Philippine stamps issued since the Japanese occupation of Manila. I gave him to sell for me four Philippine stamps for which I was to be paid a total of 65 pesos. The difference between his selling price and the price he paid me would be his profit. He said that he would try to sell them at the auction on the following Sunday.

Chapter 80.

Concerning the Arrest by Japanese Military Police of Three Prominent Business Men of Manila

On October 31, I was informed by Ramon Catala that Mr L.R. Aguinaldo, Michael Goldenberg and Mr. Hemady, three prominent business men of Manila, had been arrested by the Japanese military police and imprisoned at Fort Santiago. The military police had also padlocked the stores of these merchants. The exact nature of the charges against them were not known but it was rumored that they were accused of profiteering and buying stolen goods. It was also rumored, however, that the real reason for the arrest of these merchants was the fact that they had competed with the Japanese military administration in the buying of merchandise which the military administration desired to purchase at its own low price. It was said that Mr. Hemady had persisted in buying up galvanized iron sheets after he had been ordered not to do so. It was rumored that Mr. Goldenberg had sold at high prices khaki cloth which he had been ordered to reserve for the Japanese military administration at its own low price.

Mr. L.R. Aguinaldo was a Filipino who owned a large department store and who for several years prior to the outbreak of the war had been openly pro-Japanese. Mr. Goldenberg was a Filipino citizen born in Manila of Jewish parents. He also owned a large department store. Mr. Hemady was an Assyrian who conducted a variety of business enterprises in Manila.

I walked past Michael Goldenberg's department store on October 31 about an hour after Mr. Catala informed me that its proprietor had been imprisoned. The store was located on a corner. It was padlocked, just as Mr. Catala had said and a Japanese military truck was parked before a side entrance.

A week later, on November 6, en route to the hospital, I again met Mr. Catala, this time in front of Michael Goldenberg's department store. It was about 8.30 a.m. and, although the store was closed, there was a crowd of people waiting at the entrance. Mr. Catala informed me that Mr. Goldenberg had been released from prison and was reopening his store that day. He had been ordered, however, said Mr. Catala, to sell his goods at pre-war prices, which were much lower than the current retail prices. That was the reason for the crowd of bargain hunters waiting for the store to open.

Mr. Aguinaldo, said Mr. Catala, had also been released and permitted to reopen his store on condition that he too must sell his goods at pre-war prices. Mr. Hemady was still in prison.

Chapter 81.

*Concerning the Stagnation Which Gripped Manila
After the Japanese Occupation of the City*

As I made my way across the city of Manila to visit the hospital each Saturday after my release to my home at the end of June, I noted sadly the unkempt, poverty-stricken appearance of the city and the very evident stagnation of business. There was little, if any, improvement in these conditions during the four months which elapsed between July 1 and November 6, 1942.

Yet the Japanese-controlled *Daily Tribune* constantly proclaimed the rapidity with which the city was returning to normality. An editorial on November 6 stated: "Take for instance the city of Manila. Few are the signs of war. Peace and normality reign. The atmosphere little reflects the great struggle being waged by the Nippon Empire."

But the alleged return to normality was not evident to the casual observer. Ten months after the Japanese occupied the city and six months after the fall of Corregidor, most of the grade schools Manila and most of the grade schools and all of the high schools, colleges and universities in Corregidor were still closed. More than half of the business establishments had not reopened after the Japanese occupation started and their furniture and stocks of goods had been either looted or confiscated. Through their dusty windows could be seen the rubbish which littered their floors. The windows were criss-crossed with strips of adhesive paper, placed there at the outbreak of the war to prevent people from being injured by flying splinters of broken glass during bombing raids. Even the windows of many establishments open for business were still criss-crossed with strips of paper. Business was so poor and the future was so uncertain that the proprietors were indifferent as to the appearance of their establishments. Rubbish littered the streets. Garbage collection had been suspended when the Japanese entered the city and had not been resumed. The disposal of garbage was left to private initiative, with very unfortunate results. The people were instructed to deposit their garbage in open pits dug in vacant lots and in the parking strips which bordered the streets. A host of flies bred in this refuse. Scattered along the curbs of the streets throughout the city was the wreckage of hundreds of automobiles, abandoned by their owners when the Japanese entered the city and stripped by looters of tires, wheels, engines and all other salvageable parts. Little, other than the body and chassis, remained.

The construction of new buildings, suspended when the Japanese entered the city, had not been resumed. Weathered scaffolds protruded from the walls of uncompleted buildings. Almost the only construction during the first ten months of Japanese occupation was that done by the Japanese Army and by a few Japanese-controlled business enterprises. Temporary barracks and sheds for housing motor trucks and other military equipment were erected in many parts of the city. The campus of the University of the Philippines was littered with these unsightly structures. The Botanical Garden, formerly a public park, was enclosed with a corrugated sheet iron fence in order to provide privacy for convalescent Japanese soldiers quartered in adjacent buildings, which had been converted into a military hospital. The YMCA buildings, which had been converted into military barracks, were also enclosed with an unsightly fence made of rusty second-hand sheets of corrugated iron. The shops of the Philippine School of Arts and Trade had been converted to military use and several sheds had been erected upon its campus.

No maintenance work had been done on the streets. By the end of October the streets were in a deplorable condition. During the four months of heavy rain from June to October the asphalt surface of the streets had disintegrated into innumerable holes, many of which were more than a foot in depth. These had been eroded by the rain and by heavy military traffic.

Also all pre-war Philippine currency had disappeared from circulation. Its place was taken by Japanese "war notes" which the people regarded with suspicion and accepted with reluctance.

The Japanese financed their occupation of the Philippines with a paper currency issued by the Japanese government in denominations of the Philippines peso. A supply of these war notes for use in the Philippines was printed in Japan prior to the invasion. The Japanese army began to use these notes in payment for supplies and services which it requisitioned immediately after it landed on Philippine soil. One of the earliest decrees issued by the Japanese military administration imposed heavy penalties for refusal to accept the war notes whenever offered in payment for goods and services. "Circulate this money," counselled the Japanese military administration, "it is issued by the Imperial Japanese Government!" The war notes were issued in denominations of 1, 5, 10 and, 50-centavos and 1, 5 and 10 pesos. The 100 and 500 pesos denominations were added later when the greatly decreased purchasing power of the war notes made these high denominations necessary.

Pre-war Philippine currency was permitted to continue in circulation concurrently with the Japanese war notes but all other currencies, including emergency Philippine currency issued after the outbreak of the war, were banned.

Notwithstanding the fact that its circulation was permitted, pre-war Philippine currency began to disappear from circulation immediately after the Japanese occupation of Manila. By the end of February 1942, practically all copper, nickel and silver coins had disappeared from circulation. By the end of March all pre-war paper currency, except 1 and 2 peso treasury notes, had disappeared from circulation. By the end of October the 1- and 2-peso treasury notes had also disappeared.

The copper, nickel and silver coins, and a portion of the pre-war paper currency were undoubtedly hoarded by the Philippine people. This money reappeared in circulation immediately after the liberation of the Philippines in 1945.

But it was rumored in 1942 that pre-war Philippine paper currency was being retired from circulation by the Japanese to be replaced by war notes of equal face value and this applied to all pre-war Philippine currency which they received in the course of business. Whether or not this rumor was true, it is a fact that, although the banks accepted pre-war Philippine currency for deposit, the only currency which the banks paid out to their customers was Japanese war notes.

Of the nine Manila banks which were closed by the Japanese only two were permitted to reopen for business. Seven of these banks were liquidated by the Japanese military administration. All loans due to these seven banks were called for immediate payment; all deposits were frozen and no withdrawals could be made. Withdrawals from pre-war deposits in the two banks which were permitted to reopen were limited to a maximum of two hundred pesos per month from each account.

A decree issued by the Japanese military administration imposed forced savings upon the Philippine people. Each family was limited to not more than 200 pesos per month for its current living expense. It was ordered that any income in excess of 200 pesos per month must be deposited in a bank. Withdrawals from such deposits were limited to a maximum of 200 pesos per month from each account. The apparent purpose of this decree was to increase bank deposits but its actual effect was exactly the opposite. Because of the restriction on withdrawals many people ceased to deposit their money in banks.

The effect of the substitution of Japanese war notes for pre-war Philippine currency and of the decrees freezing many bank accounts and restricting withdrawals from all other bank accounts was to aggravate the already existing stagnation of business in Manila. Trade in some forms of property practically ceased because the owners of such property were unwilling to accept Japanese war notes in exchange for their property. This was particularly true of real estate. The restrictions on withdrawals from bank accounts reduced the purchasing power of the people and produced a dearth of capital for business enterprises. The calling of all loans due to the banks under liquidation resulted in further paralysis. In many cases the debtors were forced out of business.

The Manila Electric Railroad and Light Company, after six months of operation by the Japanese Army, was, in July of 1942, turned over to a Japanese corporation. Because of a lack of coal, coconut oil was burned in the furnaces to generate steam for the production of electricity. The policy of the operators appeared to be to spend as little as possible upon the maintenance and repair of equipment. By the end of October some seats in the streetcars had no back. For several weeks one street car was in operation with the broken back of a seat lying on the floor beside the motorman. Eventually the broken back was removed from the car, but it was not restored to the seat from which it had been removed.

The stocks of almost all large wholesale and retail establishments were either confiscated by the Japanese Army or looted, or both. As a result very few of these establishments were able to reopen after the Japanese occupation. This condition was particularly apparent in the case of hardware. The only pre-war hardware stores which I saw open for business ten months after the occupation were the Japanese-owned Daido Hardware Company and the German-owned Viegelmann and Company.

Because of the almost complete disappearance of wholesale distributors combined with the large quantity of goods which had fallen into the hands of looters, and the impossibility of importing new stocks of goods to replace those which had been stolen or confiscated, the "want ad" columns of the *Daily Tribune* were constantly filled with offers to buy and sell a vast variety of goods which under normal conditions would not have been marketed in this manner. The following want ads, quoted from the *Daily Tribune* of November 6, 1942, are typical of this phase of Manila's war economy

Wanted to buy
"Electric motors, iron plates, shafting, belting, propellers, diesel engines, check valves, welding equipment, ammonium sulphate, asbestos cloth and sheets; logging blocks and other equipment for saw mills and lumber mills; calculating machines, adding machines, typewriters even second-hand; steel safes, filing cabinets, storage cabinets and all kinds of office equipment; electric fans, lacquer paint, lacquer thinner; we buy anything except contraband; mercury, gum copal; air pistols, any quantity, good prices paid; radio-phonograph combinations, magnetic pick-ups; gold of any kind, old diamonds and other jewelries at good prices; electric refrigerators, magic chief (stove) with two burners, no oven; tin ingot, lead; cassava flour, gelatin, chocolate coating."

Miscellaneous for sale
"Furniture; asbestos packing, axes, nickel babbit (an alloy of tin, antimony and copper), hack saws, chain block, emery cloth, furniture castors, linseed oil, rubber packing, saw teeth, shoe eyelets, spoke-shaves, track bolt, lard oil, zippers; electric fans; China rugs; electric ranges, steel storage cabinet, gas water heaters; 8-tube radio-phonograph; electric generator, 76 KVA, 2300 volts, complete with factory-built switchboards and instruments, also smaller generator."

Buying and selling
"We buy and sell electric motors, generators and machinery, auto spare parts, tires, tools, grease, oil, paints, thinner, etc."

The demand for most of these goods by consumers was very small. In some cases the goods were purchased by persons who wished to exchange Japanese war notes for some form of property which would still have value after the Japanese were driven out of the Philippines. But in most cases the goods were purchased by speculators who, in turn, sold to other speculators at constantly pyramiding prices. Immediately after the Japanese occupation of the city the prices offered by speculators for their goods were but a small fraction of the pre-war value. Eventually the prices reached such heights that, in the continued absence of consumer demand, the business collapsed. This phase of Manila's war economy was called the "buy-and-sell business."

Ten months after the Japanese occupation of the city a great variety of merchandise, most of it undoubtedly looted, was still being offered for sale in small quantities by a host of sidewalk vendors. The merchandise thus dispensed included hardware, tools, toilet preparations, imported canned and bottled foodstuffs, garden seeds, sewing thread, needles, toys, pre-war imported American cigarettes, and paints.

Rents had been fixed by decree at half the pre-war rents but many buildings were unoccupied. Owners who were fortunate enough to obtain tenants accepted rents which, in many cases, were much less than half of the pre-war rents.

Ten months after the Japanese occupation there was still a great deal of unemployment. Those who were fortunate enough to be employed were receiving between a fifth to a half of their pre-war wages. The salaries of government employees had been reduced by half, or more than a half, of pre-war salaries. Salesgirls were fortunate to obtain employment at 15 pesos ($7.50) per month. Unskilled day laborers were receiving from 30 ($0.15) to 50 centavos ($0.25) per day. In the *Daily Tribune* for November 6, the

Bureau of Public Welfare announced with pride that since January 23 it had found jobs for almost half of those who had applied.

Existing stocks of cloth, almost all of which had been imported, were being hoarded. Clothing was difficult to obtain at any price. Both leather and rubber for the manufacture of shoes had become exceedingly scarce. Some shoes were being manufactured with canvas tops and soles made from discarded automobile tires, though not many shoes were being sold as people could not afford them. Wooden sandals were being extensively used instead of shoes. Many of the poorer people went bare foot.

Maximum retail prices for tobacco products and for almost all foodstuffs were fixed by decree of the Japanese. But these prices were not enforced. The actual retail prices continued to rise throughout the period of the occupation.

Philippines-made cigarettes, whose pre-war price was 11 centavos and whose lawful war-time price, as printed on the wrapper, was 17 centavos, were actually selling at one peso (100 centavos) per packet in October 1942.

Genuine ground roasted coffee, whose lawful war-time price was 1.20 pesos per kilogram, was actually being sold at 4 pesos per kilogram. A ground roasted coffee substitute was being sold as "third class coffee" at 1.20 pesos per kilogram. In order that there might be no question as to the genuineness of the coffee sold at 4 pesos per kilogram the roasted coffee beans were ground in the presence of the buyer.

Eggs were being sold at from 1 peso to 1.40 pesos per dozen, according to size and type. This was about double the pre-war price. Corn meal was being sold at 70 centavos per kilogram, seven times the pre-war price. *Camotes* (sweet potatoes) were available at 25 centavos per kilogram, two and a half times the pre-war price. Fresh vegetables were being sold at 4 to 5 times pre-war prices. By the end of October the prices of fresh vegetables had reached such heights that people refused to buy them and there was a sudden temporary drop in the prices of the more abundant vegetables. On November 6, cucumbers, which a week earlier had been offered at 45 centavos per kilogram, could be purchased for 25 centavos per kilogram; a squash, which a week earlier had been offered at 40 centavos per kilogram, could be purchased at 12 centavos per kilogram. But green string beans were still selling at 90 centavos per kilogram and dry Bermuda onions were still 3.50 pesos per kilogram.

Fresh beef was available at 1 peso per kilogram, and fresh pork at 1.20 pesos per kilogram. These prices were only about 50 percent above pre-war prices. Fish, the principal protein food in the Philippines, was also available at prices about 50 percent above pre-war prices. The prices of these important protein foods had been held down by some measure of government control.

Rice, which is the chief item of food in the Philippines, was the only foodstuff subjected to rigid governmental control. The price of rationed rice had been maintained by the Japanese military administration at 34 centavos per ganta (about 14 centavos per kilogram). This was about the same as the price which had prevailed immediately before the outbreak of the war. But the amount of the rice ration obtainable at this price was not sufficient unless a considerable quantity of much more expensive food was also consumed. The ration was fixed at 300 grams per person per day. Three hundred grams of rice have a food value of about 1,100 calories. The average man requires at least 3,000 calories, and the average woman at least 2,500 calories, of food per day. Growing children, ten years of age and older, require as much as adults. Many families purchased additional rice in the black market at prices which were more than double the pre-war price.

The only business enterprises which appeared to be really prosperous were the bars, night clubs and brothels. During the ten months of Japanese occupation there had been an enormous increase in the number of these establishments. They owed their prosperity to the patronage of Japanese soldiers and sailors. The source of the money which Japanese officers and soldiers spent so freely was frequently a subject for discussion among the Filipino people. It was said that the Japanese government paid its soldiers only about three pesos per month. It was generally believed that most of the money spent by Japanese soldiers had been obtained from looting and by robbing American and Filipino prisoners of war, who had been unable to spend the three months' pay which they had received during the siege of Bataan and Corregidor.

The Philippine Red Cross, which in pre-war days never lacked funds, found it impossible in Japanese-occupied Manila to obtain sufficient funds to carry on its work. By the end of October 1942, in spite of having greatly reduced its activities, the Red Cross had overdrawn its bank account by 10,000 pesos. My wife, who was a bookkeeper in the central office of the Red Cross, informed me that very few Japanese contributed to the Red Cross. She could recall only two Japanese contributions during the five months that she had been employed as a bookkeeper. During September and October, she said, American internees were among the chief contributors to the Red Cross. Their bank accounts had been impounded by the Japanese military administration. In August the administration issued a decree to the effect that thereafter the amount which might be withdrawn from any bank account for donation to the Red Cross would be limited only by the amount of the bank account from which it was withdrawn, provided the account was in a bank which had been permitted to resume business. Thereafter American internees were able to authorize the payment of withdrawals to the

Red Cross, although they were not permitted to make withdrawals for their personal use. Some of them were interned in their homes and were receiving free rations from the Red Cross at the time they made contributions to the Red Cross from their frozen bank accounts.

Chapter 82.

The Tide of War Turns in Favor of the Allies

To those of us in the Philippines who had hoped for an early Allied victory the news of the war during the greater part of 1942 was depressing. The Russians were being pushed slowly but steadily backwards until there was heavy fighting in the streets of Stalingrad and in the mountains of the Caucasus. On the Egyptian front there was a stalemate. General MacArthur was making little progress in the South Pacific. Internal conditions in India were chaotic and delayed the preparation of an offensive against the Japanese in Burma. England and the United States had not established the Second Front in Europe which was so desperately needed to relieve the pressure upon the Russians.

On November 6, when I went to the Red Cross Hospital for my weekly injection of liver extract, the doctor informed me that events of the war had taken a turn in favor of the Allies, although he did not give me any details. After leaving the hospital, I encountered Bill Gallin in the Quiapo Public Market. He informed me that the radio on Friday night, November 5, reported a tremendous victory for the Allies in Egypt. The Germans and Italians had been routed. The Allies had destroyed and captured several hundred tanks. The General, third in command of the Axis forces, had been killed. It was reported that the Italians had asked for a truce during which to bury their dead.

The *Daily Tribune* of November 6 published a report dated November 3 stating that "Axis and Allied tanks were locked in a great tank battle in Africa," but that "hard pressed by the Axis forces, the British troops show a tendency of gradual retreat."

A few days later my wife, upon her return from the office of the Red Cross, told me that the Americans had won a great victory in Africa, that the French welcomed the Americans and refused to fight against them. When I pressed her for details she was unable to clarify her statement. So I called on Tom Hawkins, who lived on our street, to inquire what news he had of the fighting in Africa.

Hank said that a large force of American and British troops had effected landings at five points, on both the Atlantic and Mediterranean coasts of French Morocco and Algeria and had occupied these French territories after very slight resistance. Having occupied the French territories, the Allied troops were rapidly moving east to attack the Axis forces in Tunisia. The Axis

Army in Egypt, or what was left of it, was in full retreat and attempting to effect a joint action with the Axis troops in Italian North Africa. In a desperate attempt to stop the Allied advance in Africa, Hitler was withdrawing troops from Russia, Norway and Northern France, but had been unable to transport these troops across the Mediterranean.

The Japanese-controlled *Daily Tribune* on November 14 acknowledged the Allied occupation of French North Africa, but minimized its importance. *The Tribune* declared that the Allies would encounter great difficulty in providing their North African army with sufficient supplies, that "Germany has sufficient troops to fight on all fronts," that "German troops had entered unoccupied France and had taken up strategic positions in the Pyrenees and on the French Mediterranean coast" and that "a powerful German mechanized unit landed in Tunis ... for the purpose of clearing the American troops which have invaded North Africa."

Was this the long awaited Second Front? The *Tribune* reported "... authoritative German circles declared ... that the fact that Premier Stalin neither recognizes the advance of the British troops in Egypt as the beginning of a Second Front, nor takes any positive attitude toward the landing operations of the Anglo-American forces in North Africa, clearly indicates that the so-called Allied Second Front has no influence on the Soviet Union." Nevertheless, the fact that Hitler had moved troops to strategic positions in Southern France indicated very clearly that he regarded Anglo-American occupation of North Africa as a serious threat.

The *Tribune* of November 21 reported a long cable from Tokyo in which it was alleged by Japanese naval authorities that the third Soloman Seas Battle (November 12-14) had resulted in "another great naval victory for Japan" and that the United States' report of an Allied victory was false. "America is attempting to conceal her losses while Japan had truthfully reported hers" this cable said. The same cable acknowledged that Japan had lost one battleship but claimed that the Allied naval units operating in the South Pacific had been completely destroyed. The Japanese-controlled *Tribune* had reported terrific Japanese victories in each of the three Solomon Seas naval battles.

On the afternoon of November 21, I called on Hank and inquired if he had any news concerning the third Solomon Seas naval battle.

"Yes," said Hank. "The Allies sank 23 Japanese war vessels and damaged a dozen others. The vessels sunk consisted of one battleship, 5 cruisers, 5 destroyers and 12 transports. Since the beginning of the South Seas naval engagements the Allies in the vicinity of New Guinea and the Solomon Islands have sunk over 100 Japanese warships and have shot down over 500 Japanese planes. Two Allied land forces are now closing in on the Japanese at Buni in Northern New Guinea. A force of Australians and Americans which crossed the Stanley Mountains from Port Moresby is now within 15 miles of Buni. An American force was landed in Northern New Guinea and is now closing in on Buni from another direction. Yesterday off the coast of Northern New Guinea a Japanese cruiser and a Japanese destroyer were sunk."

The news of these Allied successes caused carefully concealed, but none the less profound, rejoicing among the Filipino people. On November 21, when I called at Rogelio's book store to collect his regular weekly payment on the stamps which he was selling for me on consignment, he paid me 15 pesos (the usual weekly payment was only 10 pesos) and patted me on the shoulder saying, "it won't be long now." When I reached the hospital the doctor-in-charge said, "The news is all good. Its getting better and better every day now."

In July the Japanese military administration had prohibited listening to foreign radio stations after August 1 and had ordered all radios to be submitted to the Japanese military administration for alteration so that overseas short-wave broadcasts could not be picked up. But it was evident now that many people had not submitted their radios for alteration and were surreptitiously tuning in to San Francisco and London. We certainly did not lack news of the Allied victories.

On November 28, when I called at the hospital, I heard that the Russians had begun an offensive on November 19, and that by the end of the seventh day they had killed and captured about 100,000 Germans and at Stalingrad had surrounded a German army of 350,000 men; that the French had scuttled their fleet when the Germans occupied the French naval base at Toulon.

That afternoon I called on Hank. He had not heard of the scuttling of the French fleet, but gave me additional details concerning the Great Russian offensive. In one week the Russians had killed 63,000 and had captured 43,000 Germans. They had captured 1,300 field artillery pieces and 5,500 motor vehicles, besides a vast amount of other war materials. They had cut all of the three railroad lines leading into Stalingrad from the West and had isolated a German army of 350,000 at Stalingrad.

The next morning (Sunday, November 29) the Japanese-controlled *Daily Tribune* announced the German occupation of Toulon and stated that Vichy reported that some ships of the French fleet at Toulon had been damaged and sunk by "traitorous French officers."

The *Tribune* of November 29 also gave details, as released by the Imperial General Headquarters at Tokyo, of the alleged Allied losses in the Third Solomon Seas battle of November 12–14. Tokyo claimed that during the battle the Japanese Navy had sunk 2 battleships, 11 cruisers, 3 or 4 destroyers and 11 transports; had heavily damaged 3 cruisers, 3 or 4 destroyers and 3 transports; and had damaged 1 battleship and 3 destroyers.

The *Tribune* for November 28 reported: "Invasion of U.S. aim of Japanese in present war." … "The Japanese armed forces will not stop in the present war until they have landed on United States soil," Lieutenant Colonel Yosio Nakasima, Chief of the Department of Information of the Imperial Japanese forces in the Philippines, told a gathering of Japanese and Filipino newspapermen at the Manila Hotel yesterday afternoon. Speaking extemporaneously, he said that with the Japanese in the Aleutians poised for an attack on Alaska and Canada, with the Imperial Navy in control of the Pacific and with the destruction of the American fleet at Pearl Harbor and in subsequent naval battles off the Solomons. It is only a question of time when the flag of the rising sun will be hoisted in America."

On December 4, Hank told me that on November 30 there occurred another naval battle in the vicinity of the Solomons (Lunga) in which the Allies reported 9 Japanese vessels sunk. The Japanese report of this battle, as published in the *Tribune*, was: Japanese loss, 1 destroyer sunk; Allied loss, 1 battleship, 1 cruiser and 2 destroyers sunk and 2 destroyers set afire.

The *Tribune* of December 5 reported a Tokyo cable of December 3 to the effect that in various naval battles in the Solomon area between August 7 and November 30 the United States had lost 125 ships and 850 planes. Said this report: "The warships and vessels sunk total 87 and those heavily damaged 36. Japanese losses and damages include 41 warships and transports sunk, 206 planes which dived into enemy objectives or which have not returned, and 31 planes damaged."

Hank said that the Allied report gave the Japanese losses as being over 100 ships sunk and damaged and over 500 planes shot down.

Japanese reports published in the *Tribune* during November and early in December made it very clear that the Japanese high command was irked by American reports of Japanese losses in the Solomon Seas naval battles. One report, published in November, suggested that the United States had reported its own losses as Japanese losses. This report states that the United States figures for Japanese losses corresponded very closely to the Japanese figures for United States naval losses in the Solomon Seas battles.

I had never questioned Tom Hawkins concerning the source of the very detailed information which he often gave me concerning the progress of the war. But when I called at his home on the afternoon of December 12 he informed me that he had a short-wave radio receiver which he had not registered with the Japanese military administration and that each day he tuned in on the broadcasts from San Francisco and London. He took me to the room in which his radio was installed and tuned in on a broadcast from San Francisco.

In that broadcast was featured the triumphant return to San Francisco of the United States cruiser *San Francisco*, which the Japanese-controlled *Tribune* had reported sunk in one of the Solomon Seas battles. The San Francisco broadcast reported that the cruiser *San Francisco* had arrived at San Francisco under her own power. Her bridge had sustained a direct hit. Her captain and the admiral of the squadron, who were on the bridge, had been killed. But she had sunk a Japanese battleship and had received relatively slight injury herself. She had returned to San Francisco under the command of a 39-year-old Lieutenant Commander, who took command of the cruiser when her captain was killed.

The same broadcast reported that the Allied Forces had so far shot down a total of 585 Japanese planes in the vicinity of the Solomon Islands; that 7,000 Japanese had been killed on Guadalcanal Island and that it only remained to mop up the remnant of the Japanese force on that island; that Japan had lost a total of 306 ships during the first year of the war; that an American Flying Fortress, attacked by 15 Japanese zero fighters over the Solomon Islands, had shot down five of them and had returned safely to her base; that for every American lost in the Solomon Islands battles 50 Japanese had been killed and that the Japanese force bottled up on a 15-mile stretch of beach at Buni had tried unsuccessfully to break through the cordon of Allied troops.

The San Francisco broadcast to which I listened at Tom Hawkins' house on December 12 was the first overseas broadcast to which I had listened in five months. Although I did not know it then, I was not to listen again to an overseas broadcast for more than two years.

Chapter 83.

My Son Has a Birthday

On November 11, 1942, Leonard, my son, was ten years old. My wife was still employed at the office of the Red Cross, since her resignation would not become effective until November 15. So we postponed Leonard's birthday celebration until Sunday, November 15, when Socorro, my wife, could be present.

On Sunday morning I baked a three-layer birthday cake, using rice flour instead of wheat flour. Socorro made the frosting and put ten candles on top of the cake. We also roasted a chicken.

We had not invited any guests, but Socorro's cousin, Mr. Custodio, with his wife and their four small sons, came that morning and stayed until evening. The eldest of the four boys was only six and the youngest two years old. Mrs. Custodio was pregnant and expected to deliver her fifth child before the end of the month.

We had a rich beef and vegetable stew for lunch. The four Custodio children ate ravenously. The family had been hard pressed for some time and the children probably did not get enough to eat at home.

Early in the afternoon, Mrs. Bowers came to call on us, bringing her Mah Jong set. Mrs. Bowers, Mr. and Mrs. Custodio, and myself played Mah Jong until 5 o'clock, when Socorro announced that the birthday *'merienda'* was ready. Then we all assembled on the veranda.

Leonard began the ceremony reciting:
"Welcome is a friendly word,
A word I like to say.
So welcome to my party
In praise of my birthday."
This was followed by songs sung by each of our two servant girls.

The candles on the birthday cake were then lighted and the cake was placed on a small table at which Leonard was seated. After we had sung "Happy Birthday to You," Leonard with a gusty "whoosh" blew out the candles. My wife considered it a good omen that all of the candles were blown out simultaneously.

My wife cut the birthday cake and I carved the chicken. The menu included roast chicken, boiled sweet potatoes, corn bread and butter, hot coffee, sherbet, and of course, the birthday cake.

At Leonard's request, instead of buying him a birthday gift, I gave him one peso, to spend as he chose. It was the largest sum of money he had ever received. The peso was spent within a week.

Chapter 94.

We Again Receive News from Baguio

On December 1, Mrs. A— and the lieutenant called again. With them came Lucy, who lived next door to our house in Baguio and who had been keeping an eye on our house during our absence of almost a year. She reported that our gardener, in whose care we had left out house, had fled to his home in the Pangasinan Province when the Japanese occupied Baguio late in December 1941. He had not returned. Our kitchen had been looted of most of its contents, including the canned foodstuffs. From our garage had been stolen a large box of carpenters and mining tools and several cans of carbide. The doors between the kitchen and the rest of the house were still padlocked and apparently only the kitchen and the garage had been looted.

Lucy was a Filipino. Her husband, whose name was Elinger but whom everyone called Carabao, was an American miner employed as a foreman in one of the gold mines near Baguio. Carabao was interned in Baguio when the Japanese occupied that city late in December 1941. Lucy and her large family of children had been permitted to remain in their home. She had 500 pesos in cash on hand when her husband was interned.

In August we sent word to Lucy that she could have the firewood that was stored in our garage and at the back of our house. When we left Baguio we had on hand enough firewood to last us two years. Lucy reported that her money was exhausted and that she had used and sold all of our firewood. She had come to Manila seeking to borrow money from her aunt, who owned one of the leading funeral parlors in Manila.

Mrs. A— reported that many of the houses of Americans in Baguio had been looted. The new Filipino Chief of Police and some of his subordinates were said to be thieves themselves, who provided no protection for property stored in unoccupied houses.

My wife decided to return to Baguio with Lucy, open our house, and let Lucy live in it, rent free, in order to guard our household goods. My wife also intended to bring some of our things back to Manila and to sell in Baguio the supply of canned foodstuffs stored in the house.

On December 4, when my wife called Lucy by telephone to arrange for their trip to Baguio, Lucy reported that she had just received a letter from her servant in Baguio. The servant wrote that several Japanese had moved into our house. On Sunday December 6, my wife called on Lucy at her aunt's home and read the servant's letter. It had been brought to Manila by the driver of a freight truck from Baguio.

Since I would have to report to the Commandant of the Santo Tomas Internment Camp on December 10, when my pass expired, my wife decided to postpone her trip to Baguio until after this date. Lucy said that she must return to Baguio the next day because her children would be out of money for food.

Chapter 85.

My Wife Is Permitted to Withdraw a Small Sum of Money from Her Frozen Accounts in the National City Bank

About the middle of 1942 the Bank of Taiwan Limited, was named as Administrator of the Assets and Liabilities of the seven Manila banks which had been ordered to be liquidated by the Japanese. One of these banks was the Manila branch of the National City Bank of New York, in which my mother-in-law had a small savings account and my wife had both a savings and checking account. The Bank of Taiwan (Bank of Formosa) had established itself in the quarters formerly occupied by the National City Bank.

Early in December it was announced that depositors of the seven banks in liquidation might make withdrawals, beginning December 9. Withdrawals were to be limited to 30 or 60 pesos per month from each account, depending upon the bank in which the account was carried and whether the account was a savings account or a checking account. The National City Bank depositors, irrespective of the amount on deposit, were to be permitted to withdraw 60 pesos per month from each savings account and 30 pesos per month from each checking account. Only those depositors who were Japanese, Filipino or Chinese citizens, or who were "third party nationals," were permitted to make such withdrawals. The accounts of American, British and Dutch citizens were still frozen.

My wife went to the Bank of Taiwan on December 9, but she was told to come back the next day because many depositors had preceded her and only 100 depositors were permitted to make withdrawals each day. On December 10 she went again, accompanied by her mother, who was permitted to withdraw 60 pesos from her savings account.

My wife had left the pass book for her savings account on deposit with the National City Bank. When she requested the Bank of Taiwan to produce this pass book so that she might make a withdrawal from her savings account, she was informed that all pass books deposited with the National City Bank had been burned when the Bank of Taiwan took possession of the quarters of the National City Bank. At the suggestion of a Filipino employee of the Bank of Taiwan, my wife wrote a letter requesting permission to make withdrawals from her savings account. She was requested to return the next day to learn the decision of the officials of the Bank of Taiwan. On December 12 she was permitted to withdraw 60 pesos from her savings account and was given a copy of the ledger entries showing the balance still due to her in her savings account after deducting the 60 pesos which she had withdrawn. She requested permission to withdraw 200 pesos in order to pay the taxes on 10 acres of land which she owned in the city of Baguio. This request was refused, but she was permitted to withdraw 30 pesos from her checking account.

Altogether, my wife and her mother were permitted to withdraw during December a total of 150 pesos from their three accounts with the National City Bank. This increased our reserve of cash in hand to about 300 pesos and provided my wife with funds for the trip which she planned to make to Baguio to find out what had happened to our home and bring to Manila some of our belongings if they were still intact.

Our hope that the accounts of my wife and her mother in the National City Bank would provide us with a small source of income during the remainder of the war was not fulfilled. Contrary to the announcement made early in December, which stated that withdrawals might be made each month, no further withdrawals after those granted in December 1942 were permitted from accounts carried with the National City Bank. Officials of the Bank of Taiwan stated that the amount realized from the liquidation of assets of the National City Bank was not sufficient to permit any further withdrawals and that accounts carried with the National City Bank would remain frozen until the bank reopened for business, which didn't occur until June 1945 after the liberation of the Philippines by the forces of General MacArthur.

Chapter 86.

I Report Again at the Santo Tomas Internment Camp

My pass expired on December 10. When I reported on the afternoon of that day to the Commandant's office at the Santo Tomas Internment Camp I was instructed to report again on December 14, at 12.30 p.m., for another medical examination by Dr. Koh, the Japanese doctor. He had examined me on July 10, but the Commandant's regulations required a re-examination at least every six months in those cases where it was possible that the internee's health might have improved sufficiently to permit reinternment. A young American matron who reported on December 10 was reinterned that day.

I was very dubious about the result of my approaching medical examination. Proper food and regular weekly injections of liver extract had greatly improved my health during the five months which had elapsed since my release to my home. A test of my blood on July 9 showed only 63 percent of the normal count of red corpuscles. A similar test on December 9 showed 85 percent of the normal count. I had gained 7 pounds in weight since my release to my home, although I still weighed 30 pounds less than I weighed at the outbreak of the war.

My doctor, Dr. Orobia of the Red Cross Hospital, gave me a letter stating that I was suffering from pernicious anemia and recommending that my pass be extended because it had been found that when injections of liver extract and a special diet were discontinued my health deteriorated

On December 14, after being examined by Dr. Koh, I was ordered to report for reinternment on December 15. My wife wept when I told her that I was to be reinterned.

On the morning of December 15 my wife went to Santo Tomas to request a reconsideration of the order reinterning me that day. She took my pass and the letter from Dr. Orobia recommending that my pass be extended. At 1 p.m. she had not yet returned.

My bag, bedding, mattress and bed were ready to be loaded into the *tartanilla*. I continued to await Socorro's return with my pass so that I might start for the Santo Tomas Internment Camp. I had hoped to spend Christmas at home. But this was not to be.

There was a rumor that all American and European internees were to be transferred from Manila to Camp O'Donnell in Tarlac Province and this was to take place as soon as all the Filipino war prisoners were released or removed from Camp O'Donnell. I hoped that this rumor was not true. My wife would not be able to send food to me at Camp O'Donnell, and the rumors which had reached us concerning conditions at Camp O'Donnell were not reassuring.

I was required to report at the Santo Tomas Internment Camp for reinternment before 4 p.m. The trip by *tartanilla* from my home to Santo Tomas would require almost an hour. When Socorro had not returned at 2.30 p.m., I loaded my baggage into a *tartanilla* and set out for the camp.

At the gate of the camp I learned that Socorro was in the Office of the Commandant seeking a renewal of my pass. I was instructed to wait outside the gate until she returned to the gate.

When Socorro returned from the Commandant's office she told me that I had been given one more day at home but would have to report for reinternment on December 16.

We deposited my baggage with a Filipino merchant whose store was across the street from the gate of the camp and then headed for home.

Socorro told me that when she reached the gate of the camp that morning she was refused admission. She then went to the headquarters of the Japanese military administration, where she was very courteously received by a Japanese captain. He gave her a letter instructing the guard at the gate to permit her to enter and recommending that I be given a permanent release. She returned to the camp shortly before noon and was told that she would be admitted at 2 p.m. In the Office of the Commandant she was courteously received by the Japanese civilian clerk who had ordered my reinternment. He assured her that he would have renewed my pass if the Japanese doctor had not recommended my reinternment. No pleading on my wife's part, however, could secure a renewal of my pass. The best she was able to do was to obtain for me one more day's grace on the plea that she needed that much time in which to prepare my clothing.

Chapter 87.

I Call on Tom Hawkins Once More and Obtain from Him the Latest War News

I knew that when I reentered the Santo Tomas Internment Camp I would be besieged with requests for the latest war news. So on the evening of December 15 Socorro and I called on Tom Hawkins and his wife. Tom gave me an account of the latest war news which he had obtained from overseas broadcasts picked up by his short-wave radio receiver.

General MacArthur's American force in Papua, New Guinea, had captured Buni. The Australian force had occupied a village at the opposite end of the 15-mile stretch of beach which was the last Japanese foothold in Papua. The Japanese were still offering bitter resistance, although they were steadily being decimated. Another Japanese attempt to land reinforcements at Buni had been foiled. So far the Japanese had made eight unsuccessful attempts to land reinforcements at Buni.

In North Africa, Field Marshal Ernst Rommel's forces were retreating westward from El Agheila, where it had been expected they would make a stand. The Allies had air superiority in that sector. In Tunis the Allied lines had strengthened after some retirement during the preceding few days in the face of a powerful German attack. Tunis had been bombed, as had Palermo in Sicily together with Naples and other towns in Italy. Allied air activity in Tunis had increased. But ground activity of both Allied and Axis forces was being hampered by heavy rains and mud which made it difficult to move heavy mechanized equipment.

General Arnold, Chief of the United States Air Force, had announced that heavy bombers, larger than the Flying Fortress, were now being built and that in the near future these long-range aircraft would be used in large numbers to bomb Japan.

The Russians, with the exception of one small sector at Stalingrad, were pushing back the Germans all along the eastern front.

The RAF had bombed transportation facilities in western Germany and northern France. The RAF met practically no resistance and all its planes returned safely. It was surmised that Hitler had withdrawn planes from northern France and western Germany in order to reinforce his Luftwaffe in North Africa.

The Allies had bombed a Japanese airport in Central Burma.

The Chinese had foiled a Japanese attempt to break through the Chinese line on the Salwin River in Yunnan Province.

The Japanese position on Kiska Island in the Aleutians had again been heavily bombed.

In the first ten months of 1942 the United States had produced 8.2 million tons of cargo ships, 49,000 planes, 32,000 tanks, 27,000 field guns larger that 37 mm and much other war material. Aircraft carriers were now being built on a mass production basis. A carrier could now be completed within six weeks after the date of laying down the keel. The initial order for eight carriers was increased to sixteen before the first eight carriers were completed.

The only discouraging feature of this news was the Allied acknowledgement of their retreat in Tunis. Tom opined that the Allied forces had advanced so rapidly that it had not yet been able to bring up sufficient heavy equipment to halt the powerful German attack which had been encountered in Tunis.

The Japanese-controlled Manila daily, *La Vanguardia* (published in Spanish), of December 14 had published a cable from Lisbon, dated December 13, which claimed Axis air superiority in Tunis and asserted that heavy pressure was being exerted on Allied lines in Tunis. This cable claimed that the Allies admitted they were losing the advantage which they had gained. Rommel's retreat to El Agheila was described as masterly and the Allies were said to be cautious in Libya.

We said good night to Tom and his wife and walked slowly back to our home. Socorro wept a little. Tomorrow I would have to return to prison.

Chapter 88.

I Am Reinterned at the Santo Tomas Internment Camp

On December 16, 1942, my last day at home. I arose at dawn, as usual. Socorro and Leonard were still asleep. I started a fire in the kitchen and prepared breakfast – hot cakes made with rice flour; syrup made from brown sugar; coffee brewed from almost the last of our genuine pre-war coffee; boiled *camotes* (sweet potatoes) sliced and fried; fried eggs; and a ripe papaya from one of the trees in our garden. It was a better breakfast than we usually had because this would probably be my last breakfast at home until the end of the war.

When we sat down to breakfast Socorro's eyes were brimmed with tears. "Ask God's blessing on our food," she said tremulously. And so, as we bowed our heads, I expressed our gratitude that we still had enough to eat, prayed that we might be given strength to endure the hardships of the war and that we might have sufficient food to survive.

After breakfast I went out to my garden. A dozen old eggplants were still bearing. The huge *patola* vines and a dozen ochra planted in June were also still bearing, although their bearing season was almost ended. The *patola* vines, now more than seventy-five feet long, had overrun their arbor and had climbed into the fruit trees. The okra plants were five feet tall. The pomelo tree was still loaded with huge oranges nearly six inches in diameter. We had been harvesting about a dozen each week since early in November. Perhaps the mango tree would bloom in January. It was almost old enough to begin bearing. The cayenne peppers were already bearing. The bell peppers were doing nicely. There would be string beans within a week. Several varieties of climbing beans covered the fence around the garden. They would be bearing in January. The tomatoes and eggplant which I had set out in October would be bearing in February, the tomatoes possibly in January. The corn which I had planted on October 10 was now more than nine feet tall. Huge ears of green corn would be ready to harvest within a week. Beneath the corn the earth was covered with squash vines, which would yield a crop in March, long after the corn was finished. There were more than a dozen bunches of bananas in various stages of development. We harvested about two bunches of bananas each month. A half-dozen papaya trees were already bearing. More than eighty other young papaya trees had begun to flower. Within four or five months Socorro should have papayas to sell. Papayas were scarce and the price was high. The money received from the sale of our papayas should provide Socorro with a much needed source of income. Several varieties of greens planted in October were already yielding a crop.

There were two pigs, instead of one, in the pen now. One of them was a little fellow recently purchased. The other was large enough to butcher, but we were holding it in reserve against the time when meat would be much more difficult to obtain than it was now. Our seven hens, after a period of inactivity during the rainy season, had begun to lay again.

I would miss my garden. It was growing so well and I had so enjoyed working in it! It produced enough to supply, not only ourselves, but also relatives and friends, with the green vegetables which were now so costly in the public markets. Perhaps I would be permitted to work in the camp garden. When I entered the internment camp I would go to Mr. Boerecki and volunteer for work in the camp garden.

When I returned to the house I found Socorro busily packing my suitcase. The two maidservants were busily tying up my mattress and bedding in a huge roll.

"The war will soon be over. You won't have to stay in the internment camp long," Socorro said hopefully.

"The war will last longer than you expect," I replied.

"How long will it last?" inquired Socorro.

"I don't know, but I believe it will last at least ten more months." I replied. Even I, who was considered by other internees to be a pessimist, did not dream that the war would last for more than two more years.

"Be sure to keep on hand as large a reserve supply of food as possible," I continued. "Don't eat up your reserve supply of rice. Buy now a couple of sacks of corn for the pigs and chickens. Before the war is over food will be much harder to get than it is now and prices will be much higher."

I gave Socorro a list of the stamps which Rogelio still held on consignment and a statement of the balance still due to me on these stamps. Rogelio had agreed to make weekly payments to my wife after I reentered the internment camp. As Mr. Catala had not yet reported on the stamps which he had taken to sell for me, I also gave Socorro a statement of the amount due to me for those stamps. About a week after my reinternment Mr. Catala delivered to my wife about fifty pesos covering stamps which he had sold and returned two stamps which he had been unable to sell.

The manuscript which I had written concerning the first year of the war I concealed in our attic. I did not want the Japanese to find it. My stamp collection and our reserve supply of food were also concealed in the attic. The only access to the attic was by lifting a panel in the ceiling of the kitchen. We closed the window shutters before entering the attic so that no one would learn of our secret store.

I took a last look at our Lincoln Zephyr automobile, which Socorro had registered in her maiden name. Although the Japanese had confiscated our Ford they had so far not discovered the Lincoln Zephyr. But before the war was over, I reflected sadly, they would probably learn of it from some neighbor who had become a Japanese collaborator,.

Leonard, my son, was sent to call a *tartanilla*. When it arrived we loaded my bed and baggage into it. Socorro would accompany me to the gate of the internment camp. Leonard wanted to go also, but Socorro would not permit it.

"Daddy, I want some money," said Leonard.

I gave him two pesos. I still had ten pesos in my pocket book. I would not take more than that into the internment camp. Socorro would probably bring me food each week. There was little else for which I would need money.

My mother-in-law said good bye to me tearfully. Leonard also cried a little when he kissed me goodbye.

"When are you coming back?" he asked.

"When the war is over," I replied gravely.

"When will the war be over," he asked.

"I don't know," I replied.

The driver clucked to his horse and the *tartanilla* started. The trip across the city took nearly an hour. As the horse plodded onward I wondered when I would traverse that street again and whether things would look the same when I again emerged from the internment camp.

At the gate of the camp I presented my pass and was instructed to deposit my baggage in the compound inside the outer gate until I was assigned to quarters. I kissed my wife goodbye, while a Japanese guard looked on stolidly.

"I will bring you food twice a week," she promised tearfully.

I passed through the inner gate. As it closed behind me I looked back and saw Socorro still standing at the outer gate.

....

I re-entered the Santo Tomas Internment Camp on December 16, 1942. I did not again emerge from the camp until March 4, 1945, a month after we were liberated by the arrival of General MacArthur's First Cavalry Division on February 3, 1945.

For more than a year prior to our liberation we were systematically starved. No packages of food could be sent into the camp by relatives and friends outside of the camp. The ration supplied by the Japanese was reduced until we were receiving only about 150 grams of rice per person per day. The food value of our ration was less than 600 calories—about one fifth of the normal food requirement. Most of us suffered from beri-beri as the result of a diet consisting almost exclusively of rice. Some of us died from starvation, others from beri-beri. For two months prior to our release we were dying at the rate of three or four each day.

I suffered less than some of the other internees because, before the gate was closed in February of 1944, my wife sent me a small reserve supply of food. But even with this food in addition to the camp ration I had only about one third of the food necessary to maintain weight. My weight dropped to 125 pounds, more than 70 pounds less than I had weighed when the war began. I contracted both beri-beri and dysentery. I was in the camp hospital when we were released by the arrival of the First Cavalry Division on the night of February 3, 1945. Because of my illness and because of the heavy fighting which went on throughout the city I did not leave the camp until March 4.

During the first ten days after the arrival of the First Cavalry the camp was shelled almost constantly by the Japanese. Several internees were killed and many were wounded. For ten days, from the internment camp, I watched the city burning. Reports came to us of the terrible slaughter by the Japanese of the civilian population of Manila. I was worried about the safety of my family.

Because of the fighting going on in the city my wife and son were not able to communicate with me until near the end of February, almost a month after our release. Socorro reported that her mother's house in the southern outskirts of Manila had not been burned because the Eleventh Airborne Division arrived before the Japanese were able to set fire to that part of the city. Both my wife and son were very thin. They too had suffered from a lack of sufficient food. My son had grown very little since I had last seen him.

We had lost our Lincoln Zephyr. Someone had informed the Japanese military police about it. Everything which we had left in our home in Baguio had been lost. My stamp collection and the manuscript which I had written concerning the first year of the war were still safe in the attic of my mother-in-law's house in Pasay.

I shall never forget our journey across that city of desolation when we returned to my mother-in-law's home. There was no transportation. We pushed a heavy cart containing my baggage. Because I was weak and still suffering from dysentery, the journey took the greater part of a day. In the midst of the city was a house which by some miracle had escaped the fire which had consumed all other houses around it. My wife set up my bed in the living room and I rested there for two hours. Near the ruin of what had been the Paco Public Market we met a Filipino policeman. He pointed to the charred ruin of a moving picture theatre nearby.

"The Japanese," he said, "drove six hundred Filipinos into that theatre, set fire to it, and then machine-gunned them when they tried to escape from the burning building. All of them died."

Epilogue

On one occasion when I was with a group of Old Timer Philippine stamp collectors, the subject of Arnold Warren's internment was mentioned. They treated his confinement with contempt, hinting he had received privileged treatment with home leave because of his position and wealth. This manuscript puts an end to such nonsense.

In 2010, I received this manuscript from Bill Oliver together with a carton of Warren's correspondence from the end of the Second World War to the time of his death in 1976. Bill obtained these from Arnold's son Leonard who, having no interest in stamps, sold what remained of Arnold's Philippine stamp collection to Bill and also gave him the manuscript and letters. In the correspondence there is little mention of his internment. However, there are some references and this information follows.

In the Santo Tomas Camp, Arnold did work in the garden. There is one muted reference that he underwent an operation while there that saved his life. Socorro and his family fell on hard times. She and a friend bought and sold firewood and they had Leonard sell cigarettes on the street. However, they could not buy much to sell and they all suffered from malnutrition by the time the war ended. Leonard's growth was stunted and he grew to a height of only 4 feet 4 inches by the age of 18. Their house in Baguio had been bombed by the US during the recapture of that city. It had been totally levelled and nothing remained. Arnold lost all his carpentry and mining tools plus his personal, technical and philatelic library.

Arnold had to rest in order to regain his health. He, Socorro, and Leonard were without money at the end of the war and were shipped back to the USA in April 1945. Both Arnold and Socorro went back to work but Arnold had to rest first at his mother's house. He took a job for a year with a beet-sugar factory in California where he typed this manuscript. Arnold then accepted a job in the Philippines and for 4 years, from July 1946 to August 1950. He worked as an Industrial Equipment Engineer Salesman. He helped sugar refineries rebuild, as most had been extensively damaged or destroyed. Meanwhile Socorro rented rooms for Leonard and herself but when this became impossible during September 1946, she purchased 10 acres of land with a house in Gig Harbor, Washington. Leonard went back to school in the US but was older than his classmates because all the Philippine schools had been closed during the Japanese occupation and he now had to catch up.

Arnold put in for war claims but I have no record of what he received and whatever he did receive was not given to him until the early 1950s. They were eventually able to withdraw money from their pre-war bank account but it was limited to $218 per month. That is all the New Philippines would allow to be withdrawn from the country. I do not know when this limitation started or ended but it was effective in 1950. The gold mines gave no dividends since they had to be rebuilt. I do not know if the Warrens were able to get a monthly amount back to the US when the mines finally returned to production. I suspect they were able to get something. However, because of the war, they did lose their fortune and never again would they be classified in the "well-to-do" category. When Arnold returned to the US in 1950 he brought the maximum amount of cash and goods allowed, equal to about $10,000, when everything had been sold. As was their custom, I'm certain that some cash was invested that helped them in their US retirement. Arnold, Socorro and Leonard never returned to the Philippines but the Philippines remained in his heart as his adopted country.

Socorro's land purchase was fortunate for them. Arnold became a farmer and raised 5 acres of strawberries each year. He states, in many philatelic letters, that he has to end the correspondence now and "go tend to his strawberries." I believe he really enjoyed working outside and nature was part religion and part relaxation to him. He also raised some bulls annually for food and resale and he was also a part time stamp dealer. I don't know when Socorro stopped working but they seemed to have a modest income with the farming, stamps and whatever cash came from the Philippines and investments. Arnold was a lifelong philatelist; it was a passionate hobby for him and an outlet for his intellect. Arnold went on to become a celebrated cataloger of all Philippine revenue stamps and his work will stand for all time. In 1968, he was honored by the American Philatelic Society (APS) with their highest award—the Distinguished Philatelic Research (Luff) Award.

Addendum

Arnold's correspondence included two items related to his internment. The first was a short three stanza poem he wrote. He liked poetry and owned several books of poems that were destroyed together with his house in Baguio. In this simple iambic pentameter poem is a powerful antidote to the horrific war that had just ended. (NOTE: a Nipa is a Filipino house in the countryside.) The manuscript also refers to "Antonio's" visit to the Red Cross Hospital. This second piece of correspondence goes more deeply into their friendship. Arnold did not know until after his release that the couple was first imprisoned in Fort Santiago and later both executed near the end of the war. I hope Arnold's letter to Ford was forwarded to the Escoda's two children.

(1) PEACE HAS COME AGAIN. A short poem by Arnold written after his release.

(2) ESCODA MEMORIAL FUND. Two 1948 letters concerning Antonio and Josefa Escoda

Douglas K. Lehmann

Bibliographic Reference

Please reference this document as:

Warren, Arnold H. *War Came to the Philippines, Being an Account Chiefly of Events which Transpired During the First Year of the Japanese Occupation of the Philippines*, International Philippine Philatelic Society, 2011. http://www.theipps.org/bibliography/Warren-WWII.pdf.

PEACE HAS COME AGAIN
by Arnold H. Warren.

Down in the Land of Nipa,
On the bank of a sluggish stream.
Where Malays sit in the twilight
And dream and smoke and dream,
Down in the Land of Nipa
Darkness has fallen deep
And the voice of a tropic night
Is lulling me to sleep

Softly across the river
Comes the croon of a native song,
The wail of a tropic lullaby
Plaintive, monotonous, long.
From out of the infinite depth
Of a cloudless, moonless sky
Numberless stars twinkle and glisten
With a splendor that will never die.

Carabaos munch their fodder
After a day of toil,
Pulling the farmer's plough,
Tilling the fertile soil,
Chickens roost on the roof-top;
Pigs are fat in their pen.
Down in the Land of Nipa
Peace has come again.

Oct. 27, 1948
Mr. Ford Wilkins,
Chairman Escoda Memorial Fund,
Manila Philippines.

Dear Mr. Ford,

I enclose a check for 100.00 as my contribution to the Escoda Memorial Fund. I will contribute a like amount each year as long as the fund is continued.

I consider it a privilege to contribute to this fund.

I was one of Antonio Escoda's teachers when he was a senior in the Leyte High School in 1915–16. Even at that early date his command of English was exceptional.

I kept in touch with him throughout succeeding years and was proud of his success as a newspaper man. In 1919, when he was editor of the Sports page of a Manila Daily, he assisted me in selecting the players of the first baseball team of the Calamba Sugar Estate. That team was one of the best in the Philippines at that time and was the foundation of the fine team which Calamba maintained during succeeding years. The success of the first Calamba team was largely due to Antonio's shrewd judgement in selecting the players.

I recall the visits which Antonio made during April and May, 1942, to the Ateneo University when you and I and others were interned there in a Red Cross Hospital. From him we learned of several trips which he and his wife made to Capas to carry medical supplies to the prisoners who were arriving from Bataan. The first trip was made while the "death march" from Bataan to Capas was still in progress. He told us of seeing prisoners arrive at Capas only to lie down beside the road and die. He told us of the death of more than four hundred prisoners a day in Capas. He told us of the barracks converted into a hospital in Capas, without beds, without blankets, without medicine without bandages, without antiseptics—with nothing to alleviate the suffering of the sick and wounded who lay upon the bare floor and died.

Antonio and his wife brought in the first truck load of medical supplies and made one or two additional trips before they were prohibited from rendering further aid by the Japanese Military authorities.

Very truly yours,
(Cut off)

www.ingramcontent.com/pod-product-compliance
Lightning Source LLC
Chambersburg PA
CBHW022001160426
43197CB00007B/224